Unapologetically ME

Unapologetically ME

GERALDINE SMOTHERSON

XULON PRESS

Xulon Press
2301 Lucien Way #415
Maitland, FL 32751
407.339.4217
www.xulonpress.com

Unless otherwise indicated, Scripture quotations taken from the
Holy Bible, New International Version (NIV). Copyright © 1973, 1978,
1984, 2011 by Biblica, Inc.™. Used by permission. All rights reserved.

Scripture quotations taken from the Holy Bible, New Living Translation
(NLT). Copyright ©1996, 2004, 2007 by Tyndale House Foundation.
Used by permission of Tyndale House Publishers, Inc.

Paperback ISBN-13: 978-1-6628-2082-3
Ebook ISBN-13: 978-1-6628-2083-0

Dedication
(And A Promise)

I dedicate these words to my offspring, who have often wondered aloud what makes me tick. I could never answer them because, until I started writing this book, I didn't know for sure myself. I'm still trying to figure me out.

My children, my children... you are a hodgepodge of magnificent talent. If you could see all that I see in you, the world and all the good it has to offer would be yours. I hope you each know how much I love you and want what is best for you, including the struggles that teach the lessons of life.

One of the joys I have is that you have such fond memories of my mother. She loved you dearly. It is my desire that you also have fond memories of me. Not only you, my children, but also my grandchildren who have added so much richness and purpose to my world.

To all my beloved siblings and all your children whom I also consider mine, and to those who have become extended family, I cherish you all as well. Isn't that what God intended, that we embrace one another with love? And in doing so we enhance not only our lives but the lives of others?

I pray for divine guidance of our future generation whose days may be of a greater challenge than those of our fore-parents.

I hope that each of you knows the Lord for yourselves and that your actions are demonstrative of what Christ did for us all.

Because of my deep devotion to you all, I finally got up enough nerve to reveal a lifetime of struggle and success. In this book, I share my shame, pain, unhappiness, joy, and the gratefulness that has brought me to this point.

May God always bless and keep you safe in His arms!

Table of Contents

Foreword

My biological parents loved me dearly and I them. In most respects, that is not only normal but expected. But, how extraordinarily marvelous is it to be adopted into a family and to be loved unconditionally. I have pondered that reality over and over since I was adopted of sorts by Geri nearly 40 years ago. She didn't discard me with the broken relationship between me and her son. Instead, she drew me close to her heart and made me hers. She didn't have to, but she chose to. She chose me, cherished me, and stamped **handle with care** all over my life. For that, I am eternally grateful and blessed beyond measure.

I think of Geri as velvet over steel – simultaneously tender and strong, soft and classy on the outside, while solid and resilient on the inside. She is the epitome of grace and beauty. I'm sure when God formed her in her mother's womb, He paused to marvel at His creation. Then He set her on a course that would make her a vessel fit for His use, sharing His love and acceptance with those she encounters along the way. She has been strengthened by tragedy, fortified by triumph, and refined by fire.

I hope that you come to love and adore this lady as I do as she shares the remarkable events that wove the tapestry of her life.

Thank you, Mama Geri. Well done!

With all my love,
Zanetta

Introduction

*I*t's one thing to write a book for my own healing and another to actually publish it and make public my innermost thoughts. Where do I draw the line? At times I doubted myself, wondering what my real motivation was for this book and whether I should continue or not.

I asked myself, *Should I put my feelings on a shelf and leave them there*? My answer, *Absolutely not!* That's why I started writing in the first place.

I needed to say every word written in this book and to release into the atmosphere any sadness, disappointment, guilt, or pain. I had been suppressing my feelings far too long and wanted to move on to greener pastures. When, or if, you ever find yourself in the same or similar situation, I hope my story can help you find your way. Do I give up or do I forge ahead? I decided to do the latter. I hope that you will, too.

Originally, because of my long-time role as First Lady of our church where my husband was Pastor, my book was going to be titled ***The Making of a First Lady.*** But I could not and would not use that after Michelle Obama became First Lady of the United States. The grace and integrity with which she handled herself as FLOTUS claimed ownership to that title forevermore. She will always be The First Lady. Thank you, Michelle, for showing the world how it's done.

In writing *Unapologetically Me,* one of the more difficult questions I asked myself was whether I was wrong to disclose certain truths about my spouse, about myself, and about our relationship. When I asked friends, one said that I shouldn't publish anything that would be detrimental to the cause of Christ. In other words, will the content of my writing cause someone to denounce Christ or the church? Another friend told me there are personal things that I should not put in the book. She told me about her great respect for my husband, Melvin. I took that to mean I shouldn't include facts or occurrences one could deem negative involving him, whether true or not.

Those types of comments and thoughts gave me pause. These were people who had not lived my married life nor walked in my emotionally tattered shoes. I am appreciative of my 57 years of marriage including all of its trials and tribulations. They served as inspirations and not barriers to my triumphs.

I was at my son's church attending a meeting when a woman approached me singing Melvin's praises. She told me how wonderful she thought he was.

All I could say was, "Yes he was," because he was in so many ways.

But he also was not perfect. Jesus said no man is perfect but GOD. If that's so, I asked myself, then why can't I write about my husband's flaws in the same way I write about his strengths and accomplishments? Each of his distinctive characteristics had a direct impact on me and my children.

To everyone reading this book I am recounting the events of my life, even the ones which were somewhat difficult. It was amazing how the negative influences and occurrences invaded my inner thoughts. My generation learned not to be too boastful. We were encouraged to always be thankful even for the challenges we faced. The emphasis was placed on being humble and grateful for all that was good in life to build character and make us stronger. I lived that model but now it's time to express gratitude while also being a bit boastful. Achieving my goals, even though others saw nothing but failure in my future, was a gift from above.

From the first grade through my third year of high school, I was at the top of my class. I even became a cheerleader, which was a big deal back in my day because cheerleaders received a lot of prestige and privilege. In my Junior Year, I was elected president of my class, met the love of my life, lost my head, and had to leave school because I got pregnant. That didn't stop me. I got my GED and later graduated Cum Laude with a bachelor's degree in Training & Development. Then I earned a master's degree in Adult Education. My cup kept running over.

I excelled in a company that only accepted women because they had to and, within that company, I repeatedly became the first to do **this** and the first to achieve **that**. I was awarded two honors: the National Training & Development Award and the Diversity Development Award. I was ranked number one in my field throughout the nation and traveled the country creating and implementing programs that garnered considerable recognition.

After retirement, I began working as an independent contractor and started my own business, Training Options Plus. Now, because of God's grace and mercy, I've been fortunate enough to enjoy a healthy retirement for more than 25 years and counting.

I am the sum of every event that happened in my life. I can't take any part of it away. I am not a title or position, but a person with strengths and weaknesses; likes and dislikes. My self-esteem, my insecurities, my dreams, and even my determination hail from those experiences. Many circumstances I could not control. Others I could, but chose not to, especially when I had the chance to. In some situations I had absolutely no idea how to manage, still, there were a few occurrences in which I chose to sin willfully. I suppose if I could do so, there are events I would definitely change. Then there are those I claim with pride.

These days, I am definitely showing signs of aging, not just in my face and body, but also in the forgetful things I do. I've put eggs in a pot to boil, walked into the next room, and forgot all about the eggs. One day I put bacon in the skillet, turned on the fire, and went outside to admire the flowers. Luckily, nothing burned. These acts are so unlike me that I know that I must speed along and finish this book before I forget I ever started writing it. So here goes my story, as bravely and *unapologetically* as I can tell it. Who am I? As you will see, **I am my mother's child, my father's rejected child, and a flawed yet marvelous human being.**

Chapter One
My Mother Lula Jackson and Me

My mother was named after her great-grandmother, Easter. Later she or someone else changed it to Lula Bell. Mama was born on April 23, 1916, in Fayette, Mississippi. It's where my grandparents raised their children: two boys and ten girls. Mama was the sixth child born. Out of the 12 children, only two of my mother's sisters are still living.

There isn't much I recall or was even told about my mother's childhood or upbringing. What I do know is this... my grandparents pampered the boys while the girls had to work the fields picking cotton and doing the seasonal plowing. Both of my uncles did serve time in the military. While working on this history I was careful to tell each of my two remaining aunts that I'd be checking with them so they could help me if my memories were too cloudy or slanted toward my personal biases (of which I have many).

Everyone – Mama, her siblings, their cousins, and all the neighbors' children attended the Poplar Hill School, a one-room schoolhouse just outside of Fayette. What a challenge that must have been, all those different ages and personalities co-mingling in one tiny room. She and her sister Thelma would later teach there as well. Their photos currently hang on the wall inside the modest structure in recognition of two of the teachers who

1

taught first through eighth grade. Poplar Hill School is now a historical site thanks to the efforts of our relative, Toni Stewart.

Before I was born, Mama would travel 24 miles southwest of her home in Fayette to Natchez *(at that time a quaint little town on a hillside overlooking the Mighty Mississippi River)* where she earned her teaching certificate. She also worked as a housekeeper for a well-to-do lady to pay for her room and board. Every month a young man would come by the house in Fayette to collect insurance payments. And it so happened that this same gentleman lived in Natchez. It would have been next to impossible for this man not to have crossed paths with my mother or her nine attractive sisters while visiting the Fayette home. I would assume he and Mama had either met or at least glanced at each other before she actually moved to Natchez. But it's no assumption that while living there, it *was* my mother who lost her ever-loving mind and got pregnant by that insurance man... *my father.*

My grandmother Martha, a.k.a. *Big Mama,* was a proud and independent woman. She was the decision-maker and the person who held the family and everything else together. Big Mama raised 12 children and several grandchildren while caring for her garden, raising chickens, and selling eggs and vegetables. She even bought a piece of property with the egg money she had saved. Growing up I never knew why my grandmother shipped her daughter off to St. Louis although I'm sure she had her reasons. Over the years I tried to satisfy my curiosity using all kinds of rationale. She may have felt her pregnant daughter had brought shame to the family. It's also possible a shotgun may not have been available to aid in the establishment of a coerced marriage, or maybe my grandfather had simply killed the young man. I didn't find out the *why* until I was 74 years old. The man, my father, was already married and had been for two years when I was born. I wondered if my mother or Big Mama even knew.

I recently learned that Mama also taught at the Rodney Mississippi School about 20.4 miles from Fayette. Rodney was just three votes short of becoming the state's capital. With today's modern transportation driving 20 miles is, at most, a thirty-minute trip. But seventy-five years ago having a job 20 miles away was considered out-of-town work which also required finding room and board. When my grandfather Horace *(Big Daddy)* drove us to Rodney in his old jalopy, it took up most of his day. He wasn't about to drive back and forth on a daily basis, so we had to stay in Rodney. My grandmother allowed her youngest daughter, Florida, to travel with us to serve as a companion for me while my mother taught. I was about four years old at the time and my aunt was eleven.

My Mother and Me

I don't remember ever receiving a hug as a child, especially from my mother, a want that seems to have shaped my entire life. I loved my children but found it difficult to hold or hug them after they reached a certain age, even at the time in their lives when they needed it most. That's why it pleased me so much hearing one of my older cousins give witness to how I used to climb up into my mother's lap. She would be teaching at the Poplar Hill Schoolhouse and holding me at the same time. I can't recall that, but I felt better knowing that, at some point, she held me. I don't doubt that my mother cared for me but, growing up, there was no form of comforting that I can remember.

I was born in St. Louis Missouri on May 13, 1939, at the Homer G. Phillips Hospital. My mother and I lived on Maffitt Avenue in the home of one of my grandmother's sisters who also sheltered a lot of other relatives. Mama and I stayed until she became ill. I was two years old when we returned to Fayette so that her mother could take care of both of us. And wouldn't you know it? The young man, my father, was still the insurance man and still coming by the house to collect payments. It was my aunt Florida who told me he *(she called him West)* used to stare at me through the window. I kind of remember someone called **West** but was too young to understand the significance. And even then my mother never said a word. In fact, she never, ever talked about him.

We lived with my grandmother and grandfather for five years. My cousins Junior *(Bernard)*, Piggy *(Juanita)*, and I were the youngest children in the house. This was difficult to write about. I'll say this. A ten-year-old boy and two girls between the ages of five and seven should never sleep in the same bed. I don't know what the adults were thinking. Piggy and I didn't know enough to talk about it and Junior said we were only playing house.

From birth to age seven, Mama was the only teacher I had. I remember the books she made for me. They were well-constructed works of art. My mother would cut pictures from magazines that fit the stories she wrote and then she'd paste them throughout my beautiful book. Some pictures she even copied by hand. Her printing was perfect, every line straight as if generated by a calligraphy machine. Two of her children print the exact same way, but I am not one of them. One is an engineer and the other a gifted draftsman. I wish I had been wise enough to keep my books for they were my first learning tools.

In the summer of 1946, Big Mama's sister Elnora, I called her Aunt Nora, came down from St. Louis for a visit. Short in stature, she was a quiet sort of mousey lady, but she had a good heart and meant well. Too bad it didn't work out well for me. When it was time for her to leave she asked my mother if she could take me back home with her. Mama thought it would be okay, especially since she had planned to return to St. Louis as soon as she was able. Big mistake! At seven, I was self-conscious and insecure about everything. I'm not sure if it was due to my mother never holding or hugging me or was the result of Mama not being able to express her own thoughts and emotions. She found it difficult to talk to me. It didn't matter because to me, she was still the only teacher and sense of belonging I had known. What was I going to do in a strange land and without her? I think my aunt wanted me with her because she was lonely. That became evident not long after I got there and met her husband.

When she attempted to enroll me in school the administrator told my aunt I was too old for kindergarten. The second grade should've been the logical choice given my age because I could read and do what any seven-year-old could do thanks to my mother. But the school official decided to put me in first grade. That was probably the best decision because those second graders would've raked me over the coals. At least that's what I feared.

Ellis Banks, my aunt's husband, was a tyrant who drank too much and was abusive to his wife. Everyone else around him, including me, didn't fare well either. He called me *Chick* for chicken because I was so thin. He worked for a steel company in the daytime and made everyone miserable in the evening. They had an oil-burning heater that would heat their three-room apartment, but my aunt wasn't allowed to use it while Uncle Ellis was at work. The kitchen sat off from the other two rooms separated by a tiny bathroom and narrow hallway. As soon as Uncle Ellis would leave for work we would snuggle up around the oven and the burners on the kitchen stove to keep warm. Aunt Nora knew not to turn them up too high. That way the other rooms stayed cold and that brute of a husband and uncle would never be the wiser. She had it down to a science. An hour before he was to return home she'd turn everything off so that the stove would cool down. When Uncle Ellis arrived from work, the first thing he'd do was light the heater. Then he'd sort of look around as if he expected to spot something amiss all while Aunt Nora and I acted as though nothing out of the ordinary had gone on. That was hard to do sometimes because we were so terrified of him. I could tell by the menacing look on his face that Uncle Ellis thought he had total control over my aunt. Over both of us. He enjoyed making her feel inferior... stripping her of all her self-worth. As much as I despised him for it, I was happy when the whole house would be warm.

My uncle was sort of an entrepreneur. On the weekends he would collect empty more expensive whiskey bottles from the apartment complex's ash pit and other places then fill them with cheap whiskey, reseal the caps, and sell the bottles late Saturday evenings and all day on Sunday. Trusting souls would pay the price he set which was that of the more expensive liquor. He also ran a dice game every Friday and Saturday night which always got heated whenever he wasn't winning. Uncle Ellis would order his wife around... to bring him this or that. Sometimes, before she could turn and walk away, he would pinch her in very private places. He didn't care how humiliating that was for her, he only wanted to show off for the other drunks. When he got totally wasted, it was my turn to do his bidding. "Chick, go get this" or "Chick, make me a sandwich" or "put my house shoes on my feet" or "bring me a glass of water" were his usual commands. He also chewed tobacco and often missed the spittoon that I had to clean. One time he was so drunk he spit out his tobacco juice into his water glass then drank it and I let him. Another time I followed his order and brought him what he asked for. He got a little confused and polished his best brown shoes with liniment. And I let him.

"Chick, what happened to my shoes?"

"I don't know, Uncle Ellis!"

When I was nine years old, he made me go outside without a top on to water the garden. Everyone in the complex could see me. I begged him to wait until I put the rest of my clothes on, but he wouldn't. I had more tears flowing from my eyes than there was water pouring from that hose. No nine-year-old girl wants to be bare-chested out in public. One time Uncle Ellis chased my aunt up the alley to her brother's house. It was the middle of the night, she was barefoot, and in her nightgown. She knew that if she made it there, she could avoid getting hit again and there is where she stayed until her husband cooled down. Uncle Ellis abused Aunt Nora so much she used to write home about it. My Big Mama would travel by train from Mississippi to St. Louis to see about her sister. Once she even threatened to kill him if he ever touched her sister again. Uncle Ellis would be good the entire time my grandmother was there but once she returned home, that old devil would be at it again.

I Just Wanted To Fit In

Mama made beautiful clothes for me and sent everything that I needed to St. Louis – shoes, dresses, coats, undergarments, socks, and even handkerchiefs. I, per my aunt's wishes, was only allowed to wear them on Sundays, the other days of the week I wore clothes that she made. She would get unbleached muslin and potato sacks then dye them different colors. Aunt Nora also bought brown high-top shoes and long thick beige stockings for me to wear. High-top shoes were fashionable when she was a child and even when her son was a little boy. But my thing was why did I have to wear them? In fact, where the heck did she even find those outdated, brown, ugly, boy-looking shoes? Even in the wintertime, none of the other kids in school wore them. When you're seven or eight years old, fitting in is the most important aspect of your social upbringing. Even worse, Aunt Nora used to rub goose grease on my chest. "Oh, the smell!" Then she'd wash my hair with coffee because it was not as dark as she thought it should be. Next, she would put an ASPHIDITY BAG around my neck. Asphidity Bags contain herbs like asafoetida and other concoctions believed to ward off the flu virus, polio, and other diseases. They are usually pinned to the undergarments. Maybe we should have worn asphidity bags to ward off that COVID-19 virus. Anyway, before I got to school, I would roll the beige stockings down to hide the tops of my shoes.

I am so ashamed and not sure why I did this, but I became a thief. I needed to find a way to blend in with the other kids and not stick out like a sore thumb. What better way to not stick out like a sore thumb, right? My aunt would hide the change she got from buying groceries because she needed to have a little spending money whenever my uncle refused to provide. I'd steal a quarter, buy candy on my way to school and even let her believe my uncle had taken it. That gave me so much pleasure for her to blame him. She was constantly moving her hiding place unaware that all the while the thief was right there beside her. A quarter at that time would buy a lot of candy, enough to share with everybody including the teachers. The kids seemed to pay more attention to the candy than they did me and that was okay with me. As bad luck would have it, one of the teachers reported me and questioned where I was getting all that money... but only after she ate my candy. I don't remember what happened after that, but I did finally stop the stealing and candy buying. Probably because I got caught.

I was quiet and tried to be as invisible as possible whenever I was at school. I didn't fit in, felt lonely and afraid, and I cried a lot from all the teasing. Having the other children laugh at me was so hard to handle. I hadn't made friends with anybody yet and didn't know how to approach kids who were already paired up or in a group. Finally, one day a girl named Rosemary asked me to help her with a math problem. She was the first kid who actually talked to me and didn't make fun of me. That made me feel included. Not long after, the two of us and three other classmates became known as the five-gimmie-gats. We went around singing a song we made up begging for anything the rest of the kids had.

In our can-can kick-line formation, we'd go skipping along singing, "We're the five gimmie gats and we're happy as can be... gimmie, gimmie!"

Now, I was happy.

My Mother's Return to St. Louis

Now ten, I had been with my great aunt and uncle for three years before Mama returned to St. Louis. She stayed with us but soon realized my uncle's abusive nature was too much to bear. So we moved one block south into a basement entryway. With very little money, Mama spent most of her time looking for a job. Then one day she came home happier than I had seen her in a long time. Slaughters Cleaners had hired Mama to do alterations and repairs of incoming garments. We now had a paycheck and something to build on. As soon as things began moving in the right direction Mama realized she was pregnant again! Seems she had gotten that way before she left Mississippi. But again no mention of the father except his name, Berry Baker. She just would not talk about such things. Instead, she began to plan for the new arrival saving as much as she could afford and picking up items that a new baby would need because there was no baby shower or piles of gifts. She knew that it was all hers to do, and she did it. I have so much admiration for what my mother was able to accomplish. She never expected others to do anything for her, not even her baby daddies.

After my little sister Deborah Ann was born we moved from that basement entryway into a two-room apartment at 4319 St. Louis Avenue. We had a twin bed that my mother and I shared and a baby bed for Debbie. Although I was 11 at the time, I slept in the baby bed whenever my baby sister became fretful, sick, or wanted her Mama. I used to beg my mother to wake me up early the next morning so I could get out of that baby bed in case someone came by and saw me.

I promised Deborah Ann that, when she was much older, I would find her father. I hate that she never got the chance to meet him or get any information about him from Mama other than his name. All I ever knew was that he was from Vicksburg, Mississippi. Mama's sister Martha lived in Vicksburg all those years ago. The two of them were pretty close and Mama would visit her sister often. That's probably where and when she met Mr. Berry Baker. I haven't given up my search and with my cousin Toni's help, we remain hopeful that one day we'll find information about him or possible family members.

Somewhere around 1951 came Mr. Thomas Hill the father of my mother's last three children. I don't know where this man came from or how they met. All I do know is that Mama thought she loved him. From the outside looking in this was a complicated relationship. I say that because he would disappear every time she got pregnant and that always left my mother heartbroken and feeling abandoned. But then there he was again after the baby was born. He was good for creating that false sense of happily-ever-after and I hated him for that. Their first child was my brother Berdell Eugene. He was a happy even-tempered plump and cuddly little baby boy. Everybody loved him. I believe his first sentence was, "See the light?" He seemed so fascinated by the lights.

One day Berdell stopped talking and it seemed like years before he said another word. The doctors at the clinic thought his problem could have been caused by the measles or a hard blow to the head. Blow to the head? Where? When? Nobody knew but, when Berdell did speak again it was not with the same rhythm or tone but with choppy words and incomplete sentences. My heart bled for my mother who had to quit her job and come home to care for her son. She tried to get answers and solutions for his care but there were none. What was she to do? She was saddled with three handicaps of her own... she was poor, black, and working all the time trying to keep money coming in.

As Berdell grew older he became restless and irritable which led to her having to give him a prescribed medication. His inability to communicate effectively only added to his frustration which soon turned into anger and violent outbursts. My sisters *(there were two by then)* were often the targets on whom he released that rage. He would toss them around like rag dolls. My mother had to stay awake at night to keep him from attacking the girls. Before long, the lack of sleep and rest caused Mama to start hemorrhaging. I took her to the hospital, returned to her house, and took Berdell to a different kind of medical center.

Malcolm Bliss was a well-known mental hospital where they treated the most difficult cases of mental disorders. One thing that was important to me was that Malcolm Bliss accepted the poorest of patients, as some of the other institutions did not. The hospital received a lot of support from Washington University School of Medicine. That allowed Malcolm Bliss to open their doors to anyone who needed extreme mental care. Berdell was 15 at the time, only five years older than my firstborn. He didn't understand why I was leaving him in a strange place with people he had never seen before. The look of confusion and fear on his face still haunts me, bringing tears to my eyes even today as I am writing this. Mama could never have done what I felt obligated to do. Whatever happened to him from that point forward became my responsibility because I was the one who placed my loved one in that institution.

Berdell stayed in several care facilities over the years–some good, some bad, some near, and some far but thankfully always within the state of Missouri. My biggest concern as we both aged was what would happen to him if I died before him. God took care of that worry. My brother passed away in the spring of 2020. He was 67 years old.

Two years after Berdell was born, my mother gave birth to Wanda Diane. It's the reason she couldn't be present at my grade school graduation, January 1954. Fearing that she might not be able to attend, Mama had prepared early for my big event. The girls had to wear white blouses and blue skirts. My friends and I were super excited as we chatted about how we were going to have our hair done. I assumed the other girls would get their outfits from the local department store. Their school clothes always looked store-bought. The idea of going shopping was always thrilling to me because I seldom got the chance to do so, and this time was no different. We didn't have the money, especially with a baby coming. I knew I had to live with the fact that Mama would be making my clothes. Her sewing machine had to serve as my department store. Too bad I didn't have enough sense then to realize I wasn't missing out on anything.

My ensemble was so beautiful! Mama could work magic on that sewing machine of hers. She made me a jacket to go with my blue skirt, something the other girls didn't have. She had arranged for a neighbor to do my hair if for some reason she couldn't, even had my shoes and stockings waiting for me to wear. Sure enough, my mother was in the hospital because the baby arrived the day before my graduation. I often remind my sister that she was the cause of Mama missing my day.

I fell in love with Wanda Diane, a beautiful happy little baby who I claimed as my own. I wasn't the only one. My mother's sister, Emma, wanted Diane and became upset when Mama wouldn't give her up. I didn't understand my aunt and the odd persistent manner in which she attempted to get her hands on Wanda Diane. My mother had to keep telling her sister NO! Years later Aunt Emma developed colon cancer. She had gotten extremely ill and needed some support. It baffled me when Mama didn't respond in her usual *when-somebody-needed-help* manner.

"Mama this is your sister, why are you acting like this?" I asked. Then told her, "She needs our help!"

She eventually explained the fall-out between the two of them. It was the first time my mother opened up, especially to me, about anything. I wasn't used to that. The more she shared the more shocking it was. My mother's past feelings of anger, hurt and disappointment came pouring out. It's amazing how confused one can be when you don't have all the facts. I learned that my Aunt Emma had slept with Mr. Thomas Hill and had done so on several occasions while Mama was pregnant with his children. My mother went on to tell me how Emma had confronted her declaring Hill had but one love and it wasn't Mama... it was her. My aunt was barren. She wanted the next best thing, to take Hill's baby girl away from her sister. In her opinion, Mama didn't deserve to keep having children that she couldn't properly support. My mother's suffering was palpable, clearly visible on her face, in her voice, and in her sad eyes. My heart went out to her. I felt her pain. Something inside kept imploring me to reach out and embrace her in a way I had always longed to do but I couldn't. Instead, I thought about the Christmas Emma presented Mama with a can filled with bacon grease. At the time I wondered why she thought that was an appropriate present to give to anyone let alone her sister, my mother. Given what Mama had shared, I realized it was a **nice-nasty** gift, Emma's way of keeping the hostility going between the two of them. Anyway, I persuaded Mama to consider the love that she still had for her sister, and together we helped to take care of Emma over the next five years until her death.

Mr. Hill was back, *(and forth)* and my mother's last child was born in 1956. Together she and I named him Keith Dornell. My baby brother is only 13 months older than my firstborn, so he spent more time at my house than at home. He and Wanda Diane did have an opportunity to meet two of Mr. Hill's other children at his funeral. They've lost contact since but would like very much to see them again.

My father was George F. West of Natchez, Mississippi. My sister Deborah's father was Berry Baker of Vicksburg, Mississippi. And Thomas Hill of St. Louis, Missouri, was Berdell, Wanda, and Keith's father. I list and repeat their names because I'm sure there are relatives out there that we don't know but wish we did. It'd be nice to know if one of them was reading this book.

She Gave It Her All

It's not an indictment against her given my own indiscretions but my mother set the stage for many of her struggles. However, she maintained we were a blessing and that she didn't know what she would've done without us. She paid the price daily working day and night sometimes just to take care of us. Mama had the five of us and no husband and faced all kinds of ridicule because of it.

One day she was chatting with a couple of our neighbors just outside of our apartment when I overheard her say, "When my kids go to college..."

Before Mama could finish her statement, she was immediately interrupted by laughter as one of them exclaimed, "Your kids ain't gonna ever go to college."

I'm not sure how long they had been talking, but I do remember my mother didn't say another word after hearing the neighbor's predictions about her children. As the oldest, I saw firsthand the mockery my mother faced and how painful it was for her. Thank goodness my siblings were too young and didn't know how all of us were regarded.

To see us nobody would've guessed that we had so little. Even though we didn't have much, we did have a mother who made sure her children were spotless and well-kept all the time. She would take an old torn-up garment and craft beautiful dresses for the girls. With that same material, she'd make smart-looking shirts and pants for the boys. Mama starched and ironed everything that we wore and even made our underwear. My favorite outfit from my early teens was a two-piece green corduroy suit. Mama only had enough fabric to make the skirt and the back of the jacket. To finish the front, she gathered up all the different colored corduroy scraps she could find. I loved it! The details and patchwork design were nothing short of amazing. Not long after, garments like my mother's handiwork appeared in the clothing section of the Sunday paper. We used to tease my mother about the fact that, out of necessity, she was a trendsetter.

My mother enjoyed cooking, sharing whatever she had with the neighbors. One of our favorite meals was hot biscuits, fried smoked jowl, and syrup. The syrup always had a little of the grease from the jowl poured into it. We were as happy as pigs in mud devouring that meal and so were the neighbors.

Some would even come back asking, "Lula you got any more of those biscuits?"

If she did, she gave graciously.

Mama could cook everything except for baking cookies. They'd be so hard the kids would use them as flying saucers. Funny, but I don't remember any of the neighbors asking for cookies. Every time a neighbor needed something we would hear someone call out, "Lula, are you home?"

And of course, she would be, ready and willing to lend a listening ear or share a portion of her home-cooked meal. She was popular that way.

Mama also washed and ironed for people. I figured her specialty must have been white shirts because there were endless numbers of them hung with clothespins on a rope that stretched across the porch, each one blowing in the wind outside our door. And we knew not to touch them for fear we'd get yelled at or suffer something far worse. You could smell the fresh fragrance of shirts dried by the sun and mother nature's cool breeze. The scent was second only to that of my mother's cooking. Some of her customers took advantage of Mama's generosity. They would come to collect their laundry and promise to pay next time. Those good-for-nothing swindlers! She needed to buy groceries to feed her family. That weighed heavily on me as a teen watching my mother struggle all the time. Once I even caught the bus, went to a customer's house, and demanded my mother's pay. I didn't have a backup plan in case things went south but lucky for him *(and for me)* I didn't need one.

He shelled out the cash for services rendered then said, "Now be on your way."

I made it back home unscathed and proudly gave my mother her money.

When I turned 14 a neighbor asked Mama if I could go to work with her. She worked for a wealthy family as their housekeeper and cook. She wanted help with all the chores that needed to get done and thought some pay would be a help to my mother. I was already babysitting and running errands for people to make a little money so this seemed reasonable to both of us. Per my neighbor's instructions, I had to catch the streetcar, get off at a designated spot, then look for a tall concrete wall at the back of these beautiful mansions. I didn't even know the street I was on. I was to go through the opening in that wall and walk up to the back door of the second house on the left. And never, ever use the front door.

I dusted, changed beds, and cleaned the bathrooms, and even cooked the 98 cents a pound ground round for their dog just so I could hide his medicine in that expensive meat. This was in 1954 and I mention this detail only because my family was eating 39 cents a pound hamburger meat and happy to get it. Lucky dog! I even discovered real butter while working for this family. Everything they ate got cooked in butter, even the chicken was fried in it. At home, we had to mix white stuff (think it was lard) with yellow stuff (flavoring or food coloring) which turned all that stuff into a golden butter substitute called oleo. That's what we used.

The most difficult part of my job was serving the meals at dinner time. I had to actually hold the serving dish while serving each person. I thought, *Am I supposed to serve on the right side or the left side? How much is too much? What if they don't want it? What if I don't do it right and they fire me?*

My head used to spin from all the fears and worries racing through my mind. Even my hands betrayed me, trembling uncontrollably to the point it would almost make me cry.

This family had a daughter close to my age who was a bit overweight. They had tried all kinds of methods to help her lose weight, but nothing had worked. She seemed so lonely, sitting for hours alone dangling her feet in the pool. My neighbor told me the daughter had no friends, at least none she could ever recall seeing. The girl was always by herself and my neighbor insisted I keep it that way. Although I was 14, had some idea about how the world worked and was well aware of the racism that existed, I still couldn't understand why I wasn't allowed to go out and spend time with her. So what if I was black and she was not, or that I was poor and she was not. I was willing to be her friend and in my opinion, that should've been more important to everyone. I could have done both dusting & changing and be her friend. The two of us never even spoke to each other the entire year that I worked there.

There was something more distressing that happened to me when I was 14. Having to go work in some big ole mansion for rich white folks didn't compare to this. There was some sort of existing problem within the St. Louis Public School System. Parents received letters requesting copies of birth certificates for all their students. My mother put mine in an envelope to take with me to school. I remember I was sitting on a concrete slab in the schoolyard waiting for the bell to ring when I decided to open the envelope. I was being nosey and wanted to see what it looked like because I had never seen it before. For fourteen years my name had been Geraldine Maxine Sullivan West. Much to my surprise, or should I say horror, my birth certificate read, Geraldine Jackson.

Who?

Seems in 1939, if you weren't married, the child carried the last name of the mother. Sadly, no one told me. My mother **did not** tell me! I became the talk of the school and for a long time after, all I heard was, "Geraldine doesn't even know her name." Instead of talking to my mother about it, I just blocked it out completely. I shouldn't have had to ask; my mother should have told me.

At 16, I worked in a convenience store after school and all day Saturdays and Sundays. I say all day because the man in charge would frequently disappear, so I would have to work past the time I was supposed to get off. His name was Virgil, but it was his wife who owned the store. For my $20.00 per week, I stocked the shelves, serviced the deli counter, worked the cash register, and swept the floor. Most of the time I was the only one in the store which meant tending to everything else that needed doing as well. Late Saturday nights a truck would pull up to the back of the store. The driver would unload items stolen from the local Kroeger a few blocks away. At first, I was clueless about what was going on until one night, while I was sweeping up, I recognized the guys from the Kroger store. Then I looked out and saw the Kroger truck. No wonder Virgil was doing this late at night after the Kroger store had closed. He was buying stolen goods and I was sure his wife didn't know what he was doing. She would come by regularly during the day just to check the receipts. She had no idea what was really going on at night.

That's not all Virgil was doing that wasn't on the up and up. When payday rolled around, most times he would claim he didn't have enough money, that I would have to wait to get paid. That wait would normally spill over into the next week. Like clockwork, he would want to delay paying me again and again until I would be missing several weeks of wages. Why he thought I should believe he didn't have the $20.00 to pay me was ridiculous. I had been the one on the cash register taking in money all day, selling all that stolen stuff from Kroger's at prices higher than Kroger's. This buster even had me lying to my mother. How does a teenager tell her mother that she didn't get paid today? Every time I came home with an excuse, I also had to plead with my mother not to talk to him. Mama was already annoyed at Virgil and I can't say I blame her. Although I had set hours to work, I'd have to stay well past that time because Virgil wasn't there to relieve me. That meant getting home later than my mother expected. She didn't want her child working alone in someone else's store especially late into the evening nor did she want me out walking home alone at night. This was happening more often than not, and she was not happy about it. I assured her I would handle the situation and I meant that.

Patience is truly a virtue. There was one more thing Virgil was doing that his wife didn't know about. He had a girlfriend who did her shopping at the store. He would always tell me that he would ring her out on the days of her visits. After that happened several times my curiosity got the better of me, so I watched what he was doing. He put the cash register on *Add* to check her out. When you used the *Add* feature, entries didn't show up as a grocery tally. That meant whenever Virgil's wife checked the register receipts, his girlfriend's items wouldn't appear.

"Ohhhh... okay!"

From that day on, I never missed a payday. I too used that *Add* switch and started getting paid on time... every time. And whenever Virgil did decide to pay me... that was extra! That Christmas my mother's children got whatever they had asked from Santa. Funny but my mother thought Virgil had come to his senses.

To my knowledge, my mother's brothers and sisters never offered to help her. As a child and throughout my teen years I wondered, *why not*? Out of ten living siblings, not one of them was willing to help her and many of them had the resources and finances to do so. What I found out was that they looked down their noses at Mama the same way our neighbors did. She had us and never even had one husband. One brother had done everything immoral under the sun, *a male expectation* is how he described his sins. But Mama's transgressions, according to him, were abominations against God and mankind. I wrestled with that mindset for years. The truth is, they felt no obligation or allegiance to my mother, and it's as simple as that. They looked down on her and she felt it and, as her child, I felt it too. Shame on all of them.

Mama being the great seamstress she was, I came up with this fabulous idea of putting on a fashion show at our annual family reunion. This I thought, would be the perfect opportunity for Mama to make all the clothes for the relatives to model. None of her family knew how truly skilled and gifted she was but they would soon find out. The show was a hit. The overwhelmingly positive reviews made my heart glad and my mother a star. From that moment on she became the special feature of the family reunion. Plus, witnessing her skills and abilities, they saw how and why she was able to care for the five of us all on her own.

With Much Gratitude–It's Never Too Late to Say Thank You!

One day my mother got a notice that the building where she lived, at 4319 St. Louis Ave., was scheduled to be torn down. She immediately began looking for places she could afford. Unfortunately, what she found was a second-floor apartment that was in very poor condition. My husband and I went to look at it and found my mother there attempting to secure one of the windows that was about to fall out of the frame. To me, this was my husband's proudest moment. He said, "Oh no you can't stay here, I will find you a suitable place." Then insisted that she leave with us.

Senola was one of our church members who worked for a branch of the Human Development Corporation managing the housing for low-income clients. Melvin asked for her help in securing a place for his mother-in-law. She told him one of their apartment buildings was being renovated and that she would make sure Mama's name appeared on the designated list. One month later, my mother moved into her newly renovated apartment.

A Letter of Appreciation

April 11, 2016

Hi Senola,

Thanks to you, my mother spent her last days in a place that she loved. With tears in her eyes, her words were "I never thought I would ever live in a place like this." What was so special about a one-bedroom apartment? She had never lived in a place where everything was new, not shared with anyone else, her home, a place of which she was proud and for which she was thankful. You would understand it better if you knew the kind of places we had lived. By no means is this a pity party, I just want you to know what a blessing it was for both of us. The blessing for me was that she was happy and happier than she had ever been.

My mother was raised on a farm in Fayette Mississippi with 11 other siblings – two boys and a total of ten girls. The boys went to the army and the girls stayed home plowing the fields and doing everything a farm required. As she got older she was loaned out to a family to keep house and care for an elderly person. That's what many families did to stay afloat.

Pregnant with me, she was sent to St. Louis to stay with an aunt and her family in a very small house on Maffitt. Family members lived on top of other family members. My mother became ill when I was two, much too young to know what was ailing her, but we moved back to Mississippi so that my grandmother could take care of us.

She returned to St. Louis 8 years later and we stayed with a different aunt and uncle in a small 3 room apartment. My uncle was a tyrant and we soon found a space (not a place) but a space in a basement entranceway, right in front of the door. In the front part of the basement was a room where a family of five lived. Across from our bed in what used to be the coal bin, was a small bedroom and a man who drank all the time and came in all hours of the night stumbling and falling.

That's when I began to feel sad for what my mother had to endure. Whenever he would open the door, leaves would blow in on us, or rain or snow based on the time of year. Our bed was directly in the entrance which meant he had to pass right by us to get into the coal bin, his room. We all shared the bathroom and kitchen. My mother had to clean the bath or kitchen each time before we could use it. Since our space was out in the open, everyone had to pass us to go to the bathroom or kitchen or exit the basement. I was only 10 but I understood her need for privacy.

When she saved enough money we moved into a two-room apartment with only a toilet and a small face bowl. A tin tub was our bathtub. I didn't mind because everyone else in the building used a tin tub. I knew she wanted more, but everything she had was spent on me or anyone else who needed her help.

When news came that the building would be torn down, Mama had to find a place to live. By that time she was on disability because of blood pressure and other stressors from taking care of my brain-damaged brother and she had very little money. When my husband saw the place that had accepted my mother's apartment application, he said, "absolutely not!" That's when Melvin asked for your help.

I think often about the joy she had in having her own secure place. She finally had a bathroom with a bathtub where she could spend as much time bathing as she wanted, a kitchen where everything worked, and floors that were fully carpeted (she had never had carpet). In fact, in the house where she was raised, you could see the ground through the floorboards.

This is not a sad story but a happy one. My mother was happy and grateful. I was relieved and grateful. So, thank you again, and may God Bless you for helping her have the experience she never dreamed possible.

Geraldine Smotherson

Chapter Two
Smouthermon to Smotherson

My husband was always afraid that I would share too much about our personal life. I would then and I will now. Hence, this book. There are two things that he did ask that I not tell anyone – not a counselor, psychiatrist, or best friend. Only two things? Wow! He should have thought long and hard about that one. I have and will continue to honor his wishes. Now, let me tell you about the 101 other things I can disclose.

Melvin was born November 6, 1936, in Hattiesburg Mississippi. His parents Estelle Clark and Melvin Smouthermon were never married. Because he bore his father's first name only, Melvin was not given the title of Junior.

My husband lived with his mother and four other siblings, Annie Lee *(Ann)*, Marvin, Roosevelt *(Bobby)*, and Catherine *(Cat)*. Estelle worked at a school cafeteria which kept her away from home for long periods and after Ann left home, it was Marvin's responsibility to tend to the other children in their mother's absence. To feed his younger siblings, Marvin used to bake sweet potatoes in a black iron kettle over the fireplace. One day, he removed the kettle from the fire and sat it directly on the wooden floor. The heat from that hot iron burned a hole straight through the floorboard revealing the ground underneath. Thankfully, no other harm came to the rest of the house or the children.

The elder Smouthermon was a ladies' man. He fathered Melvin's older sister, Mattie Mae, with another woman. It is unknown if they ever married. Smouthermon *(and his daughter, Mattie)* lived with **his** mother, Elijah Cooper, and her husband, Frank Cooper, at 816 Dabbs Street in Hattiesburg. Grandma Elijah was a licensed hairdresser and Frank was a local and successful boot-legger. Melvin's family always had money, mostly from the boot-legging trade and anything he needed he knew he could get from his father's side of the family. It tickled Grandma and Mr. Cooper whenever the revenuers would raid their home. They'd come looking for moonshine, only to come up empty-handed because Frank would bury the hooch at night in the graveyard across from where they lived. There might very well be some whiskey buried there to this day.

As a little boy, my husband spent much of his time at his Grandma Elijah's often walking there unaccompanied. Estelle's house was only a short distance away and Melvin knew the route between his mom's house and his Grandma Elijah's house like the back of his little hand. Grandma and Mattie used to tell the story of how this little four-year-old boy would show up out of nowhere then without hesitation announce, "I'm hungry," upon his arrival. It wasn't unusual to see kids his age trotting up and down the streets alone in 1940 because everyone knew everybody else in the neighborhood. It was common practice and common courtesy to look out for one another, especially in those tight-knit black communities in the south.

In 1942, when Melvin was six years old, Estelle uprooted her family and moved to St. Louis, Missouri. It was Melvin's maternal grandmother, Roberta *(Mama Bert)*, who enrolled him into public school. After which his last name changed from Smouthermon to Smotherson, but no one knows for certain just how that happened.

In high school, Melvin participated in all types of sports. He was a skilled and exceptional athlete... excelling in baseball, football, swimming, and diving. Me, I hid behind books, something I could control. Melvin on-the-other-hand was extremely comfortable in the limelight. He had always worked and dressed as sharp as they came. He wore gorgeous expensive jerseys, and his Stacy Adams shoes, he kept them shining all the time. The boy looked good, and he knew it.

As a young man, Melvin was also active in the church. He was president of both the Junior Usher Board and the Youth & Young Adult Choir. Besides sports and religious affiliations, his other interest was girls. A pattern that continued after we got married.

How I Met My Husband

I met Melvin Smotherson while attending Charles Sumner High School. Sumner was one of only two segregated public high schools for black students in the city of St. Louis. The other was Vashon High School but Sumner was built first.

Melvin's best friend, Lloyd, and I were in the same math class and one day Lloyd said he wanted me to meet his best friend. He didn't say why, nor did he tell me that his friend was very much involved with someone else. At the end of the school day, Lloyd and I walked toward the gym. There standing in the doorway was this incredibly muscular black man in his gym shorts. Most striking about this dark-chocolate handsome creature were his white glistening teeth that lit up his entire face when he smiled. That smile was a ray of sunshine that fully captured my attention. Lloyd introduced us and said he thought the two of us should get to know each other. Why he thought so is still a mystery to me.

Melvin was a graduating senior and even though he would soon be leaving Sumner, he made the most of his remaining time left, often visiting me in my study room. This was the 1950's and it wasn't commonplace for students to roam the halls or bounce from one classroom to another without justification. Popular football players, however, could do whatever they wanted, with no interference from the teachers. So, instead of studying, I spent my time talking to one of the school's most popular football stars. Someone I liked very much.

It was sometime later before I learned Melvin had become a teenaged father and husband between his junior and senior year, but I didn't find *that* out until after he had graduated. It would be the summer of the following year before I saw him again. One evening, friends and I walked to Cupples School for a dance but unbeknownst to us it had gotten canceled. As we were leaving, I heard a familiar voice off in the distance calling my name. Much to my surprise, it was Melvin. He had just gotten off work and thought he would check out the happenings at the school dance. I was so excited to see him again that my head and heart were in the clouds. Melvin offered to walk me home, I offered no resistance.

As we made our way to 4319 Saint Louis Avenue I asked, "Why didn't you tell me you were married when you visited my study room?"

"That doesn't matter now because I am no longer with my wife."

"Why not?"

"It just didn't work out."

"Hmmm," I murmured.

Melvin and his wife were separated, and he was back living with his mother but still married. When we reached our destination, he asked if he could see me again the next day. I said yes, went inside, and closed the door.

Mama Meeting Melvin

The next evening when he got off work, Melvin came over around eight just as we had planned. Since our apartment was so small, the two of us sat just outside of my mother's door. There were no porch lights, which made it difficult to see but it did create a cozy even naughty setting. One where two lovers could enjoy each other's company in a touchy-feely sort of way. I eagerly summoned my mother at the start of our visit so she could meet my new boyfriend and then go back inside before the necking started. When she came to the door I said, "Mama this is Melvin!"

"Melvin?" she asked. Then said, "I can't see him in the dark."

I gasped and immediately started laughing. Melvin wasn't sure what to say or do. My mother had implied that he was so dark-skinned he couldn't be seen in the darkness. At least that's how I saw it. I knew she meant no harm but, once she caught on to why I was laughing she still chose not to be more careful with her words, proclaiming yet again, "Well I can't, I can't see him in the dark."

At that point, we all laughed. It's a good thing Melvin wasn't sensitive about his color and didn't think she was making fun of his dark complexion. Because she really wasn't. I had a problem seeing him in the darkness too but was so happy he was there. With his dark self.

The two-room apartments in the building where I lived were very close together. To keep their units cool, neighbors would leave both their windows and doors open. There was no such thing as central air in those days, not for poor folks like us anyway. During our courtship, Melvin and I would often sit on the porch where it was easy to be overheard or seen but we were always too distracted to even notice or care. I was willing to do everything Melvin wanted me to do and more. After all, I thought that was love.

Noticing how crazy I was about him, a neighbor asked me into her apartment so that she could talk to me. I suspect it was because of how giddy I acted whenever he was around, or she overheard something inappropriate that we may have said. Mrs. Womack was her name. She was always trying to explain how love worked – that no two people loved the same way. Whenever the opportunity presented itself, she'd offer up an example or two for the sake of clarification. This time it was, "He may love you, but it may not be the same as how you feel about him." I was so upset with her. She was talking about *my man* and against our relationship. In my mind, he had to be feeling everything that I was feeling. As far as I was concerned Mrs. Womack didn't know what she was talking about. Not when it came to me and Melvin. She was no authority on how our love worked! Over time and with a bit of reluctance I came to understand what she was attempting to teach me.

The Inevitable

Before I started seeing Melvin, I had done some petting but not had sex. My ex-boyfriend, Burgess, and I had planned to have sex one day when his parents weren't home. Right after he put on a condom they came home and caught us, then proceeded to give us a lecture on what we should and should not be doing. I was so embarrassed.

Melvin had a wife and had had several sexual encounters. And like all his other conquests, having sex with me was now his top priority. One time he took me to a motel which turned out to be a house that rented out every inch of its space. We ended up in a closet that had a twin rollaway cot and no space at all to walk around. It was set-up for one thing and one thing only... to get our five minutes of hanky-panky on and get ourselves out of there and make room for the next hot-&-bothered-unprotected-sex-having-sneaking-around-doing-God-knows-what-still-living-at-home teenaged couple waiting their turn. I don't know how much Melvin paid for that experience, but he seemed pretty comfortable in that closet. Even happy. I was happy for him. Condoms? No, we never used condoms because *my man* didn't like them. I guess I knew where babies came from, but I did absolutely nothing to avoid getting pregnant. How stupid can one be?

September 1956 came, and I was back at school. The halls were buzzing with the sounds of students greeting each other, lockers slamming shut, and hurried footsteps. Everyone's movements were swift and deliberate trying to get to our first class on time. Out of all the hellos, hugs, smiles, and welcome backs I'd received there was only one greeting that resonated with me. Or should I say, *warning!*

Mr. Hudlin, one of the teachers, stopped me in the hall and said, "I heard that you're going with that Smotherson boy. Not good. You're going to be pregnant before the semester is over."

And that I was, six weeks later.

At the beginning of the school year, I became president of the junior class. It was my turn to stand at the podium in the school auditorium before teachers and students and make speeches, negotiate change, and create opportunities for the class of 1958. My graduating class. Filled with a combination of apprehension, pride, and excitement, I settled into my new role.

I was busy balancing my position as a class leader while still working at the convenience store. On top of that, I had homework to do while trying to see Melvin as much as I could. By mid-October, I reflected on Mr. Hudlin and what he said to me on my first day of school. "You will be pregnant before the semester is over." Because I was! More than just pregnant, I was afraid, ashamed, and completely lost about what to do next. I knew I wasn't setting the right example for my classmates. I had no right to handle the gavel at our meetings or even speak on behalf of the student body. I felt like a fraud.

Melvin was the only one I could talk to about it even though he seemed more lost and upset than I was, offering no solutions or directions. All I kept thinking was, *How am I going to tell my mother?* I knew this would hurt her. It's possible she already knew but was waiting for me to say something. Maybe she had no idea because I was in and out of the house a lot then. Was she too busy to notice the change in me? I just wanted to vanish off the face of the earth.

When I started to show, I would look at people to see if they were looking at me differently, wondering if they noticed my body expanding. It was my loneliest time. I had no one to talk to – not Mr. Hudlin, not a classmate, not even my mother. Focusing on schoolwork was extremely difficult but what was more worrisome was knowing that soon and very soon I would have to leave school for good. I couldn't figure out what I was going to do about my education, didn't even know if an actual marriage was a possibility. I was staring at a concrete wall not knowing how to get around it, over or under it. I kept thinking, *How am I going to get to the other side of this dilemma?*

It's January 1957. The pregnant me is sitting in the classroom trying to concentrate when out of nowhere my button popped off my skirt and landed on the floor on the other side of the room. I held my head down pretending nothing had happened but knew it was time to go home and talk to my mother. The news of my pregnancy, my idiocy, did indeed break Mama's heart. The very last thing she wanted for me was to live the life that she had... full of struggle, disappointment, heartbreak, and despair. Yet it was manifesting itself right before her very eyes. I was following in her footsteps, forever altering the path that she had wanted me to follow. I'd done exactly what she had feared and what the neighbors had predicted. I was pregnant and without a husband. My mother had envisioned her oldest child going to college. She even proclaimed it when those around her mocked her words. How do you piece together your mother's broken heart after you've shattered it? How could I be so accomplished in academics, gifted in so many other aspects but so ignorant about life? I knew that my mother wanted better for me. Even though she and I never talked about it, I knew it all the same.

Mama caught the bus and went to talk to Melvin's mother, Estelle. I'm sure Estelle was curious as to what it was that my mother thought she was supposed to do. Her son was a grown man and already married. She acknowledged that he was getting a divorce sometime soon and also confirmed that he had returned to her house. Beyond that, she had no answers.

I felt bad for Melvin because he had just gotten out of a similar situation and now here he was again. I was so devoted to this man that I loaded his regret onto my already worn-out mental shoulders never holding him to account. I was so worried about his feelings I never allowed myself to acknowledge my own shame and fear. What was I thinking? He should have learned from his previous relationship and taken care of himself. But I should have learned, too. My mother's blueprint was there for **ME** to see, so why didn't I love **ME** enough to make sure history didn't repeat itself?

Melvin and I talked about getting married after his divorce became final. When that day came, he said we had to wait because he needed a car. Time was passing fast; my stomach was growing and so was my anxiety. Even my mother's heart seemed to be breaking more and more. Near the end of my eighth month, my ex-boyfriend, Burgess, came over to the apartment. That was on Thursday, June 20, 1957.

Burgess and his family lived about 10 blocks away from us. I used to walk there around dinner time and stand across the street watching them. Through the window, you could see everyone seated around their dining room table – a father, mother, son, daughter, and grandmother. They seemed like the perfect family. I admired and envied them for having what I did not.

Burgess wanted to know if I was going to get married. Of course, I hoped that Melvin and I would, but I couldn't offer a solid answer. So, this gallant young man asked for my hand in marriage. He said that he still loved me and that his parents supported him in his decision. I had never felt more special than at that very moment. He and his family loved me and would accept me, and my baby. I thought *So that's what love is!* I thanked Burgess for his gracious offer but told him it wouldn't be fair to him, and his family. I found great comfort in knowing that they all cared but I just couldn't do that to them. His proposal is the only one I ever got.

That night Melvin came over and I told him about Burgess's offer and how special it was to have someone ask for my hand. Then I told him I hadn't accepted. Early Saturday morning my baby's daddy came knocking. "Get dressed we have someplace to go," he insisted. That someplace was the East St. Louis Illinois' City Hall where we got married June 22, 1957.

My precious baby boy, and bundle of joy, was born three weeks later on July 13, 1957. His name was going to be Dwayne until I began watching the movie **Bwana Devils** on television one night. I loved the sound of the *B* and the *w* together in the word, *Bwaa-Nah*. So instead of Dwayne, I decided to name my son Bwayne. I gave birth at Homer G. Phillips, a Black hospital that trained doctors from all over the country and abroad. Bwayne was a healthy filled-out newborn weighing 7 pounds and 13 ounces. His skin, soft and smooth, had a beautiful brown glow. I fell in love with him instantly.

This was my first stay in a hospital, everything was new to me. The maternity wards at that time were full of as many as twenty to thirty mothers in each ward. It was impressive seeing so many Black nurses, each one decked out in her freshly-starched white uniform, white stockings, and white cap. My outfit consisted of a white hospital gown with a matching wristband. When I looked at it I expected to see my name. Instead, I saw the name of my husband's first wife, Gracie Smotherson. That was my first little heartbreak. After appearing to be very confused by it all one of the nurses did change my band. Gracie had had her second baby 30 days before me in the same hospital. She had not yet married the child's father and was still using the name Smotherson. I was glad that Gracie and I were not in the hospital at the same time as we may have ended up with the wrong baby.

Visiting hours were exciting times for us new mommies. I was in the seventh bed from the entrance on one side of the room. It was a great spot to be in because I could see people coming and going. At the same time, I'd be trying to figure out which father belonged to which mother. We would all watch the door from time to time hoping to see our mates who would trickle in one by one throughout the day. While the couples would be talking or sharing hugs and kisses, I'd still be waiting. Ten minutes before time was up Melvin would casually stroll into the ward. I'd be so disappointed yet happy at the same time. Again I made an excuse for him, telling myself this new-baby-thing just wasn't as exciting for him as it was for me.

I continued to focus on the other new mothers in the ward so that I wouldn't have to think about how let-down I felt. One of them appeared to have had a stroke and the right side of her face looked like she may have suffered some paralysis. I wondered how she'd even had her baby.

There was one man who was always the first to arrive at the start of visiting hours. He was very handsome which is what caught everyone's attention from the very start. On his initial visit, our gazes were in sync with his every step as he made his way through the ward. We wanted so badly to see who the lucky wife was that he was there to see. To everyone's surprise, this gorgeous hunk of a man stopped at the bed of the woman who had suffered the stroke. He took her in his arms as he sat on the side of her bed and kissed her ever so gently. Not for a second did he leave her side from the time he got there until visiting hours were over. I learned one of my greatest lessons. True *Love bears all things, believes all things, hopes all things, endures all things.*

Giving birth was new to me but taking care of a baby was not. Helping to care for my mother's 13-month-old gave me plenty of practice with diapers, bathing, and feeding a child. And yet, this was different. I was now responsible for this baby and the thought of it could be unnerving at times. Bwayne was a happy baby which made my job easier especially at feeding time. He liked everything. There were also certain shows or commercials on television he found absolutely fascinating. One was the Speedy Alka Seltzer commercial. When it came on, if he were sleeping, Bwayne would wake up, pull himself up in his crib, and dance with Speedy. Afterward, he'd lay back down and go right back to sleep no matter what time of day or night.

Mama loved my baby so much and I was worried that it might create some jealousy in my brother Keith who was only a year older. Bwayne was her first grandchild, and everyone in the apartment complex had to see and hear all about him. She made special outfits for him and showed me how to polish his white shoes, making sure to carefully polish the brown soles around the shoe with just the right shade of brown. Everything had to be perfect for *her* grandson. Of course, she did the same for Keith and I knew that. My mother made sure her son never had to take a back seat to anyone, my child included. Reminding myself of that fact removed any concerns I had. My baby brother's well-being was secure.

Playing House

In 1957 new mothers stayed in the hospital for seven days. While I was recovering, Mama and my great Aunt Delo *(pronounced Dee-Low)* were busy setting up the house for us. A two-room apartment on Labadie Avenue had become available right next door to my great Uncle Charlie. He managed the building so the three of us were able to move into it right away. Somehow they had provided all the furnishings we needed, including a bassinet for our baby boy. My mother's exquisite touch was ever-present throughout our charming little space, particularly in the handmade quilt she laid across our bed. I loved our little abode. I bought myself a cookbook and prepared every casserole in the book – tuna, chicken, beef, pork, cheese, noodle, and then some. I thought I was Betty Crocker!

Finally, my husband said, "Please don't cook another casserole as long as I live."

There I was trying to do something special thinking he was happy with the hot dishes waiting for him when he got home from work. That was over 60 years ago, and I still haven't cooked another casserole.

Chapter Three
Husband, Yes... Provider and Protector, Not Necessarily

I remember how anxious I would become the moment I saw my husband pick up the newspaper, even though I knew he was only going to the bathroom. I couldn't bear the thought of him being away from me for what seemed like an eternity. I was desperate for his attention or any sign of affection. I used to sit and stare at the door, anticipating his reappearance, as if he had vanished. The bathroom, I suppose, was the one place in the house he could go to get away from all my clinginess. Leaving home was the only other alternative. Thinking about it, he did concoct a variety of lame excuses to get out of the house. He even had some young ladies come to our door and pretend their mother needed his help with something. I suspected Melvin had begun cheating on me early on in our marriage and yet there I'd be... waiting... to celebrate his return.

Melvin always bought nice things for himself, so I assumed he would want to provide the same for me and our child. The Sunday Parade, a magazine found inside the local Sunday newspaper, listed community events and apparel. It was common knowledge the clothes were of poor quality and, after one washing, were never the same. There wasn't a nineteen-year-old around back then who would've been caught dead in those clothes, especially if they could help it. And I was certainly one of them. One day, Melvin told me to look in the clothing section of the Sunday Parade and pick out something for myself and Bwayne. I could not believe him! Advertised were these $3.99 house dresses for old ladies, and some $1.99 outfits for children. I thought, *How dare he think I was going to dress myself or my baby in those rags. Heck, even my Mama's homemade clothes were far superior.* I knew then that this man was not going to take care of me and mine.

Baby #2 On the Way

The winter of 1957-58 was a brutal one. January especially, was host to icy rains, below zero temperatures, and lots and lots of snow. My little family and I lived up the alley from my mother. Each morning I would get up early enough to get myself and my baby boy ready, then walk to my mother's so that I could drop him off before heading to the bus stop to catch the city bus. I was starting my senior year at Vashon High School, even though I lived less than five minutes from Sumner where I attended 9th through the 11th grade. In those days, a girl wasn't permitted to return to the same school after becoming pregnant and having a child. How unfortunate.

Being a newlywed and new mother presented its challenges but, like all the others I had faced in my life, I put forth my usual over-achiever's effort. Thinking back, I remember how slick the ground was that particular morning. I was walking down the alley lugging my baby, my books, and whatever else I needed for the day. Out of the blue, I slipped and fell on the ice. Everything I was carrying hit the ground... all that is, except my baby boy, he was fine. I'd held onto him for dear life or that little rascal had enough sense to hold onto to his momma. God was watching over both of us that day.

I was an exceptional student during my short time at Vashon. My grades reflected that of an accomplished individual, someone carving out a bright future for herself. I was on my way, or so I thought. I should have been paying closer attention to how bad

I was feeling; why my clothes weren't fitting the same; why my appetite had picked up; and why my energy was diminishing. Knowing me, I'm sure I tried to attribute it all to being a new wife and mother, even though I could hear that little voice in my head asking, *Could I be pregnant again? If I was, that meant I would have to leave another school with only half a semester left to complete.* Even though my grades warranted it, I was also not permitted to be part of the National Honor Society. God, are you still there?

I was so unfair to Bwayne at times. Being within four months of giving birth I needed him to grow up faster than he was pre-pared to do. I rushed him with walking and potty training. I couldn't accept the fact that I would have two sets of *cloth* diapers to wash. He cooperated with the walking but fought me on the potty training. I would leave him on the pot for what seemed like weeks at a time with nothing happening except tears and more tears. Finally, I learned to make a game of it, applauding every little progress we made. It began to work. Hallelujah!

I guess my son forgave me for the potty training drills because we went back to being best buddies. His face would light up every time I entered the room and that would always make my heart beat faster. When his little sister was born, I had to stay in the hospital for several days. Getting through them without my baby boy was hard. When I returned home with the new baby, Bwayne would have nothing to do with me. I cried like I was the baby and thought, *How could he forget me?* It took a week before I was his mommy again. It took even longer for him to accept that I was also his little sister's mommy.

August 15, 1958, was when his little sister Pamela invaded our world, and I couldn't have been happier. Unlike her big brother, I gave birth to my daughter at St. Louis Maternity Hospital. This was a time of evolution. Progress was being made and laws were being changed. African Americans with health insurance could now be admitted into a particular hospital, one that was a step up from the free clinic although it took more time for hospital staff and incoming patients to accept the change. Those who were staunch racists put up quite a resistance to this change. If it meant sharing a room or caring for folk who didn't look like them, some white people weren't having it.

My bed along with those of others who looked like me was in the basement hallway of the hospital, just one sign of the silent protest of both administration and staff. This arrangement exposed us to the constant glares of everyone who passed through the halls. Whether it was custodians moving furniture or noisy cleaning carts or food service workers wheeling meal trays, they all constantly violated what should have been our right to privacy. At first, I tried to convince myself it was because the hospital was overcrowded but that wasn't the case. The real reason was the noncompliant racists wanted us out of sight, out of mind... out of there!

I was sitting somewhere *(can't recall exactly where or when)* at some gathering and overheard a conversation between a group of ladies a short distance away.

"... and they put me down in the basement, in the hallway against the wall... and there I stayed." One of them shared.

"You're lying that didn't happen." Said another.

I politely interrupted. "She's telling the truth, the same thing happened to me in August of 1958."

A Guardian Angel For My Baby Girl

Mama knew all of her neighbors quite well. Some might argue that one, in particular, was more like family. My mother and Katie weren't just good neighbors, they had become close and trusted friends. Katie lived directly next door to my mother and was my daughter's godmother. Somewhat of a loner, she was a very generous and kind woman who would drink occasionally but only at home. Katie went out and bought a new washing machine and gave it to my mother just because Mama did her laundry. My mother even had a key to her friend's apartment.

Katie always looked forward to playing with my daughter. Pam seemed to fill a major void in her life. She bought her lots of toys and little girl dresses. She even stored hundreds of silver dollar coins in a trunk that she was saving for her godchild's future. Along with other important items in that same trunk, Katie kept a hand-written letter of intent. It stated Pamela should have everything upon her death. Because she had no living relatives, her insurance policy was made out to me to take care of her burial with the remainder going to my daughter.

One day Mama noticed that Katie had not yet emerged from her apartment as she usually did by mid-morning. A bit concerned, Mama went next door and knocked but got no answer, so she went back home. She thought Katie maybe wanted to sleep in a little while longer which did happen on occasion after a night of heavy drinking. When she failed to appear a short while later, my mother took the key Katie had given her and let herself into the apartment, my sister Debbie following close behind. There they found Katie dead. Debbie began screaming out of control. It must have been a frightening sight for someone so young. Mama immediately called the police.

When they arrived two officers quickly surveyed the scene, then told us that everything would have to go to probate after they took some items. We were instructed to notify them of the arrangements and to not enter the apartment again until everything was settled. They locked the door and left. We had no way of knowing their ill intent and honored their directives. In those days black folk were a bit intimidated and blinded by our trust in law enforcement. We proceeded to make final arrangements and, as ordered, let the police know when the funeral would be. The day that we returned from the burial we noticed a truck pulling away from our building. It didn't set off any alarm bells at the time because people were always moving in and out and around the neighborhood. That all changed when we got to the top of the stairs outside of Katie's apartment. Why was her door standing wide open? What happened to all her stuff? We couldn't believe it! The apartment was bare. The only item that remained was a single white shoe laying on the floor of my daughter's godmother's apartment. They took everything, even the curtains. I called the police precinct to find out what was going on. None of the officers could or would give us any answers.

I asked about the coins Katie had been saving and the note she'd left for my baby girl.

"Where is the trunk?" I insisted.

According to the police, neither trunk nor coins were found in the apartment, but I knew that was a lie! We had a key and should have removed the coins ourselves instead of trusting law enforcement. Two days later, an officer had the gall to return to the scene-of-their-crime asking my mother if she knew where the washing machine was. He had found a receipt for the brand-new one Katie bought and had given it to my mother. Sensing that something wasn't right, Mama told him that she didn't know and hinted he should inquire with the people who stole the rest of Katie's property. I lost all trust and respect for police officers on that day – an awful experience that took years for me to get past.

The probate court also reported that they had no record of the entire incident. Luckily, they didn't get their hands on Katie's insurance policy because I had that. We were able to give her a proper burial and there was even a little money left over for my daughter. Six-hundred dollars was a nice starter to a savings account for Pamela. However, my husband had other plans. He believed we should use the money to take care of household expenses. Even had the nerve to try and justify his reasoning insisting that our daughter was a part of the household... as if that made her financially accountable... or as if she had a choice in becoming a part of our household.

"So now a three-year-old is expected to contribute to the *house... hold*?" I was in total disagreement with what my husband wanted to do and should've fought harder for what I believed.

Time to Go to Work

I had had two kids and was not working thirteen months into our marriage. We had moved by then. I knew that Melvin wasn't going to be the sole provider of our household, so it came as no surprise when he announced, "Your mother can keep the kids and my sister can get you a job at St. Mary's Hospital."

And that's exactly what she did. The notion of working outside the home wasn't foreign to me because I had been doing so since I was fourteen and knew the time had come to do it again. About a year later, Melvin told me that we had a chance to work at the Post Office. We only needed to fill out the application to take the postal exam. He seemed excited and confident we could make more money there. When the time came he drove us both downtown so that we could take the test. I could feel the butterflies beginning to flutter around inside of my belly as he pulled up to the curb. Like a fool, I assumed this was a courteous gesture on his part allowing me to get out while he found a parking space. But, as I was exiting the vehicle, he said, "I have to make a run, and I'll pick you up after the test." Caught completely off guard, I shut the car door without saying a word. He drove off.

He must be afraid of the test, is what I told myself. Looking back I can see that I was always making excuses for him though, at the time, I didn't realize that's what I was doing. Melvin never explained why he didn't take the test, even after I inquired several times. We never spoke about it again.

This is My Last Baby!

Two years and three months after Pam was born, I was back at St. Louis Maternity Hospital. This time the experience was the complete opposite from before. The staff placed me in an actual hospital room on an upper floor, one that I shared with a young black woman who I still care about today. My roommate and I would walk down to the nursery to see our babies and, as we passed by several rooms, I began to take notice. White patients were boarded with other white patients. The same was true for all the black patients. It didn't bother me that a hint of prejudice still lingered, as I was much more comfortable around my own kind anyway. The hospital had made strides in treating patients of color with a bit more dignity and respect, and that was still encouraging to know.

Darren Keith was born on November 17, 1960, a beautiful baby boy weighing eight pounds, three ounces. He looked almost identical to my room-mate Marilyn's baby girl. One day the nurse handed Darren to her by mistake. In jest Marilyn cried out, "I don't want this big head boy, take him to his mother." The nurse did, then went and brought in her big head girl. We still laugh about the incident almost every time we see each other.

Darren's big hands and his strong healthy look were somewhat deceiving. For some unknown reason, he would be fine one minute and then suddenly develop a high fever which always led to him having a seizure. The emergency room became my second home and, with each visit, I was fearful Darren would die. Every time he got sick I swore I would never have another child. My trips to the hospital with him were so frequent that some of the doctors became concerned I may have been neglecting him. Three of them stood around my son's hospital bed discussing with me my obvious failure as a mother. Their rebuke, however, was met with my constant urging for them to watch my child. As they continued to scold me I continued insisting my baby's fever was uncontrollable, that it would elevate without warning no matter what I did. And then it happened, just as I had warned. Darren had a seizure right in front of them.

"That's what I've been trying to explain to you, his temperature rises fast without warning! Now, do you believe me?" I shrieked.

Shocked by what had occurred, all three immediately got busy. They laid Darren in a bed of ice completely covering him with only his face exposed. Then the apologies came. I could sense the doctors' embarrassment by what had just taken place on their watch. They admitted to having no idea what was happening to my baby but followed that up with the assurance that they would find out which was such a tremendous relief to me. I felt vindicated. That little boy's near-death-episodes served as the most powerful birth control ever. Never would I put me or another child through that kind of trauma again. So, Darren was and will always be my baby, all six feet, three inches, and two hundred and something pounds of him.

Charles

My husband had been someone else's husband before he became my husband. To that union a son was born, a baby boy who I knew without ever laying eyes on him would one day look exactly like his father. When I did finally see him for the first time I wanted him immediately. He was a miniature Melvin and I wanted everything and everybody that belonged to my husband. "*Hmmm*. I take that back... not everybody."

His name is Charles Melvin, a boy child who had the biggest and warmest smile that any three-year-old could have. He seemed to like me, too. Ordinarily, I would never dream of raising another woman's child but this child, my husband's child was not living with his mother. Melvin and I tried to get custody of Charles, but the grandparents blocked our efforts. They swore their daughter and her child were both living with them. That was not true. Although they were good caregivers, Charles was the only one living with them. I'm not placing judgment on Melvin's ex-wife nor do I claim to know why she chose to be away from her child. I don't even know why I thought I could handle another since I already had one and another on the way. All I know is I would have raised and loved him as my own. He's 65 now and, as I predicted, is the spitting image of his father right down to the sound of his voice. And Charles still is and always will be one of my children.

Melvin's Calling

To help with the note and upkeep, we moved into the first-floor space of the two-family duplex owned by Melvin's mother and stepfather Mr. Ernest. They lived above us along with Melvin's grandmother and Mr. Ernest's preteen daughter. As time passed, I began to witness a strange phenomenon, my husband's demeanor was changing. Melvin became more and more restless especially at night and would make constant trips upstairs so that he could talk to his mother. I thought he was feeling guilty for asking me to make such a sacrifice moving in with his mother or for him not following through on his promise that we would both take the postal exam. Yep, I was still a bit salty about that. It was neither. Those long conversations were about the fact that HE WAS BEING CALLED. Estelle wasn't at all surprised by the news, viewing it as a prayer answered. She had always believed that one day the Lord would reign her son in and plant his feet on a more solid foundation.

When he did finally tell me what was going on, I became so excited. The news that God had spoken to him, wanting him to preach, erased any ill feelings I was harboring about being hoodwinked into working at the Post Office. And even though I never saw it coming, that job turned into a blessing. I felt an overwhelming sense of relief now that I understood the shift in Melvin's behavior, no more drinking and no more staying out late. It was good having him home for a change acting as a family man. Melvin's mother may have been overjoyed and immensely proud of her son and his calling, but I was just happy for the stability. Before I knew it, I had gotten so wrapped up in my husband's future that I hadn't given any thought to what my role would be in all of this, the emotional toll it might take on me, the challenges I might have to face, or the obstacles I might have to hurdle being a preacher's wife. I was so naïve.

The church erupted in cheers and applause the Sunday my husband announced his call to the ministry. Melvin delivered a powerful message the Sunday he preached his trial sermon. I remember the day well because there wasn't an empty seat in the entire building. That day we all witnessed a dynamic speaker in the making.

Melvin and I sat down almost daily studying for his ordination, the event which would give him the authority to carry out the duties of a clergyman such as baptisms and marrying folks. When he went before the Ordination Board he was on top of his game, answering every question correctly. And so was I. I could've done a better job in that hot seat, not because I was superior, but because I had studied as hard as he did to get him prepared. Several months later we were still studying together, preparing each one of his sermons. Then one day it all came to a screeching halt. Melvin didn't need nor want my help any longer, informing me he could do it himself. And even though he did it quite well, that dismissal stung, I felt discarded. It dampened my feelings and our relationship going forward.

Family Ties

I was surrounded by my husband's family. At one point both a sister and one of his brothers stayed with us, and it was okay because that's what families do. They also had a first cousin named Reese who was around all the time. Some of you may not have ever heard of Eagle Stamps. I have. They were stamps you received from food or clothing purchases that you would paste in a book. Once the book was full you could use it to buy items. I always saved my books until the end of the year to buy Christmas presents for my children. One December when it was time to go shopping, I opened the drawer and discovered all my books were gone. We found out that Reese had come down the back stairs of the house to the first floor and taken my Eagle Stamp Books. I was so outraged! His selfishness made it impossible for me to do what I had planned all year for my children. My husband should have done something to keep his thieving cousin at bay.

"What in the world is wrong with your relatives? I asked Melvin. Then hinted, "Reese should no longer have permission to enter our house ever again! Someone should knock his block off." Reese's explanation for stealing the books was that they were *only* Eagle Stamps.

"No, you idiot! They were my children's Christmas!"

Melvin was a well-built man with a 28-inch waistline and muscular thighs. He always had to get his suits altered. One afternoon we got a telephone call from Stix Barr & Fuller Department Store. The salesperson said, "Mr. Smotherson I thought I should call you. I remember your 28-inch waistline and the challenges we had in altering your suits. A customer with your credit card has ordered several suits. He's coming by later to get them altered. Is this something you're doing?"

"Absolutely not! What time is his appointment? Thank you, I'll be there." Melvin shouted.

He made it to the store before the man showed up. As he suspected, it was Reese! He had again visited relatives upstairs and, like before, had gone down the back stairwell to our place and stolen our credit card. If you allow family members to get away with wrongdoing and never confront them they will do it again. Reese did it again and again and again. To my dismay, Melvin's cousin wasn't the only family member who hoodwinked us.

My husband's mother died from a brain aneurysm in November of 1960 two weeks before Darren was born. She so looked forward to his arrival. At the time of my mother-in-law's death, Melvin's stepfather was working for an aerospace company. Thank goodness he had a life insurance policy through his employer. Emotions were running high, especially for Melvin because her passing was also around the same time as his birthday. He felt compelled to help his distraught stepfather with funeral arrangements because, after all, that was his mother. He signed the papers to have the mortician handle the body but when it came time to pay the bill, the stepfather refused to pay. The funeral home sued me and Melvin for his mother's funeral expenses. That's exactly what appeared on our credit report *Sued for Mother's Funeral* and it wasn't removed until we finished paying the bill. That painful blemish may have gotten deleted on paper, but it lingered in our hearts for years to come.

Meanwhile, Melvin's oldest sister asked if we would buy their mother's house. Her idea was that her family would move upstairs, and she and her husband would help with upkeep and pay their share of the mortgage. Since we were all struggling, we agreed this would be of great benefit to all of us. Only to their benefit as my husband and I soon learned. Melvin wasn't too alarmed when his relatives could only pay part of their rent or were late paying at other times. It did put a financial strain on us, but we trusted that things would get better. We even gave them lunch money for their kids when they ran short of funds because we were all in this together, right? Then Melvin discovered that they were damaging the upstairs apartment and not making necessary repairs. Even worse, they fell further and further behind in their rent.

It became abundantly clear that we actually **were** the only ones struggling to pay our bills because, the next thing I knew, Melvin's sister and husband had bought a new house! They had planned to move and didn't feel any obligation to pay the back rent they owed us or make repairs to the property they destroyed. I was heartbroken. It wasn't that I didn't want better for them but why did it have to be at our expense? Now we had his mother's funeral bill hanging over us, a damaged house, and no money to make repairs. I felt betrayed and again let down by Melvin and his family. To add to our mounting troubles, his grandmother managed to finagle her way into our home. We even took in his teenage stepsister that I rescued after learning her father (*Mr. Ernest*) had been sexually abusing her since she was eleven. I found that out before Melvin's mother died. After that, I didn't want my deceased mother-in-law's husband anywhere near my daughter who was a baby then.

Fifteen Years of Roberta Clark

From 1960 to 1975 (*fifteen long years*), Mama Bert, my husband's grandmother, lived with us. Mama Bert was healthy, could bend over and lay her palms flat on the floor, had no problems going up and down the stairs, and had her own money coming in monthly. This could've been a great arrangement since I had three children, a full-time job, a husband, and no help. She should've been, but she was not. Mama Bert didn't pay rent, buy groceries, clean house, or cook, at least not for everyone in our house. And she brought with her a great-grandson, Claude, another one of Melvin's sister's child to add to our numbers. She would buy for him but not for my children who were also her great-grandchildren. Whatever she bought, she kept in her room. Claude would sneak things out of her room and give them to his cousins, especially my youngest son. The two of them would be up to all kinds of shenanigans often playing tricks on her, taking the glass stones out of her costume jewelry, and stealing her hard candy. It was my nephew's way of getting back at her because even he knew it was wrong for his great-grandmother to treat him one way and my three another. Claude was a great kid.

At Christmas time I would have to drive Melvin's grandmother to his sister's house because Mama Bert wanted to take her *other* great-grandchildren Christmas shopping. Not him, me! *I'm* driving *Ms. Daisy* over to another able-bodied member of Melvin›s family›s house in *my* car, using up *my* gas, to drop off somebody that is about to do something nice for *somebody else's* children. But they can't come to pick her up from my house so that I can tend to my children. Ain't that something! I wasn't begrudging those kids about anything. I loved them. They were my husband's nieces and nephews. But my kids knew that what Mama Bert was doing for their cousins she would not be doing for them. That's what bothered me, and rightly so. She was living with me! Having to deal with his grandmother's intrusion and flagrant disrespect was exasperating. As much as it infuriated me, it didn't seem to bother Melvin in the least. I wanted him to be the protector of his family and address the issue. I needed him to stand up for his wife. Wait! What am I saying? I should have required him to do so.

I often found myself a prisoner in my own home with Mama Bert there. She was always lurking about, always looking over my shoulder. Whenever I attempted to interact with my children there she was. And she always... always... wanted to go everywhere with me. I'd go to the closet to get my coat; Mama Bert would already have her coat on waiting by the front door. I couldn't even visit my mother or go anywhere else without my tag-a-long. It was so exhausting. To be honest, it made my blood boil. If somehow I made it to my mother's without Mama Bert, my mother would ask, "Where's your shadow?"

Melvin was free to come and go as he pleased without the hassle of a constant companion. The harsh reality was that whether he was there in the house or not, that ball and chain he referred to as his grandmother was a continual restraint around MY life.

One time she got mad at us and went to Melvin's sister Annie Lee's house. Miraculously she found a ride that day. It didn't go so well I'm assuming because the next thing I knew she had checked herself into the hospital. Over the coming days, I received several phone calls from the doctors and nurses each informing me there was nothing wrong with Mama Bert, that she was refusing to leave until Geraldine *(that's me)* came to get her. I let them know immediately that SHE was my husband's grandmother, and that I would give HIM the message. He never did go and get her. Another two days passed and the person on the phone said the same thing except with a little more urgency. "She's not leaving until Geraldine comes to pick her up." My husband then asked me, so I did.

Mama Bert was always doing mean-spirited things like telling church members that I was a nasty cook because I cooked breakfast in my pajamas or gown. Yet she was the first person at the table to eat. Melvin and I decided to put carpeting in the house and asked if she wanted to buy some carpet for her room. She said it wasn't her house and that she wasn't about to shell out money for carpet then lied to church members telling them we carpeted the house but refused to do her room. One day Melvin and I were in our bedroom arguing when we heard a sound outside our door. He snatched the door open and there she was all bent over with her ear to the door.

"You s'posed to listen if you want to know what's going on." She had the nerve to say.

Melvin and his friend Minister AC planned a trip to Los Angeles California to attend The National Baptist Convention, an event they both loved. Mama Bert wanted to go too but didn't have the money to do so, or so she claimed. She hinted to Melvin that she didn't need a hotel room because she could stay with his baby sister Catherine, still implying she had no means. He didn't take the bait, at least not right then. She moped around and moped around and moped some more before finally mustering up enough nerve to ask us to pay for her trip. I was eager to get her out of my hair for a while so we took more money out of the household funds even though we had already sacrificed

49

so much just to get Melvin there AND I never felt guilty about it because that little time without her was worth it!

As soon as Mama Bert arrived in Los Angeles she insisted my sister-in-law take her shopping. She also asked Cat to dye her gray hair black. Neither one of us knew what was going on until we compared notes a short time later. What their grandmother bought was a man's dress shirt and tie. A knock at my husband's and his friend's hotel room door produced a gift-wrapped box for the minister. Not Melvin... the other minister. Melvin recognized Mama Bert's handwriting immediately and that set off an alarm for him. His grandmother had not only purchased the shirt and tie for AC but had bought his airplane ticket and provided him with a little spending money. My husband's friend confessed that this kind of thing had been going on between the two of them for some time. If that had been Melvin's mother, she'd have been labeled a cougar. What then do you call his grandmother? Senior-Citizen Cougar?! Cougar Extreme?! Don't-make-no-kind-of-sense Cougar?!

Melvin called me on the phone and said, "So that's why she always managed to make her way downstairs whenever AC came for a visit." Before this revelation, we both thought she was just being nosey.

Melvin didn't concern himself with whatever his grandmother did or didn't do. It was only me and the kids who were enduring the inconvenience or mistreatment, so why be bothered. Not until she did something that directly affected him would he ever feel the need to say to her, "It's time for you to go!" Well, this situation hurt him. It was the straw that finally broke Melvin-the-Camel's back. Envisioning his grandmother and his best friend together romantically was too much for my husband. It was indeed time for his grandmother to go! My husband did the unthinkable and moved her out sending a firm message that she could never return. I was finally FREE!

Chapter Four
Mama Never Said One Word– George West

I met with my father for the first time when I was forty years old. My mother's side of the family held a family reunion in Natchez, Mississippi which is where he resided, so this was the perfect opportunity. He was at home recuperating from an illness and agreed to meet with me. But it had to be at a time when his wife would be at work at the funeral home they owned. My mother's brother refused to allow me to go alone. Uncle Brother, I called him, had already attempted to play the father role in my life. He was not too pleased that I wanted to meet the man who rejected me.

My uncle and his current wife had no children of their own, but they had plenty of young people who were happy to call them Mom and Dad. Although my aunt and uncle were always very loving and kind to me, I told them that I already had a mother, and I never had a father and didn't need one then. So, my aunt continued to be Aunt Dorothy and he remained my Uncle Brother. Yet he continued to exercise his God-given uncle's right to be very protective of me. On this occasion, in his most stern voice, he announced, "You don't know this man and I don't care who he's supposed to be, you will not be going to his home without me!"

We arrived at the home of George West Sr., my father. It didn't take him long to come to the door and let us in. As Uncle Brother and I stood in the front entrance of the house I thought about my mother and the fact that she had never said one word. I can't tell you anything about the home's interior because I was so focused on the man standing before me. He was no longer a figment of my imagination but a real-life, flesh & bone, as I live & breathe human being... my father. Mr. West was not a very tall man but tall enough for my mother it seems. I could tell then that I looked more like him than I did my mother and that was okay.

He shook my hand and it felt exactly like my son's small hand. That made me look down at his feet. There they were, my son Bwayne's small feet. Before making this discovery Bwayne had only his dad's side of the family's characteristics to use as a comparison. It was exhilarating to learn that I could attribute Mr. West's features to not only me but my children. I finally had the answer to the question my son had been asking me all of his life. "Who gave me these small hands and feet? Even Pam's hands are bigger than mine and she's a girl!"

I had deceived myself into believing that I was only there to meet him and had no other expectations. I shunned the thought that some unresolved suppressed emotions might rise up in me. And yet they did exactly that. That grip of his hand, the touch of my dad's hand... my son's hand *(whom I loved more than life itself)* was confirmation enough. Mr. West existed. He was my father. I had obtained another missing piece to the unfinished puzzle that was my life. Yet, deep down inside of me dwelled this little girl still in need of his love and acceptance. Much more than that, I needed a pronouncement that I was his child.

Mr. West *(that's who he was to me)* escorted Uncle Brother and me into the living room and offered us a seat. Right away he began telling us how bad his business was doing. This pitiful creature sitting before me didn't fit the description I was given at all. From the stories that I was told and the rumors that I had heard, my father was a devoted family man and prominent leader and businessman in the community. He even sent me a photo and letter showing he was a man on the rise in Natchez.

Must have been a different George F. West, Sr. because the more this man talked, the more destitute he tried to appear. His body language and mannerisms were just like those men who used to bring their white shirts by for Mama to wash. They would try and get out of paying for the work she did by using that same type of *woe-is-me* slouched over posturing that Mr. West was trying to use on me. I stopped him and asked, "Do you think I want something from you?" To protect my heart, I immediately activated my *time-to-suppress* emotional shield before quickly saying, "Because I don't! I simply wanted to meet you."

When he realized that I was only there to meet him, in a flash, he began to tell me how well his business was doing, how he was about to buy a second funeral home. His body straightened and he sat erect in his chair as if he were about to pose for a portrait. He went on about how well his children were doing, that they were all doctors, lawyers, and/or Indian chiefs. I wondered if he had any interest in how I was doing but I was too afraid to actually ask him for fear he wouldn't provide the correct healing response. I began to wonder if he felt anything at all once he saw he had indeed fathered a child out of wedlock. Was he completely detached despite our obvious attachment? I wondered, *who and what am I to this person?* The answers never came because I never asked. But I did block out the memory of his handshake after he had just lied to me. I needed to disassociate my son's precious loving touch from his. There was no love there. Not in his hands. Not in his words. At least not for me.

I wondered if Uncle Brother had any recollection of my father from years earlier, him being the family's insurance man and all. My uncle was probably trying his best to remain cool, calm, and collected. I could tell we were all having trouble coming up with something interesting to talk about because there were plenty of awkward moments and even a few pockets of complete silence between the three of us during the visit. And Mr. West seemed to be a bit distracted.

I noticed him counting on his fingers and thought to myself, *Is he doing what I think he's doing? The man ain't talking because he doesn't have anything to say, he's distracted because he's too busy fig-uring out if I'm his child!*

Then I snapped! "What are you doing? Are you counting months? It's been over forty years and you are counting months?!"

"Well yes." He replied then offered me a pop.

Of course, this bit of hospitality came only after I said I didn't want anything from him. I can't explain how that made me feel. This man, my father, after all those years, was only willing to offer me a beverage. I thought, *What about an apology or some sign that you cared about me? Perhaps even for you to inquire about me, my children, my life, or something other than offering me a pop?!* He was the only POP I had ever wanted!

Mr. West kept looking me over but it was not in a way that made me feel uncomfortable, or that suggested he was still refusing to take ownership in aiding in my conception. It was in the same way I had examined his hands and feet earlier. A way that felt as though he really wanted to embrace my actual exis-tence but was too afraid or even too proud to do so. It felt like he was making comparisons between me and his other children. I say that because he said, "You have hair like my daughter."

From my peripheral vision, I could see Uncle Brother adjusting his sitting position in the armchair he had claimed the moment we sat down. I saw him place his index finger on the side of his face thumb under his chin as if contemplating a showdown. Me, I'm thinking, *Wow! Like his daughter. Think that's because you fathered two daughters?*

It was no surprise when he went a step further and suggested I not tell anyone about our meeting or the fact that I was his child. My uncle immediately stood to his feet after hearing my father's selfish and spineless appeal. It was time to make our exit. And yet I honored Mr. West's request up until the day I found out he had died. A church member, who was also from Natchez, gave me the news.

"Yes, I was *(am)* a fatherless child but that didn't *(doesn't)* matter. I had a mother who loved me and worked hard to make sure I had what I needed." I kept trying desperately to bring comfort to that exposed little girl who still lives inside of me. In truth, I was so angry with that man, my father. He died without ever proclaiming me as his daughter.

I was happy to discover he had a sister living in St. Louis within a few blocks of where I had once lived as a child. My mother knew this but never mentioned it. A brother and his family lived two doors from my best friend's family. I was always visiting their home. Imagine that, an aunt, uncle, and first cousins all living very close to me in St. Louis Missouri and I didn't have a clue. I could have met, fallen in love with, and married a first cousin without ever knowing. Heck, my children could have dated their second cousins and so forth. That's what keeping secrets will do for you. After making phone contact with my Aunt Gladys, I explained that I had met her brother in Natchez and that I wanted very much to meet her. She didn't ask why, just said, "Come on over I'm always glad to hear from home." I felt an instant connection.

The closer I got to Gladys' door the more anxious I became because I wasn't sure what to expect. I didn't want what I thought was an instant connection to be ruined if she, too, started using her fingers to count the months as my father had done. Still, I stood there knocking lightly, willing to take the chance. When she opened the front door, I nervously blurted out, "Hi, I'm Geraldine, I called about your brother."

Gladys looked at me, laughed openly, then said, "You must be his child. Come on in and tell me all about it."

Hers was an easy-going type of spirit, nothing like my father who tried unsuccessfully to put on airs. I could tell my aunt wasn't one to deny anyone who shared her DNA as I gave her a detailed account of my encounter with her brother, my father.

"That %$@# brother of mine was always preaching to me about remaining pure and doing the right thing." She huffed. Then puffed, "He preached so much that I just left Natchez all together with the first man going north and look what HE did... that son of a b****!"

My newly discovered aunt was always so comical and full of life *(with no apologies)* that we became good buddies. Gladys had no children, just nieces and nephews. She was so very proud of them and their accomplishments, she too bragging about them being doctors, lawyers, and/or Indian chiefs. Well, she was my father's sister, so I guess they did share some personality traits. One day Gladys and I were out together when I had to stop by my office to do a few things before ending the day. She was more than willing to wait for me. I introduced her to my staff who gave her a tour of the place and treated her royally while I worked. I had no motive for taking her there other than completing my work, but she was completely flabbergasted.

"This is really your place and your people?" She asked.

"YES!" I told her.

"I knew you were a West all the time, that you took after my family. I knew it all the time!"

In her mind, that was authentication as to why I appeared to be doing well for myself. Gladys never mentioned my father's other children again except for the trouble that some of them had gotten into and how their father repeatedly rescued them. Now she had a new West she could brag about, little ole successful me. My aunt accepted me in a way that I wished her brother had.

"One day, let's go to Natchez. You can go as my girlfriend because I want you to meet the rest of the family." She suggested. So we did. We stayed at a hotel in Natchez as close to the funeral home as possible because that was going to be our next stop after checking in at the hotel. At my father's business we found Bubba, one of the sons who was now running the place. At that point, Gladys was the only one who knew that I was family.

He hugged his aunt and asked, "Who is this beautiful woman you have with you?"

"This is my girlfriend, Geraldine from St. Louis." She told him.

My brother came back with, "Well any friend of Gladys' is a friend of mine, so I must get a hug from you too."

We hugged and had a nice visit with my unaware-of-what-was-happening brother. Shortly after we returned to the hotel, the phone rang. Gladys answered. It was Bubba seeming to need to get something off his chest.

"Gladys I don't know what it was, but I felt something when she hugged me. I really need to get to know her."

In immediate reply, Gladys shouted into the phone, "Fool, that's your sister!"

I guess the news shocked him into speechlessness because he was completely silent after that. She explained that we were there so that I could meet some of the family. Bubba accepted the facts as presented then insisted I meet Teddy, his uncle, Gladys' brother. On that trip, I met several other family members including Uncle Teddy and his children as word began to spread to my new siblings that the visitor wasn't a visitor at all. She was their sister.

Outside of me, my father had seven other children, one daughter and six sons, whom I have since met. My sister, Diane *(the daughter my father said I have hair like)*, worked with me on a project in Jackson, Mississippi. She also visited my church one Sunday and sang a solo. Diane was a lovely woman who later died of pancreatic cancer. When she passed, instead of attending her funeral, I donated the price of a round trip ticket to a cause that she sponsored. The family dynamic was just too much for me to handle at that time. "Is she or isn't she George West's child?" was still a question for some, and I was in no mood to endure or respond to the speculation.

Diane's daughter, Artimese, called me not long ago. It was such a pleasant surprise because she had only recently learned about me. Diane had introduced us but at the time didn't share that I was her sister. She was afraid that if the subject came up about me it would hurt her mother, Mrs. West, and possibly her daughter. I understood my sister's concern because Artimese was so close to her grandmother.

My baby boy, Darren, is the spitting image of my father's oldest son GF. In 2008, I wanted my daughter, Pam, to go with me to Natchez so that she could meet my youngest brother of the West brood, her Uncle James. While we were there she saw GF but didn't get the opportunity to meet him face to face. According to Pam's observation, however, GF and Darren share similar mannerisms. She still marvels at the fact that there is someone out there in the world who is almost identical to her younger brother. Darren even has the same bald spot on the top of his head as some of his uncles. My brother Sam has the same hands as his father and my oldest son and I felt the same sensations when our hands touched.

Years later, during my next visit to Natchez, it was James who got everyone together for me to meet. He feels his father let me down and seems to want to make it up to me somehow. He can't, but I love him for wanting to do it. I've gotten to know three of my brothers but have only spoken to the others for a brief moment. My wish for them is that they have nothing but fond memories of the life they shared with their father. It's important to me that they also know it is not from them that I had needed acceptance. I wanted their dad to acknowledge me and he died without doing so. As a result, he left a void that I can never fill so I'll turn that over to the One who is a Healer.

Chapter Five
Future Pastor and Me – Wife of a Preacher Man

*M*elvin enjoyed visiting his friend's church in Madison, Illinois. Rev. Lonnie C. Calmese was always honored whenever my husband would stop by and share the Word of God. Pastor Calmese and his congregation liked Melvin a lot, even offered him the position of Assistant Pastor. It didn't matter that the church was on the other side of the river, three bus trips from where we lived in St. Louis, Missouri. Having no car, we had to catch one bus to get downtown, then we'd take the next bus across the river. The third and final bus would take us to the church. On one or two Sundays every month Rev. Calmese would pick us up after we got across the bridge. That first winter Melvin served as Assistant Pastor was very cold. It was near impossible to keep ourselves and our two small children warm as we waited for each bus. Spring, summer, and fall were much better and, before that next winter, we had a car.

Melvin couldn't wait to become a pastor, so he applied to several open churches that were without leadership. It wasn't long before the First Baptist Church of Creve Coeur came calling. They wanted Melvin to know they were considering him for the job but that they had some concerns about me because I worked all the time including most Sundays. It was true, I worked twelve-hour days from 6:00 PM until 6:00 AM and had one day off every two weeks. That didn't interfere with my ability to attend church on Sunday mornings so I'm not sure why me working all the time was even a concern. I wasn't the one they were considering for Pastor, my husband was.

The day had come when First Baptist Church of Creve Coeur did accept Melvin as their shepherd. It came with a whopping weekly salary of $15.00. He was so happy to finally have his own congregation that he didn't care what he was being paid. That baffled me because I had a lot of concern. I could understand why he was so excited about pastoring but was also confused by him not taking into account he still had a family to take care of. Did he think he could do that on $15.00 a week? Was his full-time job at McDonnell Aircraft Corporation going to make up the difference? I thought, *Of course, it would, no worries.* I was wrong. A short time later he quit that job claiming the Lord told him to devote his time to being a full-time pastor.

I said to him, "Melvin, you know the Lord would not tell a man with a family to quit a job for one that only pays $15.00 per week." I was even more shocked with his next move. That man walked into a Cadillac dealership and drove out of there in a brand-new car on a $15.00 per week salary. When I questioned that decision Melvin said, "Geraldine, you just don't know what the Lord will do. Oh, ye of little faith!"

My thought... *Negro, please!!*

My work schedule had finally improved, I now had every other weekend off, giving me more time at the church. So I took on more responsibility and started teaching the Junior Sunday School Class ages 9 to 11. But what I enjoyed most was working with all the youngsters preparing them for special performances for Easter, Christmas, and Annual Day celebrations. I just loved interacting with the children plus it was something my family and I could do together. The kids loved reciting poems and, whether penned or borrowed, each one had to be memorized. Performing written skits was another one of the kids' favorite activities. My favorite skit was Radio Station WMU.

WMU is an acronym for Women's Missionary Union of which I was a member. Our purpose at First Baptist was to prepare adults, youth, and children to become good stewards to those in need. We would take gifts to nursing homes, donate diapers to children's crisis centers, and visit inmates in prison. Even transported individuals to doctor's appointments whenever necessary. I had the help of some of the moms and young ladies of the church to keep things fun and interesting for the kids. Bible scriptures were our point of reference for every initiative.

We staged Radio Station WMU to look like the inside of a radio talk show host's studio, microphones and all. A disguised table and chairs served as the announcer's mixing board and there was even a set-up to interview special guests. The announcer would start, "This is Radio Station WMU, coming to you from the land of believers. Today we have Brother I-Promised-the-Lord and Sister Believe-You-Me, joining us. We're going to talk about what the Lord done done for us. And what we done done for the Lord."

The dialogue continued back and forth between commentator and guest. Bro. I-Promised-the-Lord began all his responses with "I promised the Lord," while Sister Believe-You-Me ended hers with "believe you me." Again, the kids had to commit their lines to memory. My opinion was if we allowed them to read from pieces of paper it would hinder their creativity. It also interfered with their ability to learn new concepts. My church team and I always set the bar high. We believed the children would live up to our expectations and that they did every time. When you require little from children expect to receive little to nothing. But when you compel them to be stars, they will shine as bright as any in the sky.

What I'm about to disclose is true, although you'll probably think, *that's impossible.* One time I transported fifteen or more kids in my car.

I was driving our Cadillac Deville, 1966, I think. The children ranged in age; the oldest no more than nine years old. So, this was my set-up. Ten kids were in the back. Five would take the seat in every other formation one sitting way back, the next sitting forward. Three smaller children sat on the laps of the kids who sat back. Two more sat on the floor facing them. One behind me, the other behind the passenger's seat. Okay, that takes care of that. Now for the front seat. Three sat next to me, the same formation, with two little ones on laps. There could have been one or two sitting on the passenger side floor in front as well. The seat belt laws weren't in place then and neither was my common sense.

We were rehearsing for a play and none of the children lived within walking distance of the church. Some of the parents were working and others didn't have transportation, so I volunteered to drive all of them. I wanted them all to take part and at the time it seemed like the logical thing to do. You know what they say, "The Lord takes care of babies and fools." After the rehearsal we'd pile into the vehicle again, everyone taking their assigned seat, and off we'd go. You would've thought I'd hurry and get those babies home to safety, but no. I stopped for treats, spending almost all the money I had. It was worth it seeing the kids happy as they teased each other about forgetting their lines.

I needed to get some gasoline, so I pulled into the first gas station along the way. I only had 35 cents left after buying goodies for the kids and gas at that time was 36 cents per gallon. The station attendant came up to the driver's side window and asked, "How much?" When I told him he asked, "You want 35 cents worth of gas? What, y'all going on a long trip?" Then he started chuckling and soon we all burst into laughter. I don't know if the kids understood his comment or if they were simply reacting to him laughing at us. The attendant put the 35 cents worth of gas in my car which was almost a gallon, enough to move the gauge off empty. We thanked him and continued on our way. Meanwhile, the kids decided to break out in song even though I had no idea what they were singing and was probably too tired to even care. It had been a long day and I needed to concentrate on my driving which meant blocking out all fifteen of those high-pitched squealing voices. I rolled along dropping each child off safe and sound before heading home. I guess it must have been Melvin's Lord that took care of us.

Yep, Melvin's Lord. Remember I was the *Ye of little faith* according to my husband. At that point I had but one lord whose name was not Jesus. Oh, I had always believed in God, the Father Almighty, Maker of heaven and earth but there were times I felt abandoned by the Savior. Or maybe I was too ashamed to admit to myself that it was me who had stopped trusting Him. Melvin was the one I worshipped even when it felt wrong. It was in him that I sought fulfillment, comfort, and love. A man whose every flaw I excused and every deliberate misstep I justified. I had to rationalize every matrimonial affliction to make my world all right. Lord Jesus, forgive me for I knew not what I was doing.

Speaking of matrimonial afflictions. We only had my pay-check coming into the house along with the weekly $15.00 cash the church was paying Melvin. It was routine for me to go gro-cery shopping every two weeks when I got paid but this partic-ular time I was too tired after work to do so. Rather than go to the grocery store where I could cash my check and buy groceries, I went straight home. Melvin offered to take my paycheck and get it cashed suggesting we could get groceries later. I appreci-ated the fact that *my man* was going to take care of things like a provider and protector ought. Off he went as I lay down to relax a bit until it was time for us to head to the store.

Hours went by before Melvin returned with no check and no money. After fighting back tears, I asked about all the when's, where's and why's. Oh, he was apologetic, explaining that he had used the money to get someone out of jail. I don't remember if it was a member of the church or his thieving cousin Reese but what I did know was that he had intentionally disregarded his immediate family's needs in favor of an outsider. The thought of it and the sight of him at that moment made me sick! The man didn't even offer up any solutions to remedy the dilemma he caused. No money, no groceries, no protector, and most defi-nitely no provider. There wasn't any time for me to fall apart, I had to figure something out and quick. Thank God for family. It was so humiliating having to take money from my Aunt Emma knowing that she wasn't about to just hand over her hard-earned cash without asking, "Didn't you just get paid?" *(Emma knew my pay schedule better than I did.)* I made up some lie worthy of an Oscar even as I found myself becoming more and more disheartened. This would be the one and only time I would ever borrow money from anyone again to feed our children. I didn't care in the least if Melvin ever ate again because I was tired of having to defend his reprehensible actions. My responses weren't always logical but, they usually worked for me. Not this time.

"Now where was I? Oh yeah. Creve Coeur!"

I could have spent my entire life at First Baptist Church of Creve Coeur. I thought I'd be there long enough to watch the children grow and the adults grow even older. I loved them all. The church was twenty-two miles from my house, Olive Boulevard taking us from city to country in a matter of minutes. There was only one house on the same side of the road as the church but across the way was a dairy farm, the cows no more than fifty feet away. Everything else around us was either woods or water.

On Sunday mornings Deacon Black would enter the building first to get rid of any visitors especially the snakes that always found their way inside. Sometimes there were frogs and other small creatures too, but the snakes bothered me more than anything else. Yet I wouldn't have traded the experience for anything. My husband, however, longed to pastor a bigger church. So, after nine years at First Baptist Church of Creve Coeur, Melvin accepted the position as Pastor of Washington Tabernacle Baptist Church, a prominent black church in the City of St. Louis. It so happened to have been the church where I got baptized as a ten-year-old. It was also the place where I fell in love with the song, "Jesus, He Brought Me."

Jesus, He brought me all the way. He carries my burdens every day. Oh, He's such a wonderful Savior, I've never known Him to fail me. Jesus, He brought me all the way.

Melvin was overjoyed by the opportunity. I was not. It meant having to leave everyone I loved at First Baptist, the place that had become my second home.

All That Seems, Ain't

Every Sunday for nine years my family traveled to this small community church, sometimes five days a week, and we loved it. This had been my husband's first church. We were more than a church or congregation; we were a family having a homecoming celebration each time we came together. But this time was different. It was very quiet, no one spoke a word, our hearts heavy. Nor did we look into each other's faces for fear our eyes would meet and tears would start to fall. It was our last Sunday, the last time we would make this trip! We were taking our last look at the remodeled building that had become our home and were about to share our last hugs. The goodbyes felt like huge lumps caught in our throats and I could no longer hold back my tears.

Brother Williams who was one of the older members approached Melvin and said, "Come here, boy. Now you be careful down there in that City in that big church. All that seems, ain't."

Those words had no real significance to an unseasoned young minister and his wife but, once revealed, should have been scrolled across the new church's altar.

Washington Tabernacle, a large gothic cathedral-styled building, had been the church that played host to a list of notables like Dr. Martin Luther King, as well as every other well-known Negro, African American, or Black persons of the day. Its large membership consisted of black elites, some of whom had no compassion for those less fortunate. Most had some formal education either by choice or because of a great need to belong to the inner circle, who without apology had no tolerance for those without credentials. Some created or developed their own set of criteria, which served to segregate, put down, or simply annoy others. And there were, of course, those who possessed great humanity: the ones who believed in themselves, in each other and the greater power, and who lived it.

The church board pondered several aspects of Melvin's application to become Pastor before making its final decision. We had no idea the selection committee assumed my husband would be a pawn, one they'd use for their own self-serving intentions. For starters, Melvin was young and not as seasoned as previous pastors, easy to manipulate and control *(they thought)*. We were already buying a house and because I had full-time employment, they concluded that I earned enough to maintain our household. With that underlying assumption, they decided that we didn't need the other financial perks that otherwise came with the position. They even had the nerve to insist that Melvin provide them with my pay stub, an invasion of privacy for certain. If my employer's family health plan was better than what they could offer, then the church would be off the hook. Neither my pay nor benefits were a good enough reason for them to refuse my husband *(a man with a growing family and the future shepherd of a church that size)* a fair and comparable salary plus benefits. It all felt a little shady, especially at the precise moment Melvin asked me for my paystub. I tried reasoning with my husband but to no avail. That conversation went from discussing to spilling over into fussing, then morphing into a full-blown argument. I only hoped he would see the absurdity and violation of it all... coming from that group of intrusive and self-righteous individuals. To make matters worse, Melvin turned over the paystub anyway and they later used it against him.

The devil wasn't through with us yet, nor was Bro. Williams's prophecy. Though I was certain God was never far away, I can't say I was ever prepared for the next set of challenges we would face. The warning signs were there from the beginning, but Melvin and I were too blinded by our perceived successes and future possibilities. Did we ignore the obvious? It's possible. I would come to realize our stay at that church would always be an uphill BATTLE as it was soon revealed to us the real reason why they sought after Melvin: good old-fashioned politics.

"All that seems, definitely ain't!"

That church board wanted a preacher, not a pastor. They had no plans of allowing anyone to assume real leadership. That church had a history of vacating the pulpit whenever the Pastor failed to yield all control. They wanted to continue to abuse their power, misuse people, and misappropriate church funds.

They were willing to take advantage of my husband's eagerness and inexperience by low-balling and/or retracting their original offers. These were folk whose principles were severely malnourished, who were resistant to change and determined to maintain positions of authority.

There is a popular phrase used when circumstances test and try you. These two little words can renew in you the right Spirit, strengthen your walk, and fortify your conviction. BUT GOD! The board chose to offer Melvin only a salary with no other incentives. My husband was so excited about the opportunity despite the disregard shown him. I feared he would have even taken another $15.00 a week *(just as he had done before at our first church)* if they had offered it. BUT GOD! No housing allowance was given. BUT GOD! We had a car so that meant no transportation expenses. The family medical insurance I already had was far better, so out the window went that bonus. BUT GOD! Their new young minister was not without experience nor talent and it didn't take long for the board or the congregation to discover that fact. This man of God, my husband and father of four was a gifted messenger. He also possessed a burning desire to make his church a cathedral among all great cathedrals.

I recently had a conversation with a Pastor's wife whose husband, like mine, had died. As we conversed, she happened to mention how much she and other ministers' wives envied us back then. "How fortunate that this young couple had just become Pastor and First Lady at a very popular church," she told me, convinced a lot of perks had come with the job. When I told her the real deal she was stunned. With a confused look on her face, she asked, "Why did you two accept it?"

All I could think to say was, "BUT GOD!!"

When we got to the new church there was a lot that needed to be done to the building and Melvin discovered there was no plan in place to get any of the work started. As he charted his plan of action the church's board members insisted that they approve all plans. Step by step Melvin would attempt to get the green light from board members who were frequently out of touch with the current cost of things like remodeling, replacing or updating church facilities. Not one of them was willing to admit this deficiency or their distrust of my husband's capabilities refusing to approve the go-ahead of any work. Melvin was required to present three bids from different contractors which he did. Still, the same board members would reject all three bids, claiming they were too high. That tug of war continued with each proposal my husband put before them.

Finally, Melvin had had enough. He put his preacher-slash-pastor-slash-leader big boy tighty-whities on, announced that he would choose the contractor to do the major work needed in the church, and got busy about the Father's business. Point blank and period! The selection of special contractors needed to do the repair work in particular areas was also determined by my husband. He made it clear to the entire board that if they continued to put up roadblocks, he would make the final decision himself and proceed whether they approved or not. This young pastor was coming into his own and the dinosaurs recognized it. The members got to witness the completion and installation of several projects including new restrooms and updated plumbing; new wiring throughout; a remodeled kitchen and brand-new roof; reinforced stained-glass windows; patchwork and painting – all under the leadership of Pastor Smotherson and the reluctant follow-ship of the members of the board which did finally sign off on the work to be done. In fact, many even had the nerve to brag about what they had accomplished after everything was complete.

Not wanting to actively include new members was the attitude of most of the old-timers and nothing unusual when observing the actions of the members of the church board and the congregation. Yet my husband and I found this type of flagrant un-Christ-like conduct disturbing.

"I've been a member of this church for some time now and the people still walk by me as if I don't exist" was the recurring statement of newer members voicing discontent to their young pastor. Another concern expressed by younger members was that the church had a dead spirit and needed some life, and Pastor Smotherson was in total agreement. He tried to explain how many of the older members had fallen into complacency, pointing out that they weren't always open to change. The seasoned members rarely rejoiced about improvements made to the church building or about people finding their way to Christ by joining the church. Their church. My husband and supporters encouraged people to worship with us, but closed-minded members feared strangers would take over. With a new pastor and the influx of new initiatives, some changes were inevitable. With skill, finesse, and a lot of help from above, Melvin had to find a way to merge the two opposing sides.

I think he did it quite well. We continued the existing programs, added a new members' class and all kinds of curricula for the children. The Pastor invited various gospel vocal groups to sing at the church which appealed to members of all ages. As a singer himself Melvin was partial to live concerts, featuring quartet and quintet groups male or female as long as they could sing. Rev. Dr. C. W. Clark was a well-known orator described as the preacher's preacher who Melvin had gotten to know quite well. He was even the guest speaker for our annual five-day revival several years in a row.

Preachers from churches all around would be in attendance, sure to have pen and paper handy to jot down some of Dr. Clark's clever phrasing or eloquent language. All of them, including my husband, were so taken by his style of preaching, who during his opening, never spoke above a disciplined whisper but by the time he got to his sermon's thunderous closing the church would be on fire! Affairs like that had never taken place at Washington Tabernacle. Every event drew in multitudes which resulted in the membership doubling in size. At the time I counted it all worthwhile feeling as though I could finally let my guard down a bit. I thought Bro. Williams's warning, *"All that seems, ain't,"* might finally be starting to fade.

Each step of the way Melvin continued to encourage the members to be supportive of his efforts and, for a while, they were. Early on, he wanted to bring the choir down from the loft that sat high above the pulpit. Climbing that narrow stairwell was quite a challenge, especially for the older members but descending that same staircase was even more difficult and an accident waiting to happen. He also believed we would all be on one accord if the singers were closer to the preaching and the congregation. There was plenty of room in the pulpit behind him which meant the senior choir members had to climb no more than two or three steps. In Melvin's opinion, relocating the choir was the right thing to do. At the end of his sermon one week, he stood at the podium looking out over the membership. I could tell he was gathering his thoughts. Pastor announced that on the next Sunday the choir would be singing from their new location, motioning everyone's attention towards the direction of the intended site.

A symphony of "WHY?" as if rehearsed resounded from several spots out in the audience. That set off a chain reaction of low-key sighs and whispers. Heads started turning every which way attempting to identify the nay-sayers. I never budged.

"The choir has always sung from the loft above. Why do you want to change everything?" Someone shouted without delay from an opposite side of the sanctuary.

That caused the entire room to erupt into what sounded like the swell of a rumbling ocean. Sighs then turned into full-blown squawking in reaction to the disruptors' outbursts. Those who agreed with the objectors agitatedly debated with those in support of my husband. Melvin tried explaining that the old stairwell leading up to the choir loft had become a safety hazard and that the choir would soon be singing from their new location behind him in the pulpit. Still, it didn't change the challengers' attitudes. Melvin remained determined. Those who resisted change and every good idea were not going to stop progress.

The First Lady Takes a Stand

I'm not sure where I fitted in because, even though I was the First Lady of the church, I spent several years in never-ending bewilderment. Instead of a concern for my soul, members *(particularly the womenfolk)* would bombard me with instructions, disapprovals, even nit-picks about my dress, my walk, my work, and my children. I was even told which Sunday School class I should or shouldn't be in, who I should or shouldn't talk to, or who deserved my time. I received criticism if my knees were showing when I stood up or if too much of my lap showed when I sat down.

The Women's Day committee asked me to be one of the speakers at their upcoming annual program. On that Sunday afternoon, all the ladies scheduled to speak got escorted to the pulpit. You had to take two or three steps up so to have the support of a strong arm was a nice gesture. The pulpit was an open space that had six altar chairs that sat aligned just behind the podium, facing the congregation. Sitting in that open space left me feeling exposed to the entire audience compared to when I would sit in the pew where the high back of the long cushioned bench in front of me served as a great cover.

While I was sitting in the pulpit, I looked out into the audience and noticed this woman staring at me and not the other women that were sitting next to me. Even though she was closer to the back of the church, I could still see her and there was no mistaking it, her focus was definitely on me and only me. I watched her as she went into her bag and pulled out this large handkerchief and I knew immediately what she was about to do with it. I can even remember what I thought at the time.

Oh no, she is not getting ready to do what I think she is about to do! She is about to walk down this long aisle in front of all these people and bring me that huge piece of cloth to put over my knees.

And that's exactly what she did.

When she got down to the front of the church she stood there beckoning for me to come and take the handkerchief. By now the room was completely quiet, the entire congregation's attention directed toward me and this woman. I got up, walked towards her, reached out and took the thing from her then went back to my seat. It was a really beautiful, laced-trimmed cloth. However, I knew that with it she was implying I wasn't dressed properly. Onlookers were still fixated on me and THAT HAND-KERCHIEF. I held it up in the same way a magician holds his cloth when he's about to perform a magic trick and completely captivated the audience. Then I began to fold it slowly... deliberately... from corner... to corner... before laying it... aside. You could hear the entire room exhale.

When it was my turn to speak, I took the handkerchief with me to the podium and opened it up so that everyone could see how lovely it was before I began to speak.

"Good afternoon everyone. Let me start by sharing with you this lovely gift I just received. I will treasure it always."

That was my not-so-subtle way of letting her know she was not getting it back. Then I shared with everyone how timely a gift it was, put it to my nose, **and** BLEW! The people cracked up. I could tell it was in support of me and contempt for her.

While I frequently received applause for the work I did with the children at Washington Tabernacle, I was just as frequently reprimanded whenever I spoke up for the kids who needed someone to talk to about drugs, sex, parents, suicidal urges and so much more. I expected others to share my concern for the children but some members I spoke with said that church wasn't the place to discuss such things. That was puzzling. The house of God is a place where you come seeking spiritual and emotional healing. Part of that healing comes through prayer, the other through openness to express one's truth. So why would we ever shun the truth? Especially from children trying to make sense of the world and their place in it. Those young people should've been able to talk about anything that was on their minds, a position I took with both the adults and the young people. And I'm glad I did.

One year the church paid for fifteen girls between the ages of 11 and 16 to attend a religious retreat in Kansas City, Kansas. Three adult counselors who normally interacted with the girls at church were chosen as chaperones for the trip.

A week after their return, several of the young ladies reached out to me to share their concerns about the trip. The kids and I had built a trusting relationship and these girls felt I'd be the only one who would believe them. Two of the older girls said one of the counselors, Ms. Williams, had insisted on bathing them. They went on to describe how she would come into the bathroom and begin to wash their bodies. When they objected, Ms. Williams would claim that she was only there to help, then abruptly make her exit. When it was the turn of the younger girls, Ms. Williams refused to leave the bathroom and remained until the bathing was over. I began to investigate their allegations, questioning the adult female's inappropriate behavior and asking why she was even serving as a counselor at all. It didn't matter to me that she was a member of the church, I demanded answers. All hell broke out once I did that.

"There she goes again causing trouble, making too much out of nothing," was the stance of one of the members about my whistleblowing.

Melvin's feet were also being held to the fire by those who felt I had no right to challenge their broken system. My shedding light on the situation was not what the membership thought was my role as the First Lady, but my determination to continue to investigate and support those young ladies remained firm. When my husband told me to leave things alone, I was even angrier. I thought, *How dare they – including Melvin – try to censor me?! I'll show all of you who's making too much out of so little.*

I expected support and leadership from him as both husband and pastor, but he continued to miss the mark and I continued to act. I refused to go along with any cover-up, didn't care what any of them thought, and practically dared them to try me and stop me. All that was important to me was the safety and well-being of those girls. Nothing was going to get in the way of removing that predator's access to the Church's children... and nothing did.

I took matters into my own hands and drove to Ms. Williams' house, told her that she would no longer be traveling with the girls, and stripped her of her duties as one of the youth counselors. Some of the church officials viewed my take-action approach as a threat because had I gone to the authorities with what I knew that type of exposure had the potential of tarnishing the church's good name and reputation.

There were many other battles fought, some we lost while other victories were won and, even though all was not as I had hoped it would be, through prayer I learned to cope, especially on the Sundays marred by hostility or contrived allegations. I was there dealing with folks who even Stevie Wonder could see had WOKE UP on the wrong side of the bed. My physical body was in the pew close to the front of the church as expected but it was on those Sundays when I allowed my daydreams to whisk me off to that quaint little church in the County, where my true spiritual family worshipped. First Baptist Church of Creve Coeur. With my eyes closed, a sign that you were either into the sermon or asleep, I'd be imagining familiar faces and soaking up warm embraces until the sound of my husband's booming voice would startle me back into reality. Yet his wasn't the only voice that rang loud and clear for me. "All that seems, ain't." I hear ya, Brother Williams.

That Did It!

In the coming months, Melvin did the unthinkable. He decided to run for Congress.

"So now I was going to have to be a politician's wife too? Oh, Lord!"

My husband wasn't pleased by what was happening in our City, so he thought he should stop complaining and do something about it. A world-renowned speaker once said, "There is no problem outside of you that is superior to the power within you." Melvin believed that. He thought he could and would make a difference for the better, however, many of the members were upset because he was running against a long-time beloved Congressman who in their view was already taking care of the people... black folks. They wasted no time in expressing their discontent either to his face or through nasty telephone calls. Some even sent threatening letters.

Melvin lost the election but, for someone who had never run for office, he did quite well. Even though I respected him for his conviction, I admit I was somewhat relieved by the loss. The thought of shouldering any more of his wants was more than I could stand at the time. Melvin running for office without getting the approval from the church board must have been more than they could stand because a member of the church *(who was a prominent Civil Rights attorney and friend)* came by our house to warn Melvin the members were planning a mutiny.

He asked, "For what reason?"

"You just can't keep doing what you want to do. You have got to listen to the old heads," she told him.

At first, Melvin and I thought she was there as a neutral party but, after hearing her constant pleas for him to comply, we weren't so sure what her position was on the matter. The discussion did, however, make *me* question her loyalty and our friendship.

"What do they expect?" Melvin then asked.

"That you just preach, stay in your lane, get out of politics, and leave the business of the church to them! The church, as they see it, belongs to them, not you!" Was our so-called friend's response.

I think her warning was a wee-bit too late, the church members' minds were already made up. For Melvin the warning only served as proof of their intent, and not as a directive to which he would ever follow. As I sat there listening to the exchange between the two of them and watching the light dim in my husband's eyes my heart became heavy. He was certain his commitment to being the leader ignited the flames of resistance even more. After she was done, he ended their conversation and turned to me asking, "So why fight it?"

I could tell he was coming to terms with the fact that it was the Lord's way of saying it was time to go.

I got to church late the next Sunday and as soon as I walked in I noticed how quiet it was. I had entered on the lower level of the building where most of the classes were held. Sunday School was in progress which is why the quiet seemed so strange. The adults were gathered in their designated sections out in the open space, and I expected to hear heightened biblical debate or the sound of huddled voices bouncing from wall to wall. Also, the children were in a separate partitioned room that, no matter how well insulated it was, could not contain their noise and excitement. There was no discussion of the day's lesson nor was there any other distinctive sound in the air and that made me uneasy. To make matters worse, for me to get to my Sunday School room I had to walk past other classes. As I approached, whispers would fade into complete silence. I chalked it all up to my imagination getting the better of me and continued towards my destination. Relieved I had made it through what felt like the Twilight Zone, I detected a definite chill in the air in my classroom as well. I wasn't imagining things, not in the least.

"Lord, give me strength," was all I could pray.

The end of the session was always followed by a fifteen-minute break. That's when members would drink coffee or have a quick snack before morning worship. Not this time. Folks huddled in corners talking amongst themselves while several good brothers and sisters avoided having any type of conversation with me at all. My kids standing nearby saw the shade that was being thrown my way but what broke my heart the most was the fact that the other children hesitated to even speak. I had come to adore them, and they had grown to love me.

I needed to get away from the absurdity, so I headed to the sanctuary. Other members and visitors were already assembled in anticipation of service. Melvin was in his study readying himself to preach the word. You could hear a pin drop as I strolled down that long aisle and took my seat. When it was time for the church announcements a man came forward, stood in front of the mic and announced that a SPECIAL MEETING would take place on Thursday of that same week. The agenda, he told the church, was to discuss the BUILDING FUND. This was definitely out of the ordinary and this gentleman was definitely out of order. Correspondence of any kind had to go through the church clerk, the person designated to make all church announcements.

I suspected the meeting had nothing at all to do with the building fund although I couldn't quite put my finger on what was brewing. Even the congregation reacted to this man's disorder. There was chattering all around me, as tensions mounted. The devil and his disrupters thought they had been successful before, so they came back to disrupt some more. Then out of nowhere an immediate hush fell over the entire sanctuary and stayed that way throughout the rest of the service. The atmosphere was eerily silent yet in a calming sort of way. Melvin preached his sermon as if nothing was wrong and it truly was one of his best. His scripture reference: **Do not touch my anointed ones; do my prophets no harm. Psalm 105:15.** I was at peace as well realizing what had taken place wasn't Satan's doing at all. The presence of the Lord, my and Melvin's Problem Solver and Way Maker, was in that place. That did it for me!

That Night

Between that Sunday and the following Wednesday, we must have gotten a hundred calls from folks asking, "Do you know what they're doing? Aren't you going to do something?" The *"something"* he was going to do was to do nothing at all including not attending the meeting. Melvin was ready to move on. Trusting that the Lord would make a way was comfort enough for him and for that I was grateful.

I don't remember the drive, can't even recall which of my children was in the car or whether there was any conversation between us until we got closer to the church. When we pulled up, we could see men standing at attention like soldiers. You'd have thought they were guarding a fort as they stood near the doorway on the north side of the building which was also close to Melvin's designated parking space. Memories flooded my thoughts, and images began to scroll like film credits. For nine years my family used that particular entrance to gain access into the church. For four hundred plus weeks we had pulled into that parking space every Sunday morning. But, sadly, not this time. I wasn't about to steer my vehicle into the enemy's camp, so I found a spot on the street that offered me the best escape route if it came to that. These men not only stood as guards but had armed themselves as if they expected violence.

If this was only a business meeting to discuss the building fund, what was the need for armed guards? I thought.

For fear of harm or confrontation, the children and I knew then that it was the right decision for Melvin to remain at home.

When we entered the church, to my amazement the lower sanctuary was full. Based upon my calculations, seventy percent of the audience were current members, regular worshippers. The other thirty consisted of folks who had not attended church within the nine years my husband had pastored. The reason I knew that to be true was that I recognized many of them from when I was baptized there as a youngster. Strange though, they were available to attend a fake business meeting.

How could this be happening in a church? I wondered.

The regular attendees were the same people who for nine years had hugged and kissed us, talked about the great love they had for us. Many had even invited us over to their homes for a delicious and, sometimes god-awful, Sunday dinner. The latter was a gesture that my children often dreaded, especially after their first encounter with some not-so-clean chitterlings. There it was again, that voice from the past. *Be careful boy...all that seems ain't.*

Wanting to be invisible, my children and I took the first available seats we came to which, to our relief, happened to have been at the rear of the church. From that vantage point, I could see the entire room. At the head table sat six deacons, the other eighteen on the front pews. From the second row back to where we were, people sat crowded together with their children close beside them. This was different because I had very seldom seen children at our business meetings. The playroom was always used when parents had to bring them, but not that night. How sad I thought that the children were present, to add numbers to the vote I'm sure, with their parents refusing to consider the impact it might have on them. Then, to our dismay, someone spotted us. Members began to whisper back and forth, some nodding in our direction as others looked back to see where we were. I had the urge to wave in response using only my middle finger but chose instead to keep my dignity by acting as if nothing strange was happening.

BAM! BAM! BAM! Sounded the gavel. That caused members and non-members alike to sit up straight as if at attention while others leaned forward in their seats so as not to miss a word. Deacon Brown stepped to the mic and called the meeting to order. My first instinct was to look for his wife who I saw sitting off to the side not too far from the head table. I knew she had to be close. The only power and authority Deacon Brown could have exercised would have come from his wife because he didn't make any moves or decisions without her permission. He was a very small-framed man while she, on the other hand, stood a good foot taller. That was just one of the ways she seemed to overshadow him. It was no secret that directing and controlling his every thought, word, or deed was Mrs. Brown's main purpose in life.

Before Deacon Brown could say another word, Deacon Scott (*being a bit impatient*) jumped up, rushed forward, grabbed the mic then, as loud as he could, proclaimed, "I move that we vacate the pulpit!"

There were several seconds to the motion that managed to rise high above all the rumbling going on in the room. BAM! BAM! BAM! Went the gavel again.

"Order! May we have order here," said a third deacon, pounding the gavel with greater force than that of the petite Deacon Brown.

A few people went from sitting to standing then back to sitting, others leaned forward then back, even side to side. Everyone was jockeying to get a look-see of who it was that had made such a thunderous commanding sound with that gavel. I had to stretch my upper torso and neck as if I were a giraffe because people's movements had blocked my view.

"Well, I'll be darned!" It was the Chairman of the Board, Deacon Crawford. I felt he should've been handling the meeting in the first place no matter the outcome. After it quieted down he continued, "It has been so moved and seconded that we vacate the pulpit, are there any questions?"

He repeated, "Are there any questions?"

I don't know who it was, but I heard a voice ask, "On what grounds?"

For what felt like a moment or two but was only a mere few seconds there was complete silence. I could tell some were seriously pondering that very question while others appeared resolute about their decision. "On what grounds indeed?" Another shouted. Then like an erupting volcano, the room filled with so much noise I couldn't hear the response if there was one.

BAM! BAM! BAM! "Order, please! The floor is now open for discussion and disclosure," so said Deacon Crawford.

Next to take the floor with a writing tablet in hand was Brother Fox, a deacon who had always appeared to be such a strong Christian. I was astounded by what I heard next. Lies! The deacon read nothing but lies. I knew, and he knew I knew, he was witness to the actual truth. Brother Fox had sold his soul to the devil.

The Charges

Charge #1: "Pastor Smotherson is charged with poor leadership and has not done anything in the nine years that he has been here."

The church was low in funds when we got there yet, under my husband's leadership, the building had been completely renovated, the membership increased and the church was very active in the community.

Charge #2: "Pastor Smotherson ran for Congress and didn't obtain permission from the church."

We didn't know that a citizen had to get permission from any church to run for public office. Deacon continued stating the charges against Melvin whom I thought he admired and supported. He was the one person who had practically worked side-by-side with my husband the entire nine years Melvin was pastor. So close, that if any guilt existed, he too would have had some culpability.

Charge #3: "Pastor Smotherson took $1,200.00 from the church."

Deacon Fox knew exactly what happened to the alleged *$1,200.00* because he was the one who dispersed the funds. The National Baptist Convention was in town during that time and, for an entire week, church members worked as volunteers cooking and feeding delegates. At the Pastor's direction, the deacon was responsible for paying them for services rendered. The problem, as some viewed it, was that the Pastor had no right to pay the members with the church's money without the board's approval. Guess what, hypocrites? That *$1,200.00* came from the generous personal donations of those delegates in appreciation of the hospitality shown them, not from that den of narrow-mindedness you call a church.

Charge #4: "Pastor Smotherson broke up a happy marriage."

Aldean and Herbert Boone was the name of the couple whose marriage my husband was accused of destroying. She nor her spouse were present that night to refute the allegation. I can admit that I was somewhat jealous of the attention Mrs. Boone seemed to get from Melvin. She'd always have plenty of in-depth bible questions and he always seemed just a little too eager, in my opinion, to provide the answers. I could see how encounters like that may have piqued some of the members' warped curiosity while cementing the suspicions of those who had already decided his guilt. I so needed all those hellions to be wrong about my husband even when I was doubtful myself, especially whenever I saw them together at church. All I kept thinking was, *Not again, not here of all places!* Still, I refused to allow anyone to witness my insecurity, an almost impossible feat that had almost gotten the better of me because she was just so very beautiful.

I was in an emotional hurricane, wanting and needing to believe their relationship was innocent, yet fearful that my husband's indiscretions had come home to roost. That storm, however, subsided a week before the vote when Mrs. Boone and I met to have a face-to-face. She was very upset about what the church was alleging and wanted to assure me that nothing inappropriate had gone on between her and Melvin. She also told me that my husband most definitely did not break up her marriage and that was good enough for me. A short time later, I got the news that she had become Reverend Aldean Boone and began pastoring a church of her own.

Charge #5: "For over a month Pastor Smotherson used an expired charge card issued by the church."

That accusation was more ridiculous than all the others. The church had given Melvin an unlimited gasoline credit card in support of his duties as pastor. Businesses didn't accept expired credit cards, not even a week old let alone a month past the expiration date. We learned that one of the deacons tried to bribe the service station owner where Melvin frequently purchased gas. The owner was asked to confiscate the card the next time Melvin attempted to use it and the deacon would pay a small fee. The owner opted to call Melvin instead.

The Vote

Four large speakers were strategically positioned around the room. They amplified the magnetic force of the deacon's voice as he read each charge and also elevated the frenzied chatter throughout the lower level. You would have thought those claims were a shock to many in the audience given their intense audible reaction. Oh, wait! I guess it did catch many of them by surprise since a large number of those clueless spectators weren't even current or active members. That thirty percent was only there to fill seats and affect the outcome of the vote, a ploy many hoped would result in the ousting of my husband. The increased tension in the room was palpable. Deacon Crawford abandoned the use of his gavel and opted to use a more deafening approach, yelling in the mic!

"THAT'S ENOUGH DISCUSSION, I'LL CALL FOR THE VOTE!" declared Deacon Crawford as people clasped their hands over their ears to save what was left of their hearing.

"All for vacating the pulpit, stand!"

Some folks stood immediately including those who were strangers to us. Many remained seated until their associates, angry faces-and-all, turned to them and barked, "STAND!"

Those scaredy-cats rose as ordered. Teenagers who knew the real-deal stood with tears running down their cheeks because their parents forced them. As soon as I got the opportunity I made eye contact with some of the young people. The expression on my face conveyed the love I would always have for them and that it was okay. *(Two of the young men walked out to avoid conflict with their parents and even called us a short time later to apologize for the injustice and to express how helpless they felt.)* The whole thing was so tragic. The count was taken.

A small amount of feedback from the microphone rang through the air, but the sound was less threatening than before. I guess the loudness was a bit too much for the deacon as well, but he continued, "Those voting NOT to vacate the pulpit, please stand?"

There were several who stood while others, too afraid to do so because of the obvious threats, sat and remained quiet. I had and still have great respect for the courageous few who rose with dignity, regardless of intimidation. Some members, believing they could remain neutral, stayed home hoping there would be enough do-gooders in attendance to offset their much-needed support but there wasn't.

The count this time, of those in support of Melvin, was too few to prevail so they vacated the pulpit. Our accusers were victorious even though they knew they had falsely accused us. And, just like that, we were out. We'd lost what had become our second home, a place where we not only worked hard to improve the structure but also to touch the hearts of the members. Melvin would never stand in that spacious pulpit again despite the nine years of sacrificing himself and the needs of his family in the process. Was it worth all that or had we wasted a precious part of our youth? Had we gained anything? Of course, we had. If nothing but learning, "All that seems ain't."

We took the news home, me fretting over how I was going to make my report to Melvin once I walked through our door. But it turned out that he had already received several phone calls before we got there. My heart went out to him because I could see he was struggling to be the face of strength and courage for his family. All that was still going through my mind was how glad I was that he'd stayed home. Then I began to think about all that I had just lost, the most important being the kids at the church. I would miss my Sunday School room. On one of the walls, I had painted a picture of Jesus with His arms outstretched welcoming all who would come to Him. That was very personal to me. I would also miss the older folks, wise beyond measure, who supported us from day one.

There was a lot of prestige that went along with pastoring one of the most promising churches in the city. To get forced out would have bruised the pride of even the vainest. I can't speak for my husband but, for me, the unjustified dismissal was not just an assault on him, it was an attack on my integrity as well. Prestige had nothing to do with the feeling of loss I was experiencing, especially after witnessing all the devilment that went on. It had everything to do with the fact that I had been FIRED. Sure, it was Melvin who was voted out, but my husband is an extension of me and I him, so when they fired him, they fired me, too. Never had I ever been LET GO from any job. I always gave one hundred percent when it came to my role as the first lady at that church and, believe me, that was a job! In my opinion, FIRED and I could never exist in the same realm. Ever!

I learned many lessons during the years we spent at Washington Tabernacle, but the greatest lesson and the one that was proven over and over again was, "All that seems, ain't." Most definitely.

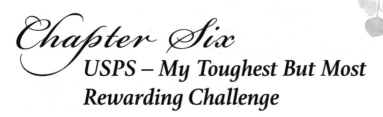

Chapter Six
USPS – My Toughest But Most Rewarding Challenge

1959–1969

On October 12, 1959, I was sworn in as a Substitute Distribution Clerk at the Saint Louis Main Post Office. But not before declaring I wouldn't have any more children. Imagine women having to swear to never have another baby so that they could get a job. It was shocking and appalling. Why were these agencies allowed to make such a demand? It didn't matter because four months later I was pregnant. I thought for sure my superiors would fire me once they found out, but luckily, that wasn't the case. But some of the male supervisors did try to make it difficult for me to remain on the job.

My duties included dispatching sacks of mail, handling parcels, and sorting mail. I was also expected to fill empty mail bags with parcels of various weights then place those sacks weighing upwards of 70 pounds onto heavy-duty push carts. On occasion, the bags would be too heavy for me to lift but most of the time I managed to get the job done on my own. I watched as men asked and received help whenever sacks were too heavy for them to pull or lift but as for the pregnant black girl one of the supervisors felt I should pull my own weight. He wasn't about to give me any help and he had no qualms about saying so. I was already carrying a heavy enough load for the man I'd married without having to deal with this jerk's B.S. too. I bet they all had hoped I would quit.

Accuracy was a major component of sorting mail for obvious reasons. I wasn't paying attention to how much, how fast, or how precise I was working, I was just doing my job. Some of my male co-workers would even get upset with me because of my productivity. Claiming I was making them look bad.

No fellas, I am trying to feed my family.

It was the supervisors' responsibility to verify our work for 98% accuracy. So they would conduct random case checks on each one of us, making sure we were sorting letter mail to the correct bins. They showed up to examine my work so much my case became their alternate workspace. I figured out they were happy with my performance and wanted all the other supervisors to know it. Even with an error or two, my rating was always well above 98%. The attention I got allowed me to become a trainer.

I loved training the new employees. Turns out I had a knack for molding their behavior and performance which benefited both the employee and the company. At the time, every aspect of processing the mail was manual with little mechanization so it was imperative to develop skilled labor. After all, inept employees could make or break the company.

Two years later the St. Louis Post Office finally incorporated the mechanized way of doing business. This meant drafting new instruction manuals and showing employees how to operate the strange new machinery. The manager of training wanted three top-performing employees who would make good instructors – one person from each of the three tours. Selected were two white men and me. Because we came highly recommended and the person in charge was confident we could do the job, we were told to report to the Training Department for a briefing on expectations. For me, I was so excited about the opportunity to learn something new which outweighed the fact that I had escaped having to do such strenuous work.

Our responsibilities included preparing lesson plans and learning to operate the equipment. Training the employees and guiding them through the transition period was also required. Within an hour of that briefing, we were told the assignment was ours. It felt like a promotion without actually being promoted. Days later, however, circumstances changed and we discovered the position wasn't ours. At least not without a price. For some odd reason, now we were being told that we'd have to pass a written examination before we could work in the Training Department.

Well, there goes my promotion without actually being promoted, I thought. Everything now hinged on passing an exam. No one in the Training Department had ever taken or had to pass an exam until the black girl showed up. That explained it! No one in that department had ever looked like me.

Out of the three of us who took the written exam, only one person did well and, of course, that person was me. I passed with flying colors. The two gentlemen went to the person in charge alleging that to pass I must have cheated. They were allowed to take the test again and *still* they both did not pass the second time. Yet we all remained in the Training Department without any mention of the examination especially to me. Once more, I had to accept the fact the rules would be different for me. Within a short time, the same guys were PROMOTED and reassigned to other departments. Everything dealing with training from developing the lesson plans and training materials to training the employees and those who would supervise all became my responsibility. It was now my operation and even though my position was not an official one, it was my opportunity to shine. I could not have been more elated.

The idea of sorting machines replacing them in their jobs created a sense of panic in the employees throughout the plant. When the jobs were posted *(seeking volunteers to get trained as machine operators)* that appeal received a lot of backlash and discourse because the workforce feared the unknown.

"What if I volunteer for training and can't qualify, I might lose my job!" many of the workers asserted.

Getting employees to volunteer presented more of a challenge than expected. So I had the announcement reposted. This time it let everyone know qualifying meant a higher level in pay. That did the trick. The workforce responded so overwhelmingly that I immediately scheduled employee orientations. It was time to introduce the new Multi-Position Letter Sorting Machine (MPLSM). During each session, the participants viewed a short film showing qualified workers sorting mail at rates of 60 letters per minute. A twenty-key keyboard module was onsite for the employees to use as a reference which did help to eradicate a lot of the worry and doubt. I could not have been more pleased with how well the orientations turned out.

My mission wasn't over yet. After briefings came training. That task consisted of developing decks of legal letter-sized training cards that would be used to simulate the process of how a letter got sorted by machine – making it faster for a letter to reach its final destination. Getting this done was no easy undertaking, but I thrived in the demands of it all.

Every once in a while, I'd get an occasional visit from managers who would come into the Training Department during orientations, stand there, and stare. In reality, they were checking out the new hires to see if any young attractive white women were in the group. The white male bosses had a habit of removing those women off the workroom floor *(some fresh out of orientation)* and then right away assigning them to an office job. A *special project* was how they described it. When my manager brought one of them into my unit to help me I took exception to it at first but it didn't have anything to do with her. I resented the fact that these men believed the pretty ones were *too pretty* to pull sacks or do all the arduous work that was required of everyone else. Luckily for me and to the dismay of the fool that sent her, this young lady came prepared to earn her keep. She was of great help to me until they found another *special project* for her.

Becoming Wonder Woman

Wonder Woman was a well-known female superhero recognized for her superior strength. That's only one of her many attributes. Speed, agility, and the ability to take flight were also noteworthy. But what's more impressive was the fact that she was well trained in hand-to-hand combat. She could even talk to animals. If I'm allowed to boast for a minute, I too could be likened to this great action figure. Strength–only by the grace of God could I have endured all the adversities. Speed–being chased around office furniture daily will get anyone in shape. Agility–they kept me on my toes, but I maintained my composure most of the time. Taking flight–did a lot of traveling on the Post Office's dime. Hand-to-hand combat–my abilities, talents, and determination did all my fighting. Talking to animals–do I even need to explain that one?

I had so many tasks to complete before I could get the trainees started. Leaving me to my own creative devices was the best thing my bosses could have ever done for me. Nobody was telling me what to do and I loved it. It was important to me that I be as knowledgeable as I could be about this new initiative, especially before introducing each phase of the training. And the only way to do that was to learn everything first myself. Take the hands-on approach. That way I'd be able to spot problem areas and make the necessary corrections or adjustments right away. It was imperative the equipment, test items, and trainees were ready for the new era of mail processing.

As the instructor, I immersed myself in every facet of the job to stay one step ahead of the trainees. I studied all the manuals on my own time because classroom preparation and teaching took up my workday. Even though I held the position of Trainer, I was still a clerk like the trainees and still required to meet the same criteria. That meant learning four different schemes plus memorize more than a few sets of addresses, hundreds of street names, and dozens of postal zip codes. Within two months I had qualified on four of the exams. Under normal circumstances that would have taken eight months to complete. I was even prepared to take the fifth and final exam just to prove to everyone, including myself, that I didn't take the role of trainer lightly.

Trucks were beginning to arrive with the massive parts for the MPLSM. That was an added incentive for me to get myself qualified. To my dismay, the manager of training refused to allow me to take the final exam. I would be the **first** to qualify and no one would understand was the explanation he gave in justifying his decision.

*I would be first? Oh! You mean I would be the first woman? Humm... or could this be about what it has always been about, **bigotry and sexism**?"* I thought.

He didn't want me, a black woman, to be the first to qualify on this exam! And the folks that wouldn't understand, of course, would be white folks, especially asinine white men. He knew how hard I had worked and that almost all my training took place on my own time. And how much FREE-TIME did he think a wife and mother of three had? All because he didn't want me to be the first. That made me so furious I went home and stayed for a couple of days. During that time I got an encouraging telephone call from my immediate supervisor, Mr. Henry Aubusson.

"Come back to work and never let anyone stop you from gaining what you have worked so hard to attain."

Everybody needs somebody sometimes to let you know they hear your voice – to assist you in your progress, especially when others try and hinder you because of their personal biases. I was grateful that the call came. It made me realize I had to get back in the fight.

David Lawson, Manager of Training, oversaw the first four exams I took. He was also the one who refused to allow me to take the fifth and final test. My immediate supervisor Henry Aubusson, however, felt Lawson's refusal was out of order. He knew other than his boss's bigotry there was no valid reason for denying me. Aubusson wanted to make sure no obstacle blocked my path even if that barrier came in the form of his boss. So he went behind his manager's back and administered the exam. The manager's office was nowhere near the exam room but we both feared Lawson would walk in on us and put a stop to the whole thing.

I devoted hours of my own time studying at the sacrifice of my family making sure I stayed ahead of the game. Practice, practice, practice is what I did day in and day out, and it paid off. I had weathered the storm, qualified, and was the first who became eligible to operate the Multi-Position Letter Sorter Machine. Wonder Woman had done it again. Three weeks later another capable black female hit the mark.

The machine examinations were not easy to pass, but so worth taking the risk because it meant attaining a guaranteed higher level in pay–*automatic upon qualification*. Even though I had earned it, for me, that pay increase was denied. Robert Dickson, who was the personnel manager at the time, received the documentation related to my pay increase but refused to process the forms. He like so many others didn't want to see a black person succeed let alone a black female. Because I *was* the *first* to accomplish this feat, he wanted nothing to do with it and that frustrated my immediate supervisor. Aubusson was sick of Dickson's disrespect, incompetence, and refusal to do his job. Left with no other choice, he called Headquarters in Washington DC and had them force Mr. Dickson to pay me the higher level. The list of imbeciles in positions of authority continued to mount, but so did my progress and influence. Two managers tried to block my advancement but couldn't. I will always be grateful to Mr. Henry Aubusson who, unlike others, looked beyond color when assigning work and shielded me when I couldn't protect myself. If you look closely there are angels all around you.

The engineering staff had to run an acceptance test on the new machine because everything needed to be in working order before the Post Office would sign off on the invoice accepting the equipment. I was certain they would be looking for me to run the test since I was familiar with the schemes and the keyboard. And I made sure I was visible and available in case they needed my help. The employees made sure they were ready as well. The first twelve who became eligible got the position and the automatic pay increase. Hallelujah!

I don't recall what exactly led to this set of events, but Mr. Aubusson came into the office one day incredibly sad. He had just lost a battle of epic proportions involving Postal politics and the highly capable, and well-trained black Lady. His superiors ordered him to return *me* to the workroom floor where I was to take my rightful place back with the other machine operators. Only supervisory personnel *(of which I was not)* could work in the Training Department. And so I returned to operations. Three white male supervisors got appointed to continue the work I alone had been doing. Although it stung a bit, I wasn't surprised to learn that they didn't have to qualify on any exam. My friends weren't too happy about the way I was treated and they made no attempts to hide their discontent about the matter. They tried to persuade me to destroy all the lesson plans that I developed. And everything else I had drafted. Especially what I had done on my time, but I didn't. It didn't matter anyway. Almost daily one of the training supervisors would come out on the workroom floor looking for me, asking **what to do with this** or **what should be next after we finish that.** My favorite was... **what report goes where?**

Question: How many white male supervisors does it take to screw in one lightbulb? *Answer:* Not those three!

1969–1980

I remained an *on-the-job-instructor* while working as a machine operator. A short time later I did get another opportunity to work in the Training Department. I loved being in direct contact with the employees... giving orientations and helping them learn new job skills. Mr. Lawson had all but abdicated his duties admitting he didn't want any more responsibility because he was retiring soon. That included attending a meeting at Headquarters in Washington DC. Seems the supervisor was just as disinterested in training as he was, so he sent me.

I was thrilled to be going to DC for a week. A tiny bit of that excitement was geared towards taking part in the Headquarters meeting. But my main focus was on getting the chance to visit one of my favorite shoe stores. When I found out there was one in the DC area, that did it for me, I was ready to go! And so was my little **she-angel.**

"Take your mind off of shoes. This is a business trip. What in the world will they be discussing for a whole week? If It's about training you can talk about that, but can you for a whole week?" *She needs to calm down,* I thought.

As usual, I was a little early for the meeting. While I was signing in at the guard's desk a petite little woman came up behind me. I assumed she was the secretary who was there to escort me to a conference room. Inside sat this large oblong table surrounded by twelve chairs. There was no one in the room but me so I hurried and picked the seat that I thought would give me a better view of everyone else. While other participants were arriving, that same petite little lady brought in coffee and danish. Food, a pleasing sight for me.

The team leader came in and introduced himself then asked us to do the same. Each person was either a Manager or Supervisor of Training. We were halfway through the introductions by the time they got to me. I was so nervous because I was only a craft employee, a mere machine operator. Right away I started lessening my worth. When I finished introducing myself to this crowd of higher-ups someone asked what happened to my Training Manager. I wanted to say he died, but my **she-angel** wouldn't let me. I sure felt like I was about to, especially after learning there was even a Director of Human Resources in the bunch. I thought for sure I was in over my head.

The team leader started talking about a new way of doing business. About an hour into the session, I realized I didn't have a clue as to what he was talking about but it appeared that everybody else did. There were a lot of questions being asked although those so-called questions were somewhat ambiguous, as was the team leader's mumbo-jumbo. He used terms not many of us were familiar with or could associate with postal concepts. However, there were a few who did nod their heads in confirmation of what was being said. I was feeling more and more inadequate by the minute and figured there was nothing left for me to do but to check out and fly home as soon as the session was over that day. After what I had just sat through, whatever reprimand my boss would issue for my abrupt departure couldn't feel any worse. At least that's what I told myself.

At the end of the day, the team leader asked for a review of what was covered. "Who wants to go first?" He asked. No one volunteered. As it turned out not one person understood what the man was talking about the entire time, not even the Director of Human Resources. He was the first to admit he wasn't clear about what was covered and everyone else agreed. What was I so worried about? We were all on the same level–team lead, manager, supervisor, and craft. Add them all up and you get STUDENT!

The team-lead worked for this high-priced management-consulting company. Some Postal head-honcho thought it was a good idea to waste money by hiring outside the organization. *Here we go again! Have we still not learned anything from our past?* He wasn't a postal employee nor did he have any experience in on-the-job training. He hadn't even been to a postal training unit to get acquainted with the process. But what I appreciated about the man was that he was open to listening. The next day the leader took a different approach. He asked each of us about our training operations. Then suggested ways we could incorporate the new concept with the old.

Everyone got the chance to share their training experience. But I had an advantage because I worked directly with the craft employees and many of them had not. *Just spotted an opening and I'm about to take the shot!* I laid out in detail the training techniques that worked well and even those that did not. By the end of the day, I had become a major player on the team. The next three days were our most productive. We came up with strategies to sell the new concept, had a plan that would provide development opportunities to all interested employees, and by day five I was tasked with implementing the plan in St. Louis. I was on fire. My she-angel said, "Now Geri, you see how the Lord works?"

One day, the *soon-to-be-pensioned* Mr. Lawson summoned me into his office and said, "I know I should leave you in charge, but I can't. I promised Jake my loyal and faithful secretary an opportunity."

Jake? This poor man in all of his 50 years of service had never shouldered the command of any operation. The pressure of the job was too much for Jake, who suffered two heart attacks before *he* even retired. But during Jake's short time as Manager of Training, I was the one who still managed the operation which was now called the Postal Employee Development Center or the PEDC. When it came time to fill the position, the Human Resources Director said I couldn't have the job. My credentials and job experience didn't matter to him.

Mr. William Holloway, Director of Human Resources, wanted someone with a Master of Educational Administration degree. The position of Manager of Postal Employee Development Center (PEDC) didn't require a degree of any kind, even on the national level. To my knowledge, our office was now the only one in the country with that prerequisite. So happens those same credentials that the Director stipulated matched those of his close friend. It was obvious to everyone what was really going on. Holloway's friend, Joel, was from the outside whose only real interest in the company was better benefits and higher pay. Landing this job was his entry point and pathway to the top.

I applied for and got the second position, that of the Training & Development Specialist when it became available. However, my real goal was to get the top job that Joel currently had and, with the right qualifications, I was certain it would only be a matter of time until I did. I would even go into Joel's office and speak with him about my enrolling in a university. Joel didn't even try to hide his condescending tone when he suggested I consider attending a *junior college* instead because he felt I wouldn't be able to handle the coursework (at the university) and would fail my first semester. It was clear he thought he was superior to me just because he was white, a man, and educated. I guess he didn't realize or care that I knew he had flunked out at one point. Me, I graduated CUM LAUDE.

I got a lot of satisfaction out of being the second in command, a position where I could affect change. I was careful not to squander the opportunity because people who looked like me, working in the same surrounding area as me, had not been as fortunate. I was always determined to rise above the norm. *"Can't"* was a word I refused to accept, especially before an attempt was even made This job provided me the freedom to explore all kinds of ways where we could improve in areas that would make things better. It felt like I had gotten a slice of heaven and I couldn't wait for the next project or challenge.

I had to drive 120 miles from my home office to a Post Office located in Mid-Missouri. There I met with union reps who had some concerns about the impact of the MPLSMs on the work-force. The machines were being installed in their facility and they feared the employees were being replaced. It was my job to convince them that was not the case. I scheduled an infor-mative meeting for anyone who wanted to hear what I had to say. I was confident I could address their concerns because this was the second implementation of an MPLSM program I had set-up. I covered information about the machine, the required training and qualifications, higher-level pay, and the fact that there would be no loss of employees. After my little song and dance, it was time for the question & answer part. First question, "How did *YOU* get that job?"

Right away my **she-angel** said, "Not again!"

I don't know why that question annoyed me, especially since it was common knowledge that this part of the state was racist. Yet I was not sure where I should begin with my answer. I wres-tled with whether to start by telling of my struggles to survive in the organization, or how I applied for the job and got it because I was the best qualified. The consequences of either would have opened up another can of worms. So, I said, "I set up the program in St. Louis which was very successful, and the Mail Processing Director asked that I do the same here."

"How can I get a job like *YOURS*?" someone in the audi-ence asked.

"Be the first one to qualify on the MPLSM and I'll recom-mend you to be one of the trainers," I answered.

At least two hours out of my eight-hour day was always wasted on me explaining how I got my job. And it was always mostly white employees who were asking the questions. They were also the ones threatening to slash my tires or warning me not to be out on the town's dark road alone, especially at night. I conducted four 2-hour training sessions from 7 PM until 3 AM which meant I had to be on the road by myself... at night and it was not a good feeling given the so-called warning. Imminent danger as far as I saw it. I took extra precautions as I traveled back and forth between the post office and the hotel where I was staying, intimidated or not. And there were plenty of times I was! Despite their initial fear of the unknown or their negative attitudes about having me as their instructor, the employees became a great team who were proud of the job they were doing. The operation was rated number three all over the country. As their development became more visible the folks in charge asked me to leave their small community and never return. That bothered me for a while, but I am grateful I had the opportunity.

Workplace Sexual Harassment

I'm glad to know that women are now empowered to speak up when or if they have been harassed in the workplace. Back during my time that was not the case, it was definitely a man's world then. Women had no one to confide in or complain to. We weren't even welcomed in the first place so, of course, there was no system in place to protect us from unwanted advances, cruelty, unfair treatment, or anything else. Men felt they could get away with perpetrating all types of offenses against us. So many sexual assaults went unreported because there were no safety measures or consequences. I remember getting chased around the office furniture by the assistant training manager. This occurred every week after all the trainees would leave the room. He was an older gentleman who couldn't move as fast as me and I would always plan my exit strategy ahead of time. Announcing I didn't want to work in the Training Department anymore was my only form of protest even though leaving wasn't really an option or the answer to the problem. So, I stayed and continued to run around the furniture until he finally gave up.

When I was part of a team from St Louis sent to the Regional Office in Chicago, we received instruction on how to prepare our District for a Regional Audit. Harry Pent was the Regional Representative who provided us with the guidelines on what to look for, how to document our findings, exactly what information to report back to him on, and his telephone number. He also needed a block of rooms reserved at a hotel near the St. Louis Post Office for the following week, which I did take care of as soon as we got back to St. Louis. The very next day after my return Harry called asking me to make reservations at a different hotel, this time for just the two of us. His presumptuous attitude disgusted me yet I remained polite *but* assertive. I made it clear that there was already a room reserved with his name on it at the Holiday Inn up the street from the Main Post Office. (*I could feel my blood starting to boil.*) And that it was the only reservation that was going to get made for him, and only him. (*I'm mad now.*) Then slammed the phone down. (*So much for politeness.*) Because I rejected his offer Harry refused to accept my audit report when I called it in as he had instructed. One of my co-workers was kind enough to submit my findings. So you see Mister, "*no weapons formed against me shall prosper!*"

While on a different audit in another city, I got harassed again but by a different regional person. I arrived at the hotel and checked in as usual. Traveling throughout the region could be exhausting at times, but I enjoyed the work I was doing so much I was willing to endure the grind. Other than the satisfaction of grooming new and reshaping old employees, what made it all worth it to me was room service, it was my favorite thing to have. I wasn't what you would call a social butterfly. No one would ever suspect how shy I was when they saw me in action in front of a group of trainees. Instructing was a skill I had mastered, plus it meant I had control over how much distance I maintained between me and them (*or anyone else for that matter*). Social settings were definitely a different animal. I was not as confident walking into them. My co-workers loved to gather in the hotel's lounge after work. Me, not so much. I relished the thought of being able to hide in my nice quiet room where I could finish adding the final touches to my next day's agenda, then order the most delicious meal from the hotel's room-service menu. It was a lovely way to end the evening.

I must have been really tired because I fell asleep with some paperwork lying right next to me that I don't think I ever got the chance to read. At about 1:00 AM came a knock on the door from the adjourning room. It was Mr. Robertson the regional person, insisting I let him into my room, saying no one would know, and it would be our secret rendezvous. I guess he knocked on and off for a good hour before I threatened to call the front desk if he didn't go away. My threat did nothing to deter him, instead, it somehow alerted this pervert that he needed to change his sleazy approach. His sexual overtures went from knocking to rendering desperate whispers and ridiculous pleas. It was hard to believe that fool was thinking that might actually work. I wasted no time in calling the front desk to report that a strange man in the adjourning room was being a nuisance insisting that I unlock the adjourning door. The young guy at the front desk seemed perplexed and told me Mr. Robertson pre-arranged for the adjourning rooms. "Do you want us to move you to another room?" he asked.

"No, I want you to warn Mr. Robertson," I demanded. Then I heard the telephone ring in the adjourning room. The knocking and whispering stopped.

When I got back to St. Louis I wrote a formal letter of complaint and also made an appointment to meet with Mr. Knopp, the District Manager. After listening to my grievance, he proceeded to put the letter in his desk drawer and said the matter would go no further. That was the end of our conversation. I was dismissed as if leaving the principal's office. Nothing else was done. Some of the men in the organization believed their positions granted them privileges beyond their job descriptions. If a woman didn't play their game there would be hell to pay, and it often was.

Years later the Equal Employment Opportunity laws had gone into effect. The Postal Service added offices to house our EEO department, a place where employees could voice their concerns and also submit their formal grievances. But women were still too intimidated by male bosses to file complaints nor did they want to be spotted going in and out of the EEO Office for fear of losing their jobs. Even the female employees from the law enforcement office would make a beeline straight to my office so that I could arrange to have an EEO official meet with them there. Imagine that! These women were federal agents with guns, they made arrests, and even investigated various crimes against the Postal Service, yet they couldn't stop the constant barrage of on-the-job harassment and abuse coming from their male counterparts.

I was also instrumental in helping female employees get job reassignments, especially for those harassed by their current male managers. Folks higher up the chain of command refused to take any action against their own. It was a classic case of the good-ole-boys looking out for the other good-ole-boys. Those hypocrites had no problem coming to my office and asking me for help, especially when they found themselves in a bit of a jam, or as they liked to call it... *a little matter*. The never-ending merry-go-round of indecent proposals and cover-ups was nauseating. Even still I would always agree to help. I had to look past what sickened me and use my influence and platform to assist those that truly needed me... women from every race, background, and job description. It wasn't easy but it was never out of the question.

An Out-of-Town Discussion With My Bosses

William Holloway, Joel Berman, and I were in Columbia Missouri a town 125 miles NW of St. Louis. We were there attending a meeting to address problems affecting our entire district, to make an assessment, then report our findings to our district manager back home. As part of our assessment, we interviewed several employees to get a feel for what might be going on. A white female employee voiced her concern about one of the male supervisors who, according to her, was having an affair with one of his female workers. A woman who, as she put it, happened to be *baaaalack*. Emphasis on *BAAAALACK*! It was something about the way she said *baaaalack* that struck me as odd.

When we go back to our hotel the three of us decided to have dinner before turning in for the evening, so we stopped in the hotel's restaurant located just off the lobby. While we waited for our food we each shared our views about the issues going on in Columbia. Issues that were not new or foreign to us. Racial biases were still affecting promotions, women were still being denied opportunities, and the good-ole-boys' network was still in full bloom. When I brought that one up they both squirmed. Older employees still felt that young folks coming into the company weren't worth their salt, or that their work ethic wasn't the same as the old-heads. Then Joel brought up the allegation made by the white female employee we spoke with earlier. Based upon the emphasis placed on some of her words Joel assumed the supervisor was also black, but he felt he needed to find out for sure. Joel had been a third-grade school teacher before coming to the Postal Service. He was also accompanied by his bigotry and misconceptions which were evident because he had never encountered both black and white supervisors until then. I asked why it was necessary for him to confirm the person's race.

"We just need to know." Was his hasty reply.

He'd soon discover there was absolutely no need for that information. Whatever biases Joel was attempting to lean towards immediately fell by the wayside. Every supervisor in Columbia's main post office was white.

"No black fall-guy here mister." my **she-devil** smirked.

I was beginning to get a bit annoyed by it all. We needed to stick to the facts and the facts alone. A male supervisor was having an affair with one of his female employees. A person's race was not the issue. It was a conflict of interest period! Our dinner had arrived just as tensions were mounting. We had all ordered something different, but the aromas that filled the air blended so well it helped bring calm to a brewing storm.

Mr. Holloway said, "Geraldine, you don't understand, you don't have an affair with just any..."

Almost choking on his words, he had to take a deep breath before starting up again. Joel seemed to understand where Holloway was going with his explanation and added...

"For example, you would be the exception, we wouldn't mind sleeping with you."

Holloway echoed they wouldn't mind sleeping with me in a tone disguised as a compliment.

"Gentlemen *(and by no means did I consider them to be that).* Perhaps you would not mind, but I **certainly would mind** being with either of you!" As I rose from the table, half-@$$ apologies ensued.

"We didn't mean anything by it. We only meant we wouldn't mind if it were you."

By repeating it, they only proved they had no idea what they had just revealed to me about themselves. As I was about to turn and exit the restaurant, I could see it so clearly in my mind. In the movies, the leading lady takes her drink and throws it in the face of the leading man in response to an insult or an improper gesture. It was what I so badly wanted to do. I began to wonder if they were EVEN qualified to assess the problems in Columbia, St. Louis, or anywhere else. And these clowns were *my* bosses.

My Detail to the Personnel Office – Don't Mess with Wonder Woman

Fred Matthews, the Manager of Personnel, was removed from his job for reasons unknown to many of us. I got the opportunity to work in his position until they found a replacement. One of my jobs included securing meeting and banquet spaces to conduct Postal business. Hotel sales teams and I would discuss government rates and hotel accommodations. Handicapped accessibility was also a must if the hotel wanted our business. The Postal Service employed thousands with various disabilities, so that needed to be a top priority to the potential facility as well. I enjoyed traveling around to all the local hotels, especially the newer ones, sampling the food and checking out the rooms.

I got some disturbing news about questionable personnel matters involving new and veteran craft employees within the unit who were being subjected to unfair treatment. The culprits were some of the management staff from that same department including the manager. Some stories I believed, while others I suspected were only excuses from employees not taking care of business. As the Acting Manager, I had opportunities to observe and review the practices of both employees and the personnel staff. It became clearer to me just how much people's biases and failure to act affected the decisions that were made.

The training department was responsible for booking hotel conference spaces and lodging for out-of-town and local Postal personnel. During the time that Fred was a management trainee, he had gotten familiar with our process of negotiating with various hotels. Hoping to gain our business the hotels would offer great incentives like complimentary rooms and free meals. Once he became the Manager of Personnel, Fred contacted those same hotels and made himself a point-of-contact under the guise of doing business for the Postal Service. In reality, he was taking advantage of the hotel's complimentary rooms, and free meals per his own personal pleasure as well as getting discounted room rates for people who didn't even work for the government.

Fred's level classification for the position of Manager of Personnel was EAS-21. He had a staff of about twenty people classified as levels EAS 11-16. There were several complaints on file alleging wrongdoing by some of the staff in the personnel office, citing the mishandling of requests for advanced sick leave. Employees could submit a written request to be advanced a certain amount of sick leave hours for things like scheduled surgeries or other medical conditions. Some employees received approval without any question while others did not. As the Acting Manager, I had to investigate the matter to find out exactly what was going on.

Cathy was a white level-14 staffer who was responsible for handling sick leave requests. She was also seven levels below me, so I figured what better place to start than the obvious. I had her come to my office and, when she arrived, I asked, "Cathy, what method do you use in determining whose requests get approved and whose get denied?"

The previous personnel managers had all been white men. She had never encountered someone who looked like me in a position of authority. Being that we were two females, I was confident we could have a professional and respectful conversation, regardless of our racial differences. Boy, was I wrong. Cathy felt she had the **white**... I mean the **right** to flaunt her contempt for my request and so she did.

"It's none of your business! How dare you think you're going to review my work or even question it!"

Here comes the final dagger.

"And anyway, this is all confidential and not yours to know."

POOF! Just like that my little **she-devil** appeared in an instant on my left shoulder and whispered, "Ohhh! So now even she thinks she can put your black behind in your place?"

I must admit her haughtiness caught me completely off guard. All I could say was, "WHAT?"

Triggered by her blatant disrespect, my veins began to swell, the adrenaline ran fast and furious through them. Instead of Wonder Woman, I felt as though I was turning into the Incredible Hulk, my anger real and justified. Through my how-dare-you gaze but in my sweet, I'm the head *you-know-what* in charge tone, I calmly issued my command...

"I merely wanted to know the procedure you were using. But never mind because the procedure is not important. From now on, I will decide the criteria for future requests. Now go and bring me the entire file!"

What I really wanted to say was, "Now begone!" But feeling myself return to normal, I said very calmly, "I'll be here waiting."

She scampered off, silenced and shocked by my refusal to take any more of her crap or insubordination.

After reviewing her files, I discovered that if Cathy liked you, then she approved your request and if she didn't, well, you know the rest. The previous manager didn't care about doing his job, that of resolving the complaints and addressing his staffer's misconduct. This type of behavior existed within the organization for far too long and *Ms. Thang* wasn't going to get away with it any longer. At least not on my watch.

Misconduct I Considered Criminal – Wonder Woman to the Rescue

I had the opportunity to review promotion packages, pay designations, and step increases while still serving as Acting Manager of Personnel. I became familiar with how much the managers *(all men)* were being paid, pay raises and all. I was confident I'd get paid in the same manner as they had been when it was time for my promotion, especially since I always received higher ratings than most of them. I wasn't concerned in the least until I opened and read my anxiously awaited letter. In it contained my job confirmation and my... pay increase?

Am I reading this correctly? What's happening here? I questioned. I was taken aback as my brain struggled to sort things out.

My anniversary date and promotion date were close to one another and according to the letter, for that reason, I would only receive the higher of the two raises. That grossly conflicted with what I knew. You're due a pay raise on your anniversary date *and* a salary increase once you're promoted. That was the usual protocol except, when it came to me, I only got one. This was troubling because I knew the process and I saw the files. The men always got both, a pay raise for the number of years in their job, and a salary increase that reflected their promotions. I wasn't about to take that lying down, so I marched into my boss's office and confronted him. Lucky for him his door was already propped open because I was going to **kung fu kick** his office door down had it been shut. I demanded to know why I was being treated differently from the two men, whose files, I reminded him, I had seen.

It had better be a good explanation buster or I'll karate chop you into little pieces, is what I was thinking at the time. I suppose my demeanor must have come across as rebellious to him. This man was the one who had signed off on every one of my outstanding performance ratings over the past year, and every year prior.

Yet on that day, he proceeds to shout at me as loud as he could, "YOU MUST BE OUTTA YOUR TREE TO THINK YOU'RE GONNA MAKE THAT MUCH MONEY!"

When he saw that his blustering hadn't caused me to move an inch, he admitted he had done that for the men for reasons he was not willing to disclose to me. His attempt to pretend he didn't understand why I would expect the same consideration fell on deaf ears. Without uttering a single word, the look on my face spoke volumes. That hypocrite knew I was fully aware of the reasons *why* and with that... I turned and walked out.

1980–1987

Quotas – *A judge assigned legal remedy to a guilty finding of discrimination.*

Around this time, there was a federal mandate requiring the USPS to put in place programs to promote qualified minorities and women. Promoting me to the position of Manager, Postal Employee Development Center did make our district appear as though they were meeting the quotas. With me, the district finally had two-in-one, a *person of color* who also happened to be a *woman* in one of the higher-level positions. When it came time to update the annual staffing reports, I was counted twice. Here's how.

The first question on the report asked: *How many **African Americans** do you have in levels 20-25?* The answer: One... me.

The next question asked: *How many **women** do you have in levels 20-25?* The answer again: One... me.

It was never indicated on the quota form that the same person was being counted twice, although I should have been. I had worked smarter and twice as hard as anyone around me. Along the way, I had already been the first female at each level and the first black person in several others. Always, always having to do more than my share just to be considered.

Manager, Postal Employee Development Center

I took pride in how the Training Department was set up. I had to. I was the new Manager, Postal Employee Development Center. My staff needed to be proud of their surroundings so, like my mother, attention to detail was a must. We scrounged around the building until we located items we could use for our office. The best stuff was on the lower floors and in the basement where we stumbled upon tables, chairs, cabinets, and bookshelves. There was even some beautiful furniture crafted from wood. It appeared that a lot of it had long been sitting or discarded, for what reason I didn't know. An executive and friend who worked in the Data Center let me have some furniture out of one of his offices as well. Seems they didn't need their unused stuff either. Many of the pieces were actually quite lovely and you know what they say, **one man's trash was indeed another training unit's treasure.** We were in business!

The training staff's goal was to inspire and help further the employees' development, talk about possibilities both personal and professional if necessary, and motivate and encourage those types of discussions. But for us to do that the place couldn't look like a dump. It had to reflect the message and promote that which we preached. So, we created a professional space for the employees in which to grow. Now, here comes the boom!

Office Communication: *Effective Immediately! Only offices on the third floor are allowed to have wooden furniture.*

As if they were a herd of buffalo, the executives from the third floor stampeded the second-floor offices taking whatever they wanted from us. We lost our favorite conference table that stood in the library, along with all our other favored items. I contacted the regional office to see if there was currently a local or national policy in place regarding the use of wooden furniture. Of course, there was none. *Time to play ball,* I sensed.

Over the weekend I pondered what to do next but luckily, I didn't have to ponder long. As soon as I arrived at work on Monday I reached out to Clarence, a friend, and co-worker in the Chicago office to inquire about furniture. I put him on speakerphone so that I could put my purse down and hang up my jacket. But before I could do so, he started telling me there was plenty of old wooden furniture in their storeroom and that they would be glad to get rid of it all. *Watch God work!* That next week I got a call informing me a large tractor-trailer from Chicago had pulled up to the loading dock full of wooden office furniture and that I needed to come right away to sign for it. You would have thought I was ten as I skipped from my office down to the loading dock.

My entire staff got wooden desks (*and so much more*). Not those old metal contraptions that the executives tried to give us. The powers that be took our stuff then refused to even buy new metal furniture for us. They felt it was only fitting that we use whatever was in the building as long as it wasn't wooden or new. My job as a manager was to look out for my staff and that's just what I did. If I could have sent out an inner-office communication of my own, it would have read... **Third-floor execs–welcome to the newly furnished Postal Employees Development Center.**

The Token Me

As I navigated through a sea of endless BS I continued to move upward in the system. But again not without a cost, tons of sacrifice, unfair prerequisites, or disguised intent from whoever was in charge at the time. Speaking of disguised intent. I was often used as the token and mostly always in a dual capacity. Token Female and Token Black.

When my bosses needed to add a little color and a female I would be the one they'd ask to sit on promotion boards or speak at various affairs. That would give the appearance of racial and gender equivalence in the workplace. It took a couple of times for me to catch on to what was happening especially concerning the promotion boards. They were generally made up of five members: three white men, one female, and one person of color each having one vote. But because I was black and female, those two votes became one vote at which time another member, usually a white male, would be added to the board.

The promotion board's responsibility was to make a recommendation to the selecting official of the top three candidates for the job. Here's where the tomfoolery comes into play. Managers would sit in while we conducted interviews, then suggest whose name we should send to the selecting official *(a.k.a. the Manager)* with no regard to who was best qualified. The board would then sign off on a letter of recommendation and send the applicant's name to that same selecting official. I was new to the process but seasoned enough to know that what was taking place was corrupt. I thought *if the manager was telling us who to recommend for the job then why were we holding interviews?*

I met with the Director of Human Resources to discuss and reaffirm the proper procedures the promotion board was to adhere to and to also inform him of what had been happening. This type of unethical conduct was so egregious, and I needed to speak up. I made it abundantly clear that I would no longer sit on any board where a manager was present or was able to have any input during the process and, each time it happened, I would be filing a written report. My resolve was clear, my stance firm. Going forward, as a safeguard, I asked for clarification on the exact selection criteria, to make sure our recommendations were per the guidelines and to get my request added to the record.

At one of our promotion board interview sessions, I insisted we keep things fair and on the up and up. We used tallies to score the interviewees. There would be no manager allowed to sit in and pick the candidate they wanted before giving everyone else a fair shot. And wouldn't you know it? When we added all the tallies, it was a black female who scored the highest. This didn't sit well with any of the white men, especially the selecting official once he got the news. I was accused of somehow signaling her right in front of their very eyes *(by using my skills as a magician I supposed)*. The men couldn't describe how I had accomplished such a feat but did manage to convince themselves I had to have done it and that was why the black female candidate did so well. But everyone knew that wasn't the case at all. They had their shorts in a knot all because the top score belonged to someone who looked like me. These racist and sexist individuals had no other choice but to adhere to the rules and regulations set forth or they were going to have to contend with me. Someone no longer willing to look the other way.

Tokens All Around!

While I was on an assignment in Washington DC, I got a call saying I had to attend a special headquarters event. One they were going to video.

"Why me?" I asked.

"They didn't say, only that you needed to be there, so find something to wear and get there on time," said the voice on the other end of the phone.

I got dressed, caught a cab, and made my way to the venue. After paying my fare, I rushed from the taxi and hurried inside so that I could find a seat. I hated walking into large rooms full of strange people. Heck, I wasn't that comfortable doing it with people I knew. I gave my name to a nice elderly gentleman dressed in what appeared to be a theatre usher's uniform standing by the big entry doors. To my surprise, they were expecting me. I should have known right away it was a set-up. An usher escorted me to a table where seven other people were already seated, six white people and a black gentleman. The only seat available landed me between a white female on my left and a white man on my right. Across the table was my black counterpart which luckily for me gave us direct eye contact.

Cascading crystals hanging from the ceiling decorated the event space. There were floodlights and cameras at the front of the stage, and some postal paraphernalia was there as well. A huge ice sculpture in the shape of an eagle sat in the middle of the room, an area normally reserved for dancing. *More than likely they'd remove it when it was time for people to let down their hair,* I thought. These types of post office events almost always included music and dancing which was fitting because the room's atmosphere almost felt wedding-like.

Throughout the evening, none of our white table companions bothered to talk to us or even acknowledge our presence.

When I attempted to converse with the man on one side of me there was no interaction at all. The black man looked at me and smiled. I recognized that look because I had seen it so many times before. My mother used to give me that look and then say, "Geraldine is so special." It was that **this child ain't got a clue** look. I was already feeling apprehensive about having to attend the event, before, during, and after I had arrived so I'm pretty sure I did seem a little out of sorts. What's worse I still didn't know why I was there. I just wanted it to hurry up and be over with so that I could get back to the peace and quiet of my hotel room.

His gaze did make me start to pay closer attention as I began surveying my surroundings. It didn't take long before I realized the two of us were the only people of color in the entire room. That was definitely an **uh-oh** moment for sure. We didn't know anyone there, didn't even know each other until our introduction at the table. The familiar faces weren't because we knew the people, it was because we recognized them from photos of the top executives in the organization. Later, after the event was over and we compared notes, my table companion said he noticed I hadn't caught on to what was happening around me. One thing we both agreed on was that we had been hoodwinked. It seems we were only there for a photo op and a video-staged event to make the company appear to be engaged, concerned, progressive, and inclusive. The token female and the two token blacks *(counting me twice again)* had saved the day. The gentleman didn't appear to be as bothered as much by everything that took place as I was. It had happened to him once before and no one at that event talked to him either.

> *The word* **token** *can be defined as a similar set of people in an organization who include a person from a minority group to give the impression of diversity. People with* **disabilities** *are also considered members of a minority group. They are often forgotten or excluded from, among other things, community life. This particular occasion touches on both.*

In recognition of the new handicap laws, established in the '80s, and to show support for people with disabilities, Headquarters hosted a Handicap Awards Banquet in Washington DC. Sarah, one of our Postmasters, was to receive the first National Handicap Award. She had lost the use of her legs following a severe automobile accident on her way to work. She was extremely popular in her community and highly admired for her determination to work using her wheelchair to get around. Because she was so highly revered, Mr. Holloway asked me to escort her and her family from St. Louis to the event, again I'm thinking, *why me?* I wanted to believe he selected me because of my commitment to doing the best job possible no matter what, and not because he needed to give the appearance of inclusion in the workplace.

We arrived at the hotel only to discover there was no handicap-accessible entrance from the outside. When we got to her hotel room we discovered Sarah's wheelchair couldn't even fit through the bathroom door and to make matters worse, there were no handrails or any support features around the toilet or tub which meant Sarah's husband had to pick her up to take her to the bathroom and support her while she was on the toilet. The entire situation was extremely distressing to me so I could only imagine how it made them feel. Turns out, the hotel had not yet complied with the national guidelines for people with disabilities.

What was my boss thinking? Didn't he know the accommodations weren't suitable for anyone in her condition? I thought.

I was completely incensed by the whole ordeal and Sarah's husband was just as infuriated. At one point he wanted to leave and take his wife back to St. Louis, but she rejected the notion even with the accommodations or lack thereof. With her husband and two other family members there who could assist her, Sarah was determined to see things through to the very end. But all I could think of was, *what if her husband had not been there?*

As the couple continued with the inspection of their temporary housing, I walked over to the room's only phone that was sitting on the desk near the big picture window overlooking the nearby park, picked up the receiver, and began dialing not even bothering to take in the picturesque view.

The Director of Human Resources came on the line. Like a speeding train, the first words that came racing out of my mouth were, "We are moving!"

I needed to get his approval to move the honoree and her family to another hotel, one that was handicap accessible and I didn't care if he could sense how upset I was. I didn't even care how great of an idea it was to host a celebration for someone with a disability. She was one of our own, and to have it at a hotel that couldn't even accommodate the person we were trying to pay tribute to was absolutely ridiculous!

"No, you are not moving!" he barked. "Don't you realize whose hotel that is? It's owned by a Bigwig who is well connected!"

"Bigwig?" I sassed.

"...and the celebration will go on. Geraldine, your job is to make the best of it, take care of the family, and don't cause any problems!" He ordered.

After a bit more prodding, Mr. Holloway revealed that the **Bigwig** who owned the hotel was the man running the Postal Service. I was so engrossed in our tug-of-war I hadn't realized the family's full attention was now on me, each one absorbing my every word. After I hung up the phone, Sarah and her family told me they understood the awkward position I had been put in. They were so polite. Hoping to help relieve some of my frustration, Sarah and her family reassured me that they would be alright. But it wasn't all right, at least not to me. It was completely unacceptable. All I kept thinking about was Mr. Holloway. He knew that the hotel did not meet guidelines and he still chose to make Sarah the *disabled token* and me the usual *token black-female* just so that he could impress his boss and make the man-in-charge feel like he was giving the appearance of valuing a diverse workforce.

Just when I thought it couldn't get any worse, it did. Propped against the stage where the award ceremony was to take place was a long plank of wood. To my horror, this was the hotel's facsimile of a handicapped-accessible ramp. The hotel staff was going to lean that big ole piece of wood against the stage but had absolutely no idea how they were going to secure it. I felt as though I was trapped in this ghastly nightmare and couldn't wake up. I had learned a little something from watching all of the construction work going on when my husband was renovating our church building and knew the hotel staff didn't have a clue what they were doing.

Sarah and her entire family weren't shown the type of hospitality they truly deserved. Still, that night at the ceremony, Sarah remained focused waiting with great anticipation for the awards part of the program. When it was time, Sarah with the help of her dutiful husband, made her way up that makeshift ramp onto the stage and proudly accepted the first United States Postal Service's National Handicap Award.

I had been put in another awkward situation. The entire ordeal made the organization look completely incompetent and hypocritical. But we got through it and the family was grateful.

Dealing With the Male Ego At Work

In the St. Louis office, several units fell under the umbrella of the Director of Human Resources: EEO, Safety, Personnel, Employment, Labor Relations, Training, and the Medical Unit, yet each division operated as an independent entity. The managers did their own thing with no consideration of the impact it had on other offices. I often reflect on my experiences with many of them who I had worked for and there are only two words that would pop into my visual cortex... **male ego!**

These guys were extremely self-absorbed and had no problem using me or anyone else to get what they wanted. They always saw themselves to be more worthy or better than those that they managed, particularly women and especially me, a black woman. In meetings, my suggestions would either get ignored or left on the table, because the idea came from me and not them. They would sacrifice real progress/change rather than take the advice of the little-black-know-it-all. Even if it appeared they were adhering to sound advice, rarely if ever did they follow it, and opening themselves up to receive constructive criticism was simply out of the question as was admitting to any flaws personal or departmental.

There was also a breakdown in communication between the various functional areas. So, the HR Director brought us all together to discuss the issues, which resulted in us having to come up with a resolute plan of action to fix the problem. Even though I wasn't recognized for many of my contributions, I knew exactly how we could turn things around. Most of them had taken advantage of me far too many times but I wasn't about to let those past assaults discourage me. When the Director asked if anyone had any ideas, I didn't hesitate to speak up.

I made my way to the front of the conference room once the HR Director yielded the floor to me. If those piercing stares I received could have burned a hole right through me, I think they would have. None of these egotistical half-wits were ready or willing to put their necks on the line, and none were willing or able to come up with a workable solution to the problem. They were comfortable with continuing down the same non-productive path because that required no effort or innovation. Each in his respective role felt his way of managing or *mismanaging* was the right approach. Their male egos needed to show off individual accomplishments instead of team successes.

The HR Director wanted us to work as a team, and I believed my concept was perfect for such a cause. I explained that it had occurred to me that none of the managers had any knowledge of the others' roles and, in my opinion, that was what contributed to the communications barrier. I suggested a rotation schedule that would give each manager the chance to detail into his or her peer's job temporarily, then explained in detail the benefits of my plan-of-action. First, it would give them insight into their counterpart's position and responsibilities and, second, it allowed for transparency and critique. Finally, it had the potential of alleviating distrust, resentment, or departmental conflicts.

I was so engrossed in what I was sharing that I didn't realize people had started to sit up in their chairs and take notice. Their usual posturing, whenever I spoke, was to put elbows on tables and heads in hands. Not this time. This time they all repositioned themselves, like preschoolers seated at their tiny desks anticipating a snack. Finally! I had everyone on board the *can't-we-all-just-get-along-train*. Or, so I thought. Dissension soon took shape after I finished my presentation and, even though I had expected as much, I did remain hopeful if only for a second or two.

It didn't sit well with some of the managers who felt threatened or somewhat uncomfortable by the idea of someone else coming into their department and possibly making changes to their current procedures. Others objected only because they didn't want the rest of us to discover what they WERE NOT doing. One of the managers who objected the loudest did so without giving a valid reason, just that he didn't think the whole thing would work. He was the type of guy who would complain if silver dollars were falling from the sky and somebody else was lucky enough to get one even though he had all the rest. Flustered by his staff member's disruptive outburst, the HR Director ended the meeting. My idea got sidelined again. As we were all exiting the room the little voice inside my head began screaming, *You're the DIRECTOR for goodness sake! You should have told that fool to sit down and shut up so that you could comment on what you had just heard!*

That same unruly individual presented my idea as his own at a different staff meeting when I was not in attendance. The HR Director, who had tabled the idea a month earlier, thought the concept was brilliant. He praised the thieving culprit right there on the spot in front of everyone, all the while pretending it was the first time he had ever heard of it. The nerve or EGO of these guys was too much!

Even the Nicest Guys Have the Biggest Egos

My co-worker John was not the kind of guy women would notice right away although he was an okay-looking fellow. He just wasn't the kind of man that found it easy to approach unfamiliar women, unlike a lot of the men that strutted around the building, their body language metaphorically displaying the words HUGE MALE EGO for everyone to see. Not John. He was extremely well-mannered and, once you got to know him, very likable. Yet his ego, as harmless as he was, could get a bit annoying in a slightly less intrusive or offensive kind of way. His head would start to swell from the attention he did receive from the opposite sex, even when that attention had no real objective. We both worked nights as distribution clerks and often our schedules would overlap. One day I was eating my daily lunch of a boiled egg, one piece of toast, and a small carton of milk. John stopped at my table and asked if he could join me. I was usually alone, so I welcomed the company.

"Is that all you're eating?" was the first thing he asked as he took his seat.

"Yes, I'm watching my weight." That was the lie I told him. The truth is that it was my way of stretching my money to make sure my three hungry mouths at home got clothed and fed. There was also an added benefit to starving, I didn't gain an ounce of weight. I was looking good.

John and I ate together for two years so I guess that gave observers the impression we were more than lunch buddies. This is where his male ego starts to inflate. John would do things like pull out my chair especially if someone were watching, or he would lean in closer during our conversations as if we were whispering sweet nothings to one another. And it was just that... nothing! I had no interest whatsoever in John and I'm sure he had no desire to be with me. He was just happy he was getting some attention. He didn't mind the rumors or the false impressions because, in his mind, it showed the ladies he was the man! We talked about why he wasn't bothered by the misperception others had of us. It was more important to John (and his ego) for it to have appeared that he was having an affair with me, than for us to have had one and nobody knew it. We both agreed he had a real problem and laughed about it each time the subject came up.

Our lunch arrangement served me well because I had someone to eat lunch with even if it was someone from the male persuasion. He was the total opposite of the brazen personalities

I had to work with which was a welcomed change. I'm not sure why he would do this, but John used to fold money and place the bills inside chewing gum wrappers, then give them to certain ladies. I was one of them. What was in that wrapper the night before, provided lunch money for my kids the next day. He didn't realize it, but his thoughtfulness was a blessing to me. Then again maybe he did realize it given the fact that he watched me eat the same pitiful lunch every day for two years. Perhaps John was one of God's angels.

Not Recognizing a Good Thing Right Under Our Noses – Channeling Wonder Woman

It was important to me that my counterparts saw me as not just a female but their equal, a member of the team, and an individual who was more than qualified to be in charge. Despite my best intentions, some of the men's egos always got the better of them whenever I took the lead on anything. Instead of addressing the problems, they often alleged that I was the problem, accusing me of speaking out of turn or sticking my nose where it didn't belong. I was only upholding my belief that everyone in an organization should be working toward the same goal and that having a well-trained, unified workforce with everyone advancing in the same direction was what our goal should've been. That was not the case once the USPS transitioned from mechanization to automation, a system that would now scan and sort the mail by machine. With that change also came the need to have qualified electronic technicians *(repairs and maintains the electronic equipment)* on staff.

The managers knew the change was coming, yet we didn't do anything to prepare our current employees for the role. We were going to need qualified people to handle the new job. Instead of training our own, we hired people who were already mechanics, electricians, and technicians from the outside as trainees, and it cost us dearly. I'm sad to even have to include myself as one of the components in that entire fiasco. Even though I often found myself on the opposing side of things, I was still a part of the team, and equally responsible.

We had a long list of committed and hard-working career employees who expressed an interest in obtaining one of the new positions. They took the related written exams and met the qualifications but were still not allowed to take part in the training. The idiot hiring manager told our in-house applicants they lacked experience. That egotistical moron displayed more allegiance to the outside folks, for what reason, I don't know. Other than their field of expertise they didn't have the necessary experience either. His methods made absolutely no sense whatsoever. Just a thoughtless individual if you asked me. On top of that, he sent the outsiders to our elaborate training operation in Norman, Oklahoma where they received instruction on how to handle the new equipment thus gaining a new skill. Wait! The saga continues and gets even more ironic. Not only did the recruits take full advantage of the tuition-free education we provided and collect a USPS paycheck every two weeks, corporations and competitors recruited our trainees right under our noses. These outside treasonists would resign once they completed the training and move on to more lucrative positions with other companies. This wasn't just happening on the local level either. It had become a nationwide problem that needed some major strategies to remedy.

This is what happens when you allow your over-inflated ego to cloud your better judgment, was my thought.

Several career employees filed EEO complaints, and for good reason. After all, they weren't afforded the same opportunities as individuals from the outside. Employees would even come into the PEDC asking about related training because they wanted to be better prepared in case the technician jobs were offered again. For many of them, the chance to become a mechanic or electronic technician would be life-changing.

As the PEDC manager, I couldn't ignore their concerns, especially since we were hiring outsiders as fast as we were losing those same outsiders-turned-skilled-technicians. We were spinning our wheels, wasting our time and resources on people who had no plans of staying with the postal service in the first place and all while continuing to ignore the needs and aspirations of our own employees. We needed to do something, heck, I had to do something about what was happening. So, I met with the Plant Manager to see if I could join his team to help solve the problem. By the way, there was, NO team. The only plan was to continue hiring from the outside and ignore the interests of the employees inside. The Plant Manager asked me why I was inquiring and what I thought I could do about it. I resented his inference; his tone was condescending and dismissive as if somehow he was convinced I couldn't do anything to help.

I could just imagine him saying something like, *"Woman, who the H-E-double hockey sticks do you think you are and why are you all up in my business? This is a problem for the menfolk to fix, not some pie-baking mishap! You just leave it to us, little lady. Go on now, git!"*

I hated it when managers gave up before even trying. Besides, had he known what I was capable of, he would not have hesitated to have me... Wonder Woman, on his team. *The time would come when he would get to witness first-hand my superpower,* I thought. He did thank me later for not giving up.

Next, I met with the Manager of EEO and found him to be more difficult, rude, and obnoxious than the Plant Manager. At least, with him, I was able to put a crack in the wall of his rough exterior. BUT this old buzzard I was standing face to face and eyeball to eyeball with had me feeling a bit uneasy. As I began to explain the reason for my wanting to meet with him he immediately started talking over me.

"I cannot and will not discuss any of my EEO cases with someone who has absolutely nothing to do with EEO. This matter is between me, this office, and the complainants. It is none of your business Geraldine." He took a deep breath then started in on me again. "How dare you question anything that I am doing. I've been in this job since its start, and no one knows the job better than me."

With the show of as much contempt as I could muster, I asked, "What action if any have you taken to resolve the matter? If you don't mind me asking!"

He must have assumed I was there to lecture him. I guess he thought he was going to school *me* on how it was or put *me* in what he perceived to be my rightful place. Or maybe a little of both. It didn't matter because I wasn't going to back down from him.

Watching his blood start to boil was somewhat entertaining, so I continued with my line of questioning full steam ahead. I wanted to know if he still had all the complaints that were filed by the employees. I could feel my **she-devil** awaken. I knew she'd have my back if this clown were to push me too far. I was the one who was going to do the pushing this time. Then I hinted that I knew exactly where he kept *(hid)* those files. The man still sat there with that look of superiority and contempt on his face.

I told him the employees' EEO complaints were in his lower right-hand drawer. Bingo! I hit the motherload with that one! His staunch-like expression went from arrogant to worried. Divulging the location of the files not only made him angrier, but I could tell he felt exposed and vulnerable. I wasn't accusing him of anything, I only made a simple statement. His reaction confirmed what the employees had said. Those files were indeed in his lower right-hand drawer, out of his sight and off of his list of responsibilities. I found out later he accused me of trying to usurp his authority and that I had my nose where it didn't belong. It seems then and now, that's the only weak or go-to-excuse threatened men with power ever resort to using. *That a woman with some intelligence and authority always has her nose where it doesn't belong.* Well, all I have to say is, "Silly rabbits, TRIX are for kids and so are fragile egos!"

We all should have been on the same team trying to solve the problem but the EEO Manager's bias prevented that from happening. So, I obtained permission from the employees to get copies of their complaints so that I could take them to my next meeting with the Plant Manager. You know, the one I had won over.

My question to him was this, "What can we do jointly to resolve these complaints?" Then I went on to explain how our employees had been with the organization for years and that they had no desire to work anywhere else. With them, I told him, we had a loyal following. Individuals from the outside we hired had but one intent, to launch a well-strategized exit plan once the training was over in Oklahoma.

"We are losing skilled workers faster than we can hire new outside trainees." I said to the Plant Manager. I was trying to stir him up in a way that he would want to take some kind of action.

Then I asked, "If we can bring our current employees' skill levels up to where they need to be, will you accept them as qualified technicians?"

Hoping he wouldn't catch on to the set-up, I pushed even harder for a commitment. "Will they be able to go to Oklahoma and take the advanced training class?"

He said yes! So, without delay, I took my next step and requested an airline ticket to Norman, OK. I used the time during the flight to review my notes. That way I could clear my head of any doubts I was having about my purpose in going. Especially not knowing how I would be received. When the plane landed, I hit the ground running. Once I got to the training site, it seemed the Lord had ordered my steps, gone before me, and straightened the path. *Thank You, Jesus!*

When I met with the team in Oklahoma they were already ahead of the game. They had identified outside companies that were taking advantage of the Postal Service and had talked to some of the trainees who admitted they had only joined the Postal Service to receive the free training and get paid for it in the process. Some even said that other organizations had promised them a better job once they got their certification. We were developing skilled labor at no cost to our competition but on behalf of our competition. Unbelievable! And why not? We were the ones dumb enough to foot the bill. A fact that never sat well with the staff at our training facility. They were glad when someone finally started paying attention and addressing the problem. That, someone, determined and *unapologetic...* was me!

I left Oklahoma with a plan of action. The team there assured me they would do their part by developing a two-phase process, each to prepare employees to meet the challenge of the job. Phase one included six weeks of classroom and simulated training in the PEDC. A skilled electronic technician would be the instructor. Those who completed phase one moved on to phase two advanced training in Norman Oklahoma. Employees who met the qualifications were then reassigned to the maintenance department. The program was so successful that Headquarters implemented it on a national scale. Postal employees were the first to be considered before anyone got hired from the outside. We stopped losing our well-trained and highly-qualified technicians to other companies. Lesson well learned!

My relationship with the Plant Manager improved over time. Our trust-level even grew to the point that he would drop by my office on occasion just so that he could, as he put it, run a few things by me. As for the EEO Manager, he never got over himself, but I got every one of his related EEO complaints settled. All except one employee qualified and got reassigned to the maintenance department. Wonder Woman had struck again. Only because the Lord promised that if I did my best... He would do the rest.

Women Managers in the Workplace: Wonder Woman Kicks Butt

Women were finally being promoted as supervisors and managers within the St. Louis District. That should have been a cause for celebration, but it wasn't because we were still working in an environment where the men expected us to fail. If we had a question, the retort would be, "You're the supervisor, don't you know? Didn't you learn anything in that class you took? The manuals are right there, look it up!"

Pouty men felt we were taking what belonged to them, and they were not about to provide help on any level. Even some of the craft employees seemed irritated by the presence of a female boss. They would make stupid comments like, "I just can't work for a woman."

Getting promoted but not having the support needed was an unexpected challenge that caused some of the women to regret even taking that step. The initial pay wasn't that much different from what they used to make, and the loss of overtime-pay made them question their decision even more. I completely understood their plight and felt we should be doing something to support each other. As the person in charge of training, I considered myself to be a possibility guru, one who refused to accept the status quo, a change agent, and a problem solver. I invited the women from all the functional areas, black and white, who were promoted to managerial positions to my home for a private off-the-clock gathering.

As I was putting the final touches on the little house cleaning I was doing, my mind was racing with all kinds of crazy thoughts. *There you go again stirring up the pot. Not knowing what the result will be but feeling somebody's got to do something and that somebody is always you!*

I had to take my peach cobbler out of the oven and check on the chicken that was frying. Yes, we had to have food! The smell of my yeast rolls circulated throughout the house just the way I planned. The macaroni salad needed a little more paprika on top to make it look festive, and the olives had to be added to the relish tray. *Don't forget to go downstairs and get the ice cream,* I reminded myself before the first guest arrived.

The discussions got underway amid whispers about how delicious the food was. The sounds of "um, um, um" came from all sides of the room. We talked about the challenges that plagued us and how we should address them without damaging our relationships with the men... our bosses mostly. Everyone agreed it was best to keep our conversations and strategies under wraps. There were benefits to establishing this type of network: improved job performance, a great support system, and personal growth.

This meeting took place on a Saturday. When I returned to work at 6:30 AM that following Monday I found a surprise waiting for me outside of my office. One of the male General Supervisors stood there blocking the doorway. I thought, *This man had better be glad I'm not having a hot flash cause, if I were, this would not go well for him.*

Without showing any signs of getting out of my way, he asked, "What are you and the women up to, and why were they at your house?"

It turns out a female General Supervisor had gone back to work and told her male peer all about our meeting. I don't know why she did it, but I can only guess she felt more loyalty to him than to us... even to herself. Or maybe she did it to upset him. He and some of the other men feared we had some type of advantage over them. Not sure why they felt so threatened by smart and capable FEMALES. A short time later, the Postal Service launched an initiative called the Women's Program. It was designed to do exactly what we were planning to do on our own... eliminate challenges and barriers for women at work.

Formulating a women's group was not the only effort that had gone sour, and I had dedicated months of my time and energy to that cause. The St. Louis Main Post Office is a 24-hour operation, seven-days-a-week. During the time I was employed there, employees struggled to find and keep reliable babysitters, especially single mothers who worked evenings, nights, or weekends and that caused an increase in absenteeism. Mandatory overtime was a problem for parents as well. Getting sitters to stay past their time created more of a challenge for everyone. So I interviewed employees to see if a 24-hour childcare center would be of interest. The responses were encouraging so I forged ahead with great vigor.

There was a parking garage across from the post office that only utilized two-thirds of the building for parking. The other one-third was for rent. So, I arranged for a well-known childcare agency and the garage owner to join me on a tour of the building. We needed to determine if the place was suitable for what I had in mind. The childcare director was very interested and thought a downtown center was an exciting possibility. The owner of the garage also liked the idea for two reasons: the potential increase in the building's value *(especially after renovations)* and the guaranteed monthly revenue.

Employees would be able to park their car and drop their children off all at one location. It would also be ideal in case of wet and snowy weather. It seemed like a win-win situation for everyone involved. When the director asked if I had canvassed the people, I immediately handed over all the data from my research, including the number of employees who had expressed an interest. After careful negotiations, the garage owner agreed to certain modifications at no cost to us. The Childcare Director promised she and her team would turn the space into a state-of-the-art facility, at their expense. We only needed to get fifty employees to enroll their children. The pre-enrollment included paying for the first week as a show of real interest. I can't even describe how thrilled I was, and I had no doubt the employees were as eager to jump on board. I passed out sign-up information to all the ones who had expressed an interest. We were going to open in 90 days, so I told them they needed to respond within a week.

By the end of the week, I had only received a handful of applications and payments. I was so disappointed and couldn't understand what had happened. Where did all the excitement and enthusiasm go? I needed to know so I started searching for the employees who I felt had misled me. I made my way through the halls and even walked across the workroom floor looking for them. When I located some of the employees they told me they had changed their minds. Others gave no reason at all. One of the employees I stumbled upon said she wanted to hip me to a few things. I'm thinking, *okay!* She pulled me to the side and explained, "Just because people work together doesn't mean they want *their* children to mix with *other people's* children."

I did notice that the few applications and payments I did receive were all from black employees who lived in the Saint Louis Metropolitan area. They, of course, had no apprehension about coming downtown. Other non-black rural and County employees only came to the City because of the job and for no other reason. They didn't even interact with people of color outside of work. I can be so naïve at times. That thought never crossed my mind until that instant.

A lot of people laughed at me and thought the idea was unrealistic from the beginning. There were quite a few others who even wanted my efforts to fail. But I saw so many possibilities with the downtown location. Parents could walk across the street at lunchtime to see their kids, improve their timeliness on and off the job, and handle emergencies, if any, almost immediately. To top it off, it would be a brand-new facility at no expense to our company. I was a progressive thinker all those years ago. Today many companies provide on-site childcare facilities and gyms for their employees. All the conveniences of a one-stop-shop. The Main Post Office to this day is still behind the eight-ball.

It Ain't Always Them Against You, Sometimes It's Them and Us

I had grown accustomed to leaping over the hurdles that the white Postal establishment set before me. Even some attempts by them to sabotage me were too trivial to entertain. Soon, I had to deal with a horse of a different color. They'd be similar situations only they were created by people who looked like me.

I've had only three EEO complaints filed against me by black Postal employees. That in contrast to the many unfair practices and bogus complaints conjured up by mostly white men throughout my career at the Postal Service. For all practical purposes, they really didn't have to file a formal complaint against me, they could just flat-out disapprove, disagree, or disallow my very existence. White privilege was all the excuse they needed. A false claim against me was never challenged by one of their own. If a white employee, especially a white male, suggested I cheated on a test then it was true. Didn't matter if the facts disputed the accusation. This was almost always the case whenever one of them failed an exam. Their egos and bigoted attitudes wouldn't let them accept the facts. I passed...you guys failed! But black folks had to do more than make a verbal complaint against my achievements, they had to submit their bogus grievances in writing. Says a lot doesn't it?

The first grievance alleged that I got the training job because I was lighter-skinned than the complainant. I was busy working in the training room one day when I noticed two strangers standing in the hallway just outside of the classroom looking at me through the glass window on the door. They would stare at me for a few seconds, then start to laugh. I had no idea what was going on or who the people were. Towards the end of the day, I discovered they were from the Chicago Central Region sent to investigate an EEO Complaint. They came, eye-balled me, chuckled, and retreated to Chicago. That was the full extent of their investigation. They had expected to find a black person who looked white based upon the information contained in the filing. To their surprise, there was nothing about me that even came close to resembling a Caucasian. The case was dismissed.

The second EEO case dealt with the issue of education. The complaint came from an African-American female employee who was upset because I had gotten one of the training jobs having only a GED on my educational resume at the time. It didn't matter to her that I had set up the entire training program. She had had some college but never disclosed how much college she had completed. I earned my Bachelor's and, if I'm not mistaken *(and I'm not)* and Master's before she did. Case dismissed again!

The third and final grievance had to do with the Supervisor's Exam. Like the white men before him, a black male employee named Hampton, accused me to my face of cheating on the exam and all because I passed, and he didn't. There were six of us preparing for this particular exam, five females and one male, Hampton, a cocky guy who thought he had it all together in so many areas of his life *(poor deluded thing)*.

The supervisor's exam involved considerable logic, problem-solving, and memory. After work, we would regularly meet in the training room to drill each other on the material we were studying. Hampton didn't see the importance of devoting that much time to preparing but the women did. I passed the exam with a score of 93-point something. When I got the results of my passing score, I was excited and relieved at the same time, so I went to the workroom floor to share my good news with one of the women from our study group. Her reaction was not what I thought it would be. The way she saw it, I was showing off and she accused me of flaunting it in her face. Later I found out that her test score was 63. I didn't share my news with the others after that encounter and it's a good thing I didn't because I also learned that only two out of the six of us passed.

Whenever someone scored high on the exams, the news would spread all over the building like wildfires. Joseph was a white management trainee who took the exam at the same time as the six of us. He also challenged my test score since it was identical to his and he wasn't shy about voicing his skepticism. He acted as though my high score lessened the value of his grade, challenged his intellect, or threatened his standing as a white man and couldn't reconcile the fact that a black woman possessed the same greatness, an attribute I'm sure he thought was unique only to him.

To add insult to injury, rumors were circulating throughout the company that I was sleeping with the bosses. Women whom I believed did sleep-with-the-enemy still didn't advance much further in their careers, yet they were convinced that was the only way I had moved up in the organization. What, in their weak and easily influenced little minds, did they think set me apart from all the other women including them?

"Honey if it didn't work for you what makes you think it would have worked for me?"

1988
I Had Enough

Taking that ridiculous oath not to have any more children is how I entered the Postal Service all those years ago. Since that time I have been fighting my battles with discretion, as well as the battles of those who could not or would not speak for themselves *(for fear of reprisals, I suppose)*. Why? Because I continued to believe, until this incident, that things would get better. After all those years of putting up with so much nonsense in the workplace, I had finally had enough of the games that my current superiors were continuing to play with me.

I journaled the following sometime later, after one of those horrific days:

> *Wow! They said I have great potential! After all this time my bosses now admit out loud that I have great potential. Really? Why now? They go on to point out that my talents are being wasted, that I should be in a higher position because my contributions would be beneficial to the company. Yet none were willing to admit the number of times they denied me the chance. The pretense got on my last nerve. I could feel my anger rising. It was time to call it quits for the day because I*

was about to explode!! Tears blinded me as I drove home... my brain was overloaded with emotions. It felt as though I was having an out-of-body experience.

*On my right shoulder appeared my soft-spoken, forgiving, and accepting **she-angel**, who I knew that instant was there to try and reason with me. Even comfort me. She, in her calm and collected voice, asked, "Why are you so upset? Weren't those the words that every up-and-coming employee such as yourself wanted to hear? And if you are a Black female in these here United States of America, were those not the words that drove your desire to excel, to be all that you could be and get recognized for it? Let's try and calm down, shall we?"*

*I hunched my shoulder in an upward motion as if to try and knock my **she-angel** off while at the same time blurting out, "Ah, shut up!" I didn't want to calm down. Didn't want to play Miss Nicey-Nice. I was mad and I didn't want to talk to another person that would not understand what I was going through.*

*Then suddenly in my left ear, I heard a fiery voice that sounded a lot like my feisty Aunt Gladys. "You're a 52-year-old, Colored, Negro, or whatever the popular term is these days, Black woman! You came in fighting battles when our people were rarely promoted in this organization, and you're too old to be toyed with." This wasn't my **she-angel**, it was a miniature me in a red suit with a tail and horns, standing proudly on my left shoulder. I thought, What the heck is happening here?*

*With all the attitude she could muster, my little **she-devil** continues. "You were the one who took every written exam and passed, even while the rules continued to change. And the reason why the rules changed was that a female and Negro met the challenge every time. You, who to benefit her white peers, got subjected to Quota over Qualified. You, who as a* *female, had to submit an idea through male peers just to get it through the system. But not before making the little boys believe it was their idea. That was you wasn't it?"*

The last thing I heard her say as I pulled into my driveway was, "After 29 years they say you have great potential. What does that mean? A bunch of crock! That's what it means!"

I put the car in park, turned off the ignition, leaned back in my seat, then took a deep breath. Before I exited my vehicle, I remember thinking, Finally! Someone or some THING, who understands.

I was so tired! Tired of pretending that all was right in my world. Tired of acting like those events had not been damaging. Tired of picking up and starting all over, and reaching out for support that was never there. I was so darn tired! All those events had taken their toll. It's like I'd been beating my head against a wall, knocking it down many times only to see it rise again, and each time a little higher and more resistant than before. Still, I refused to let those occurrences reduce my career to a miserable and non-productive one. That would have been a waste of true, enthusiastic and proven talent.

I used to conduct a workshop that I called **Games People Play**. In it, I would stress the importance of the participants becoming aware of the game. I also encouraged them to become smarter players if they chose to play. I knew someone was orchestrating a master game designed especially for me just so that they could continue to deny me opportunities. However, the time had come when I was no longer willing to play. Following those rules would have required giving up all that my mother taught me about loving God, having integrity, and respecting my fellow man. And that I just was not willing to do! Instead, I continued to remind myself that God could turn trials into tranquility. I was proud of who I was and all that I had accomplished. Those years of quality performance were worthy of much praise so I congratulated myself on a job well done. Thank You, Lord, for all You've done for me!

GERALDINE SMOTHERSON

1988–1992

Let us not grow weary in well-doing, for in due time we will reap a harvest if we do not give up – Galatians 6:9

I didn't give up. I'd met every challenge set before me, passed exams that were not required of others, and made one of the highest grades on the supervisor's exam. I established the new training program, managed the entire training operation, and had even gone back to school. Knowing I had paid my dues it was time for me to, once again, apply for the job above me. My boss's job.

In 1988, I interviewed for the position of Manager, Employment and Development but was not selected because of political reasons. I wasn't given any further explanation. My job performance was what they should have reviewed instead of concerning themselves with my political affiliation. Postal Regulations clearly stated that external politics were not supposed to influence the outcome of their hiring decision, and that selection of a potential candidate was supposed to be based on one's demonstrated ability to do the job. It was a well-known fact that my performance was always outstanding.

In 1992, I found out exactly what the political reasons were as to why I didn't get the job four years prior. My husband had run for political office against a career congressman who had loyal Postal executive followers in the company and I just happen to have the same last name. The selecting official's boss felt he was not required to adhere to the rules and said that his selection or non-selection of a candidate **did not** have to be based on performance. I was the designated person grooming management employees to serve on promotion boards, so I knew exactly what the regulations asserted.

When the Director of Human Resources decided to retire he gave me two letters which he typed himself. I still have those letters to this very day.

Ms Geraldine Smotherson
1247 Perdue
St. Louis. Mo 63130

Ms Smotherson:

This is to confirm our prior conversations regarding the reason I
did not promote you to the position of Manager Employment and
Development in 1988 and 1992.

In November of 1988 when I appointed Louis Moore to the position
I was called into Mr. Goodman's office and given a lecture on the
fact your husband had run against William Clay for Congressman.
It as stated their was no way you and Mr. Clay's office could
work together. In addition I was told you were not loyal to Mr.
Goodman but to Mr Vito Reid and Mr T. Charles. It was made very
clear to me that I could not place you in the position.

In 1992 when I promoted Mr. Paul Lee to the position I was called
into the Mr Goodman's office and instructed not to place you into
the position.

William E. Holloway

Geraldine Smotherson

This is just a note to thank you for the many years of loyality you
have given me. Your are truely a person to be admired.

I have had a lot of bad days in my life but I think the worst two
was the day I was instructed not to select you as Manager,
Employment and Development prior to me even recieving the package
and the other one was when I had to tell you you did not get the
position because I had been instructed not to select you. I was
wrong in not protesting that instruction and as a result did a big
injustice to you. I apologize and hope you have forgiven me for my
weakness.

Bill

The Lord Will Make a Way – Just Trust Him

Those were sad and disappointing times for me but luckily, I
had far more victories than defeats during my career. Holloway's
letters freed me from the hurt and somehow from the guilt and

shame I was carrying that wasn't mine to even shoulder in the first place. I was the victim. The wrong was done to me and for what? For being BLACK and FEMALE? For being smart, capable, and determined? Or kind and considerate, even when some would have if they could have, spat on me?

There may have been times when they thought I was caving to the unfair treatment. Nothing could have been further from the truth. What they failed to realize was God had a higher purpose for me. A plan that none of them could disrupt even when they felt triumphant in their attempts. It was in those times that I had to step back, take my hands off of it, pray, and wait for God to show up. I found myself doing that more times than I can count, and things worked out every time. Every door that was slammed in my face, denying me access, the Almighty provided an open window that I was always able to climb through. God had my back as I forged new avenues by which to triumph over the elitist culture that surrounded me.

> But you give us victory over our enemies, you put our
> adversaries to shame. Psalm 44:7

I finally got the chance to work temporarily in the job of Manager, Employment and Development. The physical office was located on the third floor of the Main Post Office, which is where all the top executives were housed. Mr. Goodman, the District Manager, didn't block my interim assignment, but he did make it crystal clear that I was not to use that office or work on that floor. If I wanted the assignment, he told me, then I would have to find myself an office on a **lower floor**. It wasn't because he thought I couldn't do the job, it was his way of keeping me in my place by sending me to the back of the bus, away from the white folks in charge.

I wanted the opportunity even if it was short-term, so I started looking around the building for the perfect office space. My search yielded one dead end after another with every logical room I came across. Then it hit me like a ton of bricks. In that great big old building had to be another little hole-in-the-wall that could serve as my new office. If my mother could make a small entryway livable for the two of us, surely I could do the same. In a matter of a few days, I located a storage room on the second floor that seemed plausible. The talk of this situation spread all over but, when the maintenance staff got wind of it they came to my rescue, without my even asking. They cleared everything from the entire storage room, slapped on a couple of coats of paint, built a closet, and added shelves and racks just for me. Then they brought in the most handsome office furniture that only they knew about and that I had ever seen.

Claudia, one of the maintenance crew, was a tall stocky woman who had worked in maintenance for years. The lady was a meticulously hard-working, and dedicated employee. She was, as we liked to say, *Postal Proud*. One morning I walked in and saw her down on her knees cleaning the baseboards along the floor. That struck me as odd seeing a woman her size comfortably down on all fours but there she was making it happen. I was standing there watching while fighting back tears when Claudia looked up and said, "We gotta do this *thang* right." And that's just what she and the others did. Their efforts and eagerness to help were awe-inspiring and when the folks from maintenance got done transforming the space, I had an office that many, especially those from the **upper floor**, envied.

There were several projects left undone that my team and I completed, all while I was in my temporary position. We recruited, tested, and trained individuals who were hearing impaired as Letter Sorting Machine Operators. They were so eager and appreciative of the opportunity that was afforded them. I can't think of a more worthy and capable group of individuals. No doubt, they rose to the occasion.

The training staff took sign language courses as did many of the machine supervisors. Even our instructor was hearing impaired which I felt was most appropriate. I had learned to sign well enough to recognize those interpreters whose skill levels were not up to par. Some couldn't even sign what was being spoken and that wasn't acceptable to me. So I challenged the selection process and was successful. We were able to choose more competent translators from then on.

I made a personal commitment that I would use as many people with challenges as possible. Trainees that did not qualify as machine operators became part of the maintenance staff. I was so proud of the outcome of that initiative.

My superiors couldn't figure out how I continued to excel, succeed, overcome, or even thrive, despite their many attempts to derail me. Maybe they saw my achievements as defiance. It was only God, moving mountains that were impossible for me to push aside and if any of them had an ounce of faith they would have known that. I pitied them for always being so blinded by their hatred, jealousy, and need to dominate. All I was doing was using the gifts God gave me for good, as they should have done. I even tried to instill that mindset in my staff. I would always tell them, "No does not mean no. It simply means not now!" And I had faced a boatload of not now's. I wanted them to understand that situations and circumstances change day-to-day, that the timing might not be right at that moment for whatever it was they were hoping to achieve. But, if what they believed had logic and purpose and was for the good of us all, to wait for it and, at the right time, their **NO** would turn into, "Why didn't we think of this sooner?" But never, ever, respond with, "We did!"

Perks Along the Way

My first time in New York was for a meeting that was held in a high-rise office building that seemed to ascend into the heavens. Mesmerized, I was so busy looking up as I walked along that I stumbled and fell flat on my face. I hadn't visualized New York with broken sidewalks, only skyscrapers. I showed up for the meeting with ripped pantyhose, a torn skirt and bleeding knees.

"You must have been looking up at the building." Was the first comment the receptionist made as she watched the blood trickle down my leg. Then she began searching for band aids in her desk drawer.

It didn't make me feel better learning I was not the first bruised person to have ever approached her desk. Empathetic to my situation she attempted to apologize for the busted sidewalks. I think she was fishing for a little understanding too, claiming New York was like so many other cities. There were good parts and not so good parts she explained. Then using a bit of light-heartedness she asked that I not judge everyone there. At least not by the broken-up pavement surrounding the building. I promised as long as she didn't judge me for not looking where I was going. We both laughed and promised.

My second trip to the Big Apple on a work assignment was with a team of three. Me from Missouri, Henrietta from California, and Marlene from New Jersey. Being from the east coast, Marlene knew her way around New York like the back of her hand. We decided to take advantage of our time there and made the Statue of Liberty the first stop on our siteseeing tour. We got on a train that was so crowded we could hardly find a spot to sit or a handrail to hold on to. The scene was exactly the way I remember seeing it on TV – people were everywhere!

As the train pulled up to the stop Marlene alerted, "This is where we get off."

I attempted to make my way through the jam-packed car politely asking, "Excuse me please, may I get by please, excuse me please?" No one seemed to move.

All of a sudden Marlene came out of nowhere, grabbed me, pulled me through the crowd and snatched me off the train. Then she started laughing her head off after that. "I know you're from Missouri but you're a New Yorker now." Still cracking up.

I thought the people were going to let me off once I said, "excuse me." As we stood there, I was trying so hard to pull myself together. That was such a terrifying incident. Marlene with a hoot added, "You will never get to the door to get off the train just by saying, excuse me, please. Especially in that sweet little voice of yours."

"Neither would it work in Oakland," chuckled Henrietta.

Both of them loved to tease me because I was from the Midwest and it seemed we talked so much slower than folks from the east or west coast. Henrietta claimed she could say four or five sentences in the time it took me to form one, and Marlene kept suggesting I never go anyplace else alone in New York. She couldn't let what had happened to me on the train go. After all that jesting, there was no way I was going to share my first New York experience with them.

The train was only our first means of transportation. To get to our destination we then had to board a double-decker tourist boat of which we took the top deck. Unlike me, Marlene and Henrietta loved how the wind blew the water off of the Hudson. That must have been an east coast/west coast thing because I was just thankful the day was warm enough to offset the chill created by the drifting mist. Suddenly there it was, the Statue of Liberty! Coming from my humble beginnings I never dreamt I would ever get to stand near or even view such a site, a symbol of freedom, hope, and opportunity. That was such an emotional time. My team members were already making fun of my midwestern idiom, so I hid my tears for fear they would ridicule me yet again. They'd never imagine how deep an impact the whole experience had on someone like me.

1992-1994

I spent the last 18 months of my postal career as a Diversity Development Specialist, a position that was a first for me as well as the Postal Service. Biases blocked progress and thwarted individual and organizational growth and since we had a diverse workforce, for the company to acknowledge that fact was major. I was proud to be part of the effort. It was a rewarding experience. I hope that the organization continues to learn from past mistakes. I also pray that my retirement check continues to hit my bank account on the first of every month. For this laborer was worthy of her hire. To God be the Glory!

Retired June 3, 1994... but not from life.

Chapter Seven
Wannabees and Other Shees

*M*elvin always had the gift of gab and the most pleasant and joyful personality of anyone I knew. A real charmer, women were drawn to him in much the same way I was years earlier. Those qualities were best displayed whenever he performed. Throughout the 1960s, Melvin was a member of a local group called the Gospel Keys, one of the most talented gospel singing groups in our city. They, like all popular male groups, had a following which included lots and lots of women, even girlfriends. Churches would be at full capacity whenever the Keys were in concert, mainly with those same women who could care less if the wives were in attendance. I remember it well. All the wives would be together on one side of the church and all the girlfriends or **wannabees** would be sitting together on the opposite. Each wife knew who the girlfriend was of the other husbands but not her own. I knew who Melvin's wannabee was and the **other shees**, who supported her. Her name was Dorothy Tailor.

Like me, Dorothy also worked for the Postal Service. She knew who I was but I'm not sure if she knew that I knew who she was. I never let on, but I knew. Whenever she would come into my work area, she'd start bragging about her new boyfriend, making sure I was in earshot. Her boasts always included facts about him being a local preacher. I could be going to get a cup of coffee in the cafeteria and if Dorothy spotted me, she'd be sure to get close enough to me so that she could disclose even more intimate facts about their affair. She didn't miss an opportunity to taunt me and, each time she did, I pretended not to hear.

Sunday afternoon and evening programs were a common occurrence way back when. The Gospel Keys were always in demand, always on a program or in concert. And I'd always be there unless I had to work. This particular Sunday was one of those instances. As I was leaving the program some of Dorothy's friends followed me out of the church and started making fun of what I was wearing. The mocking continued until I got in my car and drove off. I couldn't help but think about the hypocrisy of it all. The men had just sung songs of praise to God while watching their girlfriends shout all over the church. Then, the same *glory-hallelujah-shoe-throwing-wig-losing-so-called-women-of-God* would pull it together long enough to harass me just outside that same church. I was no better because turning the other cheek was the furthest thing from my mind and certainly was not in my heart. Even though I enjoyed hearing God's word through song, at that moment I just wanted to run over each one of those hellions with my car for how they had treated me.

Days later, my telephone kept ringing and ringing. Each time I answered, the person on the other end would hang up without saying anything. This went on all day long. Where was Caller ID or Star 69 when you needed it? It rang one last time and, again, I answered but this time there was a voice on the line, a woman's voice. She asked, "Mrs. Smotherson has your phone been ringing all day? Well, it was me, and I called to apologize." Then like before she hung up. I recognized the voice immediately, it was Dorothy! I tried to tell Melvin about the phone calls and even the apology but all he did was yell at me. "She did call and apologize!" he snapped. I asked him why he had gotten involved with Dorothy in the first place. Trying his best to sidestep the issue he said, "I needed some new shoes." The wrong person got snapped on that day! I should have beat that fool with a stick.

The Gospel Keys always ended their performances on a high note. And this particular occasion proved to be no different.

Much to my surprise and afterward, much to their dismay, the men asked me to come forward and give remarks. Why? Could have been divine intervention, I don't know. I stood before the audience and began. "One day these gentlemen are going to live the lives that they are singing about. On this side of the church sit their girlfriends and, on the opposite side… the wives." The room went up in applause as I took my seat. I was never asked to speak again.

My Cheating Husband and His Cheating Friends

There's something every cheating husband should know. Keep your infidelities to yourself and, whatever you do, don't tell your male friends. Bragging about your prowess clears a straight path to but one thing, your wife. These men will be eager to fill what they perceive to be a void left by you. Hoping, praying, even expecting her to surrender to their indecent proposals, they will call just to see if your wife is okay. Even come by the house when they know you're not there and she's all alone, possibly feeling sad, lonely, rejected, or weak. And, when she starts to question why the calls or the unexpected visits keep coming, your buddies will use that all-time player line, "I was just checking on you."

Husbands take this sound advice if not from me, then from Johnny Taylor. *Who's making love to your old lady, while you are out making love?* Most likely your best friend.

Melvin's friend and church member propositioned me when we were at First Baptist Church of Creve Coeur. Hal was a prominent businessman in the Missouri-Illinois region, even owned and operated a car dealership. For some reason he thought we should get to know each other better, this after his news informing me that Melvin was seeing a member of the church, named Cheryl Lee. He goes on to tell me, "I don't know what your husband sees in that woman, with her nappy hair sticking out from under her wig."

Was that comment supposed to benefit me in some way? Did he think insulting her would make me feel he was on my side, or that I appreciated his back-stabbing advances towards me?

Was he hoping my body language would suggest I somehow thought myself to be better than her? Even if she was some NAP-PY-HEADED WIG WEARER? His words, not mine.

Another incident occurred when a member of my husband's gospel group dropped by the house. This on the pretext of wanting to discuss a family matter. I was home alone and uncomfortable about having any man in the house with me without my husband being there, so I told him we had to have that discussion on the front porch. "Since both of our spouses are cheating, I see no reason why the two of us shouldn't get together," he rationalized before revealing he liked me. He didn't see why I should endure what was happening to me all alone, that he could help me. I thought to myself, *Did he think he could raise me from ground zero or that we could rise out of the miry clay together?*

On a separate occasion, a different group member came to the house to pick up my husband. Melvin was still in the shower, so I had to let him in. I didn't think anything of it when I told him he'd have to wait, invited him to have a seat, then went about my business elsewhere in the house. I remember being on the phone when suddenly this man approached me and started rubbing my hair. In my house! With my husband close by! To say it shocked me is an understatement. I could not move. Regrettably, no reaction was a bad reaction. Why didn't I say something, scream or hit him? I should have told my husband or just put his behind out of my house... something. Instead, I froze.

You would think one member of the Gospel Keys hitting on me would've been enough but oh no! Didn't these boys keep some type of scorecard? How about a checklist or a cheat-on-your-wife-with-your-friend's-wife playbook? Anything so's not to get their paths crossed or prey mixed up. Weren't there enough **wannabees** or **other shees** they could've pursued? Did they think I was an easy target? I had so many unanswered questions.

Melvin wasn't home at the time I got this unusual phone call from yet another would-be admirer. I picked up the receiver after about the third ring. All I could hear was this unrecognizable voice whispering, "I need juh, I need juh, I need juh."

"What?" I yelled into the phone.

Still, a bit baffled by the undertone in this voice, I allowed him to continue. That's when I figured out who it was. This man grew up with my husband and was also a preacher. He told me that, for us to talk, it had to be in person so I agreed to meet him on the steps of the neighborhood high school. He was already there by the time I arrived and what he said next was all too familiar. It was the same tired line Melvin's other friends used on me. "I was just checking on you." Then he told me how much he needed me.

Oh! So that's what he was muttering, I need YOU! I laughed to myself.

Not only were he and Melvin friends, his wife and I were too but that didn't seem to matter much to him. He probably had no idea how close he came to ruining a life-long friendship. I told him I didn't have the slightest interest in him and thankfully he let it go right then and there. I heard through the gossip mill that I was the one who had been flirting with him, but nothing could've been further from the truth. I never ever had a carnal thought about this man on any level. He was and had always been my husband's friend. That's it.

I had driven to Washington, Missouri to make a presentation for work. It was still pretty early when I arrived, so I made my way to the assigned meeting room to get set up. Already seated inside was my co-worker Sam. My husband and I knew Sam well, and we were all friends. Sam was on his second marriage to an acquaintance of mine and was the father of eight children from his first wife. He had even once lived close to where Melvin and I stayed. I had always been comfortable around Sam and didn't think anything of it when he walked over wanting to talk to me. It's what he said that completely threw me for a loop. Sam started talking about the possibility of us having sex. Immediately I said NO! and expressed my disbelief that he would even be thinking something like that. He became a little incensed and demanded to know why I wouldn't consider sleeping with him. I looked that fool dead in the eyes and asked, "Did you think the long-distance made you more appealing?" I told him I thought he held me to higher esteem as a colleague and a friend. Instead, his behavior made me feel cheapened and devalued. His proposition was disappointing, and it hurt.

I had always promised myself that if I ever strayed it would never be with a church member or any of Melvin's friends. Only one time did I almost break that promise and not because I was the aggressor. I was fooling myself by thinking I could maintain a relationship with someone of the opposite sex and no harm would be done. No matter how innocent it is, once you let your guard down, someone is bound to get misled. And when I saw where it was going, I stopped it immediately.

Me and Mama

I was so proud to be holding my first grandchild, Jaymi. My mother was holding her sixth grandchild, LaKeisha (Right).

Poplar Hill Schoolhouse
(Before and After)

Mama with one of her sisters, my Aunt Thelma.
They taught at Poplar Hill School.

Me

Winners All in City Women's Bowling

By a Post-Dispatch Photo

This group includes team and other division winners in the St. Louis Women's Bowling Association city championship tournament. Front row (from left) are Mrs. Isobel Smith, Mrs. Irma Kuhn, Mrs. Marge Bornemann (all members of the Kutis A team winner, score 3081) and Mrs. Irma Moore. Back row—Mrs. Cathy Shine (also a member of the winning team), Mrs. Mildred Staud events winner with scratch 1768), Mrs. Marilynn Ca (singles winner, 712), and Mrs. Geraldine Smot Mrs. Smotherson and Mrs. Moore won the doubl 1369. Miss Jeanne Reitz, captain of the team, v presen' when picture was taken.

I was on an outing with some of my husband's church members. We were supposed to dress casually. I guess the Pastor's wife missed the memo on "church casual."

147

Me and Melvin

Melvin at age 19 and his
first child, Charles (Pictured Above).

My Children

Bwayne   Pamela   Darren

My Postal Career

I'm running an acceptance test on a mail-sorting machine.

My staff member and friend, Tillie, teaching sign language.

My Passion and My Purpose

The Academy's East Entrance
543 Walton Avenue
St. Louis MO 63108
CIBC Westend Academy Children's Corner
Dedication & Ribbon Cutting Ceremony

Members of the National Phoenix Association and
Supporters of the CIBC Westend Academy

I love these two photos that show off the kids' artwork on display and feature some of the Academy's most ardent supporters.

Top photo: My best friend, Mary (left); Ella Banks (middle); and my
sidekick, Mildred Boyd (right). Bottom photo: My baby boy and CIBC
Westend Academy Board President, Darren (center) greeting guests and
shaking hands with my granddaughter, Sydney. Her dad, Charles (left) is
videotaping.

Every year the Summer Camp Program concluded with a grand performance.

The Wiz

Barbara E. Huck photo

The Tinman (Elbert Jaquess on left), the Cowardly Lion (Dominic Harris), Dorothy (Jaymi Smotherson) and the Scarecrow (Alexia Rowe) ease on down the road during the CIBC Westend Academy's recent summer production of *The Wiz*. The private, not-for-profit academy, located at 543 Walton Ave., provides educational programs for children of all ages.

My Aunt Emma had a coupon for a free photo that was about to expire. She wasn't going to use it so she gave it to me. I had a black dress (I called it my "Grown-Up Dress") and some pearls that I thought would be the perfect outfit for such an occasion. I was 21 years old, married, and had three kids when this picture was taken.

Chapter Eight
J. W. Logan

$\mathcal{S}$omewhere around 1980, I did fall in love with a gentleman whose name was J. W. Logan. He was **Logan** to me. I still have a photo of him hidden in one of my file cabinet drawers that I used to look at when I needed to remember our time together. In that relationship, I learned more about what love should be and how it should feel than in any other relationship I had ever had, including my ex-boyfriend, Burgess and my marriage to Melvin. When we first started talking, the conversation was about his brother who, years earlier, when I was 13, was my summer program counselor. All the young girls were head over heels for his handsome brother who went about his business not noticing any of the girls which only made them even more interested. I remember telling Logan that he was a lot like his brother because he, too, didn't seem to take in all the attention that was being thrown his way. He laughed and said it was his job to do the hunting when and if he decided to hunt.

"Are you hunting now?" I cunningly asked.

"Maybe!" he replied smiling as he walked away.

It had become quite obvious to the both of us that we had a spine-tingling attraction to one another. Most of our time together was spent talking about any and everything, including whether or not we had been with other people and of course about my marriage. One day we were walking out of the building on our way to lunch when he noticed my hands were bare. It was a cold and bitter afternoon and in this extremely caring tone, he asked, "Where are your gloves?"

"I don't have any."

"Do your children have gloves?"

"Yes."

"Does your husband have gloves?" he scowled.

I could tell he already knew what my answer was going to be. Shamefully all I could do was answer with a pathetic, "Yeah."

He appeared a bit more annoyed at having to even inquire about what my husband had, a man he felt didn't give a rat's you-know-what about me than at my pitiful answer. Yet again he asked, "And where are your gloves?"

His piercing gaze and the scripted frown lines on his face said it all, and I knew he was hoping I had gotten the message, that I deserved better than that. And I did. He took off his gloves that were double the size of my hands and put them in his pocket even though it was freezing outside.

"You don't have to do that." I insisted.

Valiantly he responded, "Oh, yes, I do."

The next day I had gloves and he had my heart.

One night in a hotel room, *(Yes, the hunter captured the prey!)* he asked, "Why aren't you being faithful to your husband?"

In an attempt to justify my crime I told him, "Apparently a **faithful relationship** was not the kind of relationship my husband wanted."

Logan and I had no secrets between us, always answering each other's questions truthfully and without hesitation. I told him things that I had never shared with anyone. My innermost secrets and thoughts were never met with judgment, only concern. He would even make suggestions on how I might handle future situations differently to avoid crashing and every critique resulted in me becoming more aware of ways in which to better take care of myself. For example, I was going to use a check to pay for some items I had picked out for my kids. Logan was watching me fill in the payee line but stopped me just short of writing in the amount that was due. He could tell I was going to write it out in cursive but told me to always write it out in print instead because cursive could be easily altered. To this day, I continue that practice and still fondly think of Logan with each check that I write.

We didn't have sex... he would make love to me. He spent a lot of time talking to me about making love and asking me what I liked. I'm embarrassed to admit this, but I had never experienced a man who displayed that type of interest or even engaged in that kind of conversation before Logan. When it came to intimacy, getting me to talk about what I liked had its challenges given the fact that I had suppressed so many of my feelings. He was extremely patient and that helped to ease my inhibitions. His explanation as to why the talk was so important made me pay close attention.

He said, "If I can't please you then you don't need me."

With practice, we found several ways he could please me.

It didn't take long for Melvin to notice the change in my attitude. I was happy, in my own world, and just taking life as it came. I had no complaints, didn't even ask why he was late, where he had been, or any of those questions that never got answered truthfully anyway. Except for my children, I was numb to what was happening around me especially if it had anything to do with Melvin. My head was so far up in the clouds it took a while before I even noticed my husband was staying home more. The change in me did one thing, it led to Melvin saying, "We've got to talk."

He demanded to know if I was seeing somebody.

My answer was, "Yes!"

"Why?" he asked knowing full well his cheating and neglect had driven us apart.

"Why not?" I snarled. I had found someone who cherished me and wanted to treat me like a queen, so I wasn't about to let Melvin off the hook this time.

"Who is he?"

"Why does that matter?"

"Do you love him?"

"Yes!"

We went back and forth until he hit me with the big one.
"Do you still love me?"

While I was struggling with the answer, Melvin started making all kinds of promises and asked me to give up that relationship so that we could start anew. He said all the right things and made all the right promises I had been longing to hear. He apologized for all the cheating and neglect and told me his bad behavior had nothing to do with me, that he loved me beyond the moon and back, and that his life wouldn't be the same without me.... and on and on and on. I said that I believed him even though my insides were screaming NO!! So, I asked permission from my husband to allow me to go to Logan to end the relationship. Melvin asked where I would meet the gentleman and I told him a place that was at the opposite end of the city from where I really would meet Logan. I'm glad I did because Melvin left right after I did and headed in that direction. Logan and I met in the garage of the Famous Barr Department Store in nearby Clayton, Missouri. How ironic that I would break up with someone I knew loved me to stay with someone I knew would lie to me.

It was something so tragic. I cried, Logan cried, I cried even more because he cried.

"Are you sure you are doing the right thing? How can you continue living with him the way he treats you?"

With that we said goodbye and it was over. My heart was ripped to shreds. Two hours later I was back home, watching Melvin as he was pulling into the driveway.

"Where did you go?" He asked.

"To break it off!"

He never confessed to being out looking for us, but I knew he was.

I was grieving the loss of Logan but was still hopeful about my marriage. All I ever wanted was a husband who loved me. The next two weeks were like the honeymoon Melvin and I never had. It was so exciting to finally have my husband's attention short-lived as it was. One day past the two-week mark, on **day 15**, my husband was back to his same old lying and cheating ways.

I was so distraught but what made my situation much more painful was that, when I tried to get my friend and lover back, I couldn't.

Logan wasn't going to allow me to play that on-again-off-again game with him. He didn't want his heart toyed with and he meant it, something he made clear to me early on. I was sick for days to come at the thought of never seeing him again. Melvin thought my despair was brought on by him betraying me again but that didn't come close to describing the torment I was feeling. For two years, after suffering those devasting blows, I was only able to muster enough strength to do what I had to do for work and the church. The rest of my time was spent in bed mourning the loss of the one I loved, and I don't mean the one at home. My children were on their own or away at school, so I slept.

Chapter Nine
The Start of Something Amazing

Paul's words in his epistle to the Romans are among the most well-known and most quoted in the Bible.

> *And we know that all things work together for good to those who love God, to those who are the called according to His purpose. Romans 8:28 NKJV.*

Our phone rang non-stop that Thursday evening in 1979 following my husband's removal from the pulpit. Every caller asked the same question, "Rev. Smotherson, Sister Geri, where are we meeting on Sunday?" Astounded as we were, those inquiries were the spiritual medicine my husband and children's father needed. I had no doubt there was a *Balm in Gilead* and He brought healing to what seemed a hopeless situation. Melvin was ready to start anew and, before long, the dark days of Washington Tabernacle were but a distant memory. Our Heavenly Father had truly intervened, and we were about to experience firsthand God working things out for our good.

Cornerstone Institutional Baptist Church (C.I.B.C.)

By the time Sunday had rolled around Smut *(that's what I called my husband)* had acquired a space for his followers to meet. The Pastor of a Seventh Day Adventist Church was gracious enough to allow us unlimited use of their sanctuary until we could get our footing. They worshipped on Saturdays so our presence on Sundays didn't cause a disruption. Sixty-six members gathered under our new name, Cornerstone Institutional Baptist Church, but there was yet a sixty-seventh person in attendance that fateful day. This young man had managed to slip away from his family and worship service at the previous church so that he could be there in celebration with us. Ashamed of the way they used falsehoods against my husband, he again offered apologies for the behaviors of his parents and others. I wanted to sweep him up in my arms and hug him so tight the gesture would have rid him of any guilt or doubt about my love for him. I so admired this sweet and kindhearted soul. The presence of that kid, who found the courage to rise above the muck and mire to represent the truth, was a gift to me. He will always have a special place in my heart. I hope he knows that.

We were allowed to bring in whatever we needed to carry out our service at the Seventh Day Adventist Church. Music was central to us having a good time in the Lord, so we purchased a small organ which the chairman of our Deacon Board, Deacon Ben Stewart, kept at his house throughout the week. He lived only a couple of blocks from the church, and the men would always help transport the organ back and forth every Sunday. Melvin noticed how much the movers were struggling to try and get that organ in and out of the building, so he called a brief meeting after church one Sunday to discuss an alternative because this situation had the potential of damaging the sanctuary. The Seventh Day Adventist Church had been much too generous for us to damage their property and my husband was not about to destroy a personal friendship with their pastor in the process. We were brainstorming other available spaces when a member asked, "While we're looking for a permanent place why not rent the Viel for now?"

The Viel Auditorium sat near the northwest corner of Page Avenue and Union Boulevard. Most of us in attendance agreed it might be worth looking into while others were a bit hesitant at the thought. You could rent the space for almost any occasion, but it was mostly known for hosting events that some considered unsavory.

"That's a party house with smoking, drinking, and all sorts of things happening in that building," expressed another member who was brave enough to speak out.

My husband told us, "There will be no smoking, drinking, or doing all sorts of things except for praising the Lord." He also talked about the possibility of the church buying the property if things went well which seemed to put everyone's worries to rest.

Melvin called the Viel hoping to find out that there wasn't some type of Saturday night shindig on their calendar that week, but there was. He then asked if the facility had a clean-up policy which they did. The manager even assured Melvin that he would make sure the place was cleaned from top to bottom by the time we got there on Sunday and my husband seemed to be okay with that. However, nothing could have prepared us for what we stumbled upon once we got inside the building early that Sunday morning. Although the look of horror and disgust on everyone's face said it all, we were still speechless. You could tell we were thinking the same thing even though nobody said a word, except for Sister Boyd, our church clerk.

"What in the world went on in here last night?" shaking her head at what she was seeing. "Isn't this a business establishment and shouldn't maintenance have cleaned up the place?" Then as she looked down at herself she exclaimed, "Honey, I'm not dressed for this!"

We were all dressed in our *Sunday-go-to-meeting* clothes, but that no longer mattered because somebody had to clean up before Sunday School started at 9:00 AM.

The place looked and smelled like a landfill. There were empty beer and whiskey bottles everywhere, and waste cans, overflowing with trash, sat at every exit. Used paper plates and napkins were strewn all over, and dried spilled liquor mixed with cigarette butts and ashes covered the sticky floor. The restrooms were worse than any you'd find at a corner gas station. We each picked a task and from there everyone got to work.

The women's bathroom is where I spent most of my clean-up-time because I couldn't allow anyone, especially our children, to come in contact with the filth that was left from the night before. The fact that women could be so nasty... leaving toilets unflushed and soiled sanitary napkins exposed made me ashamed. I agreed with Sis. Boyd, the facility should've had a custodial crew on hand to clean up the place plus the manager gave Melvin his word that everything would be in order. Guess we were wrong.

Members came in and out checking on me, making sure I had all the supplies and deodorizers I needed to make the space usable. My mother used to take a toothbrush and scrub the collars of her customer's white shirts to get them pristine because that's how serious she was about doing a good job. I wasn't about to scrub those toilets with a toothbrush, but I sure did approach the task with the same mindset my mother had. When I got done, I said to myself, *Melvin sure is lucky the members and I love him.*

After what turned into a two-hour cleanup, Sunday School finally got started. It was a struggle trying to ignore the aroma of perfumed air freshener layered with the smell of cigarette smoke and liquor, but we managed to soldier on right into morning worship after Sunday School. The building had no windows which restricted ventilation, and only the front and rear entry doors provided natural light and fresh air, but they were seldom opened. So, when my husband concluded his sermon, like always he would say, "The doors of the church are now open." That was when those who were seeking the Lord were invited to become a member of our church. Only this time, probably because even my husband couldn't take that awful smell, the doors were opened... literally! I wondered if it was even feasible for Melvin to consider doing business with these people.

As I was driving my usual route to church this particular Sunday morning, it struck me how ominous the skies appeared. It's weird because, when I exited my home and made the short steps to the car parked in the driveway, I never noticed the atmosphere. Not until I was on the road did I start to pay attention. Given the appearance of the clouds above, I was relieved that I had made it to the Viel before mother nature could unleash the obvious rainfall that was coming. Something felt off as I sat in my car thinking about what was awaiting me inside, but I couldn't put my finger on what was gnawing at me.

The thought of being drenched by pouring rain wasn't the issue because I had an umbrella, and I had assumed everyone else who was coming to help did, too. But I was certain the rain did have something to do with the anxiety I was experiencing. One by one people pulled onto the parking lot just minutes apart from me. Once everybody had arrived, we greeted each other with our usual, "Praise the Lord," and "Good morning sister so-and-so," or "God bless you brother you-know-who," then we all hurried inside just as the rain came. Like clockwork everyone moved to their designated cleaning areas and immediately got busy washing, wiping, or sweeping so that we could get on with our worship.

A few minutes into our service the force of the rain grew more intense and, as it was pouring down outside, to our dismay a torrential downpour was now happening inside! *That explains my premonition*, I thought. Yet there we were, confronted with another set-back, hurdle, obstacle...TEST! *(It turned out that the building's roof had major cracks in it, something we knew absolutely nothing about before renting the place.)*

While the service was going on it was kind of funny watching people sitting in their chairs holding umbrellas as the rain trickled down upon them. From the visual, we could have been the poster child for the quote, *When it Rains, it Pours*. Refusing to be deterred, members went out to their cars and brought back anything to aid in the wipe-up while the choir kept singing and the Reverend kept on preaching. Deacons searched the entire building, trespassing inside of unmarked closets and rooms that appeared to be off-limits, trying to locate whatever they could find to slow the incoming flood. As the waters continued to come down, I know prayers were going up.

I was going over some old paperwork of my husband's from when he tried to buy the Victory Center. At the time, it was under new management and the name had been changed from the Viel to the Victory Center. Melvin didn't like the fact that I had started having some reservations about him trying to go after that property. Whenever he would tell me about the conversations he and the owner had I would say to him, "Melvin, something's not adding up." The owner was trying to pull the wool over my husband's eyes, but Melvin couldn't see it and he refused to entertain my concern. My husband was still reeling from the injustice he suffered months earlier and he needed to have something work out. I couldn't blame him for that. But, given the fact that the building had too many issues and just wasn't worth the trouble, I wanted him to approach the situation with a bit more caution.

Melvin went ahead and put a deposit down on the building as a good-faith gesture but, before they could seal the deal, he found out the seller wasn't even the true owner of the building. I was no longer privy to much information after that but I did, on several occasions, overhear my husband on the phone discussing the matter with one of the deacons. The agitation in his voice told me all I needed to know. That building was no diamond-in-the-rough, just a darn money-pit not worth our time or finances. The guy pretending to be the manager-owner was a professional conman and thief. He and his accomplices were attempting to pull off an illegal transaction and, had they been successful, Melvin would have not only lost a tremendous amount of money but the building as well. As always, God stepped in and shielded us again.

The Corner Market

Next door, east of the money pit, was a vacant building that used to be a neighborhood grocery store. Per my suggestion, after church one Sunday, Melvin and I took a short stroll down to the corner of Page and Union which meant we'd have to walk right past the abandoned market, my intention all along. I sort of slowed my pace, looked to my left at the site, then began hinting that the store would be perfect for a church.

"What are you talking about?" he asked as we walked along nearing our destination.

Melvin didn't seem that interested in what I was yapping about or having to walk anywhere. I had forgotten that he had preached one of those fiery sermons a few moments earlier and that usually left him sweaty, dehydrated, and exhausted. It appeared he wanted to go home. Me, I kept right on walking, right on talking, and right on dreaming aloud. My imagination had already placed a red carpet at the store's entrance ready to greet all who crossed the threshold. For the outside, I envisioned a steeple that would stand tall atop the structure and serve as a beacon for miles around. What was so special about the building, I shared, was that it sat on the corner of a busy intersection. You could see it clearly from all four directions. He still didn't say anything, but I could tell by his expression that he was either pondering the notion or doubting my theory. I needed to prove to him that you really could see that location from every direction, so I suggested we stand on each of the four corners. He conjured up a bit more energy and continued to tag along. I thought, *At last! I had gotten his attention.* This time I pushed the envelope a little further and suggested he find out about that building. It was hard to tell what he was thinking, and I was convinced he was about to do what he usually did, object to my idea. I may have been worrying for nothing because he did inquire and made arrangements with the owner for us to tour the site.

Unlike the Victory Center, the store had a flat roof that was well-maintained. The foundation was strong, built to withstand any storm that might arise. There were no steps to climb which made it accessible to everyone. When we went inside and walked on the smooth level concrete floor, I said to my husband, "Let's have a skating party before we open it as a church." Melvin didn't feel like entertaining my whims, his focus was on liability and calling the insurance agent to see what we needed to do to get the building insured.

I visualized all kinds of possible uses of the store's interior. There were rooms, large and small, perfect for my office, some classrooms, a meeting space, and a dining area. I wanted the largest side room for the women and had even designated a special room with a great closet specifically for the choir. A nursery for the babies and a playroom for the little kids would be located on the other side of the building. But what was more ideal was the open space in the center of the edifice, large enough for a 1000-seat sanctuary. Everything I thought of was what I wanted never considering what any of the other members or even Melvin might want. Excited to share my wish-list, my husband asked, "And exactly where will my office be?"

Immediately I snapped out of my self-imposed hypnotic spell and said, "Oops! You do need an office, don't you."

It was best to have a planning committee anyway. I only needed one seat on Sunday morning and didn't care where that seat was as long as we were all together. I'm not sure how hopeful Melvin was about this being our new home after that Victory Center fiasco, but I was still filled with enough optimism for the both of us.

Let the Fundraising Begin

Deacon Ben's wife, Sister Retia Stewart, sought the advice of a close friend about how to raise money for our church. Her friend, who was a busy laborer at her church suggested we open a childcare center. "People are always looking for a good childcare center. You all have plenty of space and the right location for one," she explained.

Sister Retia got busy and, before we knew it, we were in the Monday through Friday... 10 hours a day... daycare business. We had an entire staff of the most incredible willing workers who, along with Sister Retia and Sister Harriet *(another eager member)*, took great care of the babies. I had a granddaughter and a niece enrolled who started out wearing one size then quickly grew into two fat little darlings. Kids, whose parents described having the most difficult time during feeding times at home, ate everything that Sister Retia fed them. Twice a day the children and staff enjoyed some of the best home-cooked meals around. Heck, I even ate several of her delectable meals with no thought to counting calories. Retia wasn't the only great cook in our church. We also had king and queen grill masters waiting for a chance to show what they could do.

To raise money, we also sold bar-b-que every weekend... the best in the city according to our repeat customers, and we chose to believe them. Our secret weapon was none other than Sister Retia who had some secret weapons of her own... great recipes. That woman used to make the best potato salad using a box of instant mashed potatoes. One time we ran out of potato salad during a busy BBQ rush and customers were frantic. A new batch would have required peeling potatoes, putting them on to boil, chopping vegetables, and mixing all of the other ingredients. An hour max–time we did not have. So, she put a small pot of water on the stove to boil, grabbed a big box of instant potatoes from the pantry along with some other secret ingredients, and in less than 15 minutes... POTATO SALAD! I'm still in awe at the thought of it. Grateful and ever mindful of all that God had done for us, we adopted a practice of never turning anyone hungry away. If you had money, of course, we expected you to pay because it was for a worthy cause. But those who couldn't afford a sandwich got one anyway especially if I or Sister Retia was around. It was such a great fellowship and time for us to all be together.

Sister Malinda Franklin was one of our most faithful senior members. She had been a years-long congregant of Washington Tabernacle until the vote. I remember the colorful expletives she used especially after the horrible way the former church had treated her pastor. That's the day she moved her membership even though it meant leaving her sister and the church she had been a part of for decades. It was Malinda and her sister Martha who first welcomed Melvin when he became the pastor there. Sister Franklin was also my son Darren's first love. She showed tremendous affection to my entire family.

Malinda was a big woman. She walked with a cane because of her stooped-over posture resulting from years of hard labor but you could tell she once was tall in stature. She wore her beautiful gray hair in two buns, one on each side of her head behind her ears. Her stockings were always rolled down under her knees and knotted on one side, a somewhat comical view you could only see when walking behind her. Sister Franklin was a strong advocate of my husband and was never afraid to speak her mind even to him. She would threaten anyone if they said something derogatory against her pastor. Quite the character that one.

Ms. Franklin was always so proud to be able to help raise funds in support of any initiative we had going on. She lived on a limited income but operated on a never-ending supply of sheer willpower. Every Saturday Malinda would set up her makeshift stand a few feet from where we sold BBQ to sell her candy bars. Customers received a free dessert whenever they bought a full meal but that didn't apply to the purchase of a sandwich. Those sandwich buyers became Malinda's target audience. To show off her entrepreneurial skills, she'd stop customers as they passed by and suggest that a candy bar would be the perfect ending to a great lunch. Malinda sold almost as much candy as we did dinners and turned all the monies over to her church. Sister Franklin was also known as the candy lady in the senior living facility where she lived. She would sit in the lobby of her building and catch people coming and going, many of whom never made it to their intended destination without buying a candy bar or two. That old lady showed us that her limitation didn't define her determination. We were Cornerstone Institutional Baptist Church, the underdogs out to prove a point. We may have been down but we would definitely get back up one candy bar at a time if Sister Franklin had her way about it. Like I said, quite the character.

My husband was a great preacher who documented all of his sermons. I thought we could sell them as another source of church revenue. Other preachers would call in hopes of borrowing one or two of his texts, so why not have some writings available for a reasonable fee? I even tried convincing him to sell them at various conventions but that was my vision, not his. Anyway, he was always off and running with other new and different ideas, which kept something going on all the time. Even though we weren't successful in purchasing the store and had to return to the Victory Center, those were some of our joyous times.

The Voices of Cornerstone

That joy carried over into our service through the singing. Melvin loved music and his choir. He wanted them to be the best of the best, and they were one of the finest choirs in the City. At my husband's insistence, the Voices of Cornerstone rehearsed at least twice a week, a regimen that helped turn them into a well-oiled singing unit. Whenever necessary, choir rehearsals were even held at our house. Melvin was driven to excellence.

Say Amen, Somebody is a gospel music documentary featuring Cornerstone. Melvin is the young preacher seen with his congregation and his choir, the Mighty Voices of Cornerstone. I have never told anyone about what happened to me the day the loaded movie cameras were filming at our church. I wanted to be in that movie so badly that all week leading up to that day I worked on putting together an outfit that was sure to get the camera's attention. I picked out my favorite color knowing that the yellow would highlight my skin just so. I chose the perfect sparkling gold jewelry to place around my neck to add to my marvelous glow. I decided to do a better job than normal with my makeup so that my eyes would appear larger as they shimmered in the camera's light. Even practiced making my face up every day so I would look amazing. I stepped out of my house the day of filming not needing anyone to say I looked good because I knew I did. I was going to be in that movie, and everyone would look at me and shout, "Say Amen, Somebody!"

Well, the Lord teaches us lessons all the time, some harder than others. I took my seat and positioned myself in the most obvious spot, knowing the camera crew had to pass me more than one or two times. The organist started playing, and it was time for the choir to march in. Then I noticed one of the choir members running around trying to find someone to care for her young child. This was a challenge because she was the parent of a child who had several disabilities. No one was willing to help her, so I reached out and grabbed Shona. Her mother really wanted to sing, and I couldn't in good conscience take that opportunity away from her. The cameramen did walk around me several times but never once turned the camera on Shona and me. *Lord, I hear you!* I had gotten so wrapped up in being cute and seen, the Lord had to force me to think about others. That baby needed someone with enough compassion to care for her... to ignore all the metal braces and apparatuses required to support her delicate body. Her mother also needed at that very moment to be a choir member. What I was wearing would have added nothing had I been in that movie.

Over the years it had become too difficult to deal with the temperament of some of our musicians. In response, Melvin decided the choir would sing without the help of a pianist or an organist for a while. Church members raised objections that our service would suffer from the absence of music. Some of the choir members who were less confident in their vocal abilities also agreed. We didn't know it at the time, but it was the best thing that could have happened to our church and our choir. Their well-blended and uniquely-gifted voices produced the sweetest sound many of us had ever heard. That made it easier to deal with the fact that our piano and organ sat unoccupied for over two years. Those were some of the proudest moments I had of my Voices of Cornerstone, I relished every a cappella note. It was a true test of our faith and a reminder that, with God, nothing was impossible.

Singing without music made believers out of not only *us* Cornerstonians but others who had the pleasure of hearing our choir sing. Many church choirs began to trust themselves without a musician as well. Believe me when I tell you that they couldn't do it like the Voices of Cornerstone, and they knew it. We had gone to the First Baptist Church of Creve Coeur to help celebrate their current pastor's anniversary, and our choir was asked to sing. The pastor of FBC said, "I heard about the Voices of Cornerstone and, you might be good, but my choir is the greatest." His choir's president begged him to stop making that declaration because she knew choirs didn't want to sing after the

Voices got through setting the church on fire. Pastors around the city had this friendly rivalry when it came to who had the better singing choir. At the end of the service, she said to me, "I wish he had not embarrassed us like that." She too was a fan of the Mighty Voices of Cornerstone.

One year I was in charge of a Regional Postal Convention that was held at an exclusive hotel in downtown St. Louis. Any time I booked a hotel it had to be top quality with spacious conference rooms, upgraded sleeping quarters, and fantastic food. I was under a lot of pressure because local managers wanted our convention to be the best, so I asked my church choir to be part of the entertainment. They loved to sing at different venues. I arranged for them to have breakfast in the hotel's restaurant while our opening session was taking place. At 9:00 AM, the national president had just finished her presentation and my choir was next on the program. The audience became more and more excited as they watched a seemingly never-ending-parade of professionals entering the room in single file.

Our pianist took his place and started tickling the piano keys in a way that got everybody's attention. And then the Voices of Cornerstone started singing. The melodious sound filled the room in such a way that the mouths of some of the most dignified folks flew open. Most of the audience stood on their feet in appreciation of what they were hearing. When our pianist saw their reaction, he became even more animated than he'd ever been. Folks started clapping and, before the song was over, everyone was on their feet applauding. The locals were well pleased.

The choir's final number was a song that my daughter taught them and one that every Postal manager recognized... WE DELIVER, the Postal Service's theme song. The sound of the harmony was rich and the words resonating throughout brought tears to the eyes of some of the most bureaucratic Postal Managers. The choir received their final standing ovation as they exited the room singing...

You know we're gonna be there, don't think twice. Service is part of our name. We're the people you rely on to get it right, and no one else does it the same. We're a part of the country, we're a part of your town, we're faces you see every day. Though practice makes perfect, we got it down, and we're gonna keep it that way! We deliver ...

Not only was my choir good, but they also made me look good as they so often did.

The Voices also sang at the habilitation center where my brother, Berdell, lived. This particular audience didn't seem to care about the choir's melodic sound. The clients booed them after each song until they sang one of their favorites... Jingle Bells. I get tickled by it still. And, to support me at my next visit, the choir put on a full concert for the entire facility. The Voices received rave reviews and got invited to return the following year.

At Melvin's funeral in 2015, every person who had ever been a part of the Voices took the choir stand. The singing filled the church with the melodious sound of angels. You would have thought they had rehearsed for days when, in fact, most of them had not seen each other in years. They were together again as I had remembered and that comforted me, I was so grateful. My husband would have been overjoyed. I'm sure he was because, above where he lay resting, sang his VOICES OF CORNERSTONE.

Worshipping Amongst the Dead

Before purchasing our current building we held services at five locations with the last being Ted Foster's Funeral Home. Rev. Foster was a good friend to Melvin and he was always very supportive of anything we wanted to do. People would ask us how we felt having church service in a funeral home and the reality was that we weren't bothered by the caskets of dead bodies that were in the adjoining rooms. We didn't have to be quiet and those who slept continued to sleep. If you thought I was talking about the deceased, I'm not. I'm talking about the members who fell asleep each Sunday and awoke in time for the benediction. The only time anybody became alarmed was when one of us discovered we knew one of the decedents and had been unaware of their passing. We had some of our best services in the funeral home's main chapel, some so spirited we almost brought the dead back to life.

Over time, however, I became increasingly concerned about holding service at Rev. Foster's because members often failed to watch their children. Kids would pretend they had to go to the restroom only to dawdle in the vestibule, play in the hallway, or sneak around looking for dead people. My feeling was that they either belonged with their parents or needed supervision the entire time. One Sunday I went to the restroom and found kids sliding down the handrail. This for me was the turning point. Ted Foster had been so accommodating and could reasonably expect that we would treat his building with care. So, on the way home, I told my husband that it was time for us to leave the funeral home before we damaged it and Melvin agreed that it was time we had our own place of worship. As we headed home, with Melvin driving, I looked at several vacant buildings along the way. A week later we were leaving a meeting at the Masonic Hall and, before Melvin could drive even a block away, I noticed a vacant building, one that had been empty for quite a while. Melvin said he would check it out and, after he inquired, he reported that the building wasn't for sale.

"Not for sale? What building are you talking about?" I asked. Turns out he had been looking in a different direction at a completely different building.

"That's not the building I was talking about." I scoffed. When he checked on the one I had originally suggested, he learned that it was available and that the owners were willing to work with us. I'm putting this in the book because **I** told **him** where to look and which building to buy. Melvin said, no, the Lord guided him to the building.

"Then what role did I play?" I asked.

"You were the conduit the Lord used to give me the message." Melvin was always so full of *s*ugar, *h*oney, *i*ced *t*ea.

My Husband the Contractor–Our New Church Home

The building I had selected for our new site was the old garage of Albert H. Hoppe Funeral Home. *(Mr. Hoppe was a well-known white businessman, funeral director, and licensed embalmer.)* How ironic was that? We were already holding our Sunday services in the Ted Foster Funeral Chapel and here was a building on the grounds of another funeral home. It may have been a coincidence, but I choose to believe that nothing happens by chance. It was all a divine decision to place us in that spot. Melvin thought so, too, and we were ready to take the next step. He called the owners and made an appointment for us to see the inside of the building. Together we toured what was to be our new church home. We didn't know what to expect, but I don't think it mattered because Melvin had already made up his mind.

A greater part of the building had previously housed the limousines and hearses and Melvin thought it was the perfect area for our church sanctuary. As we walked through each section of the building, Melvin would say, "This is where the classrooms will go" or, "this area will be the restrooms." Everything he visualized seemed plausible except where the kitchen would be. The owners told us it was the space they used to embalm the bodies. It was still the best location so, at the risk of losing all of our cooks, I suggested we not share that part of the building's history with any of the church members.

The price for the building was reasonable as it was old and had not been used for several years. There were cracks in the concrete floors throughout the building, and it had a flat roof that needed replacing. The place was a mess, but Melvin was so elated because we would finally have a place of our own. All I could think was, *work and more work, so get ready*. The building had two separate sections which meant we could remodel one side and wait on the other until funds became available. We, Melvin & I, applied and got approved for a loan because the church had no money at the time.

"Melvin, who are we going to get to do the work?"

Using his distinguished preacher's voice he announced, "I'm going to do the work myself."

You have got to be kidding, I thought to myself. My husband was someone who had never fixed anything in our house. The only painting he had done was to our bathroom and that was after I hung wallpaper. *(The pattern was beautiful yellow flowers that I thought added a special touch... a lovely view since that's where he spent a lot of his time.)* One day Melvin painted over all my beautiful flowers with white paint but some of them were still visible because he didn't remove the wallpaper first. His excuse was that those yellow flowers would have driven him crazy. That was never my intent but, at that moment I seriously thought about hanging yellow-flowered wallpaper throughout the house.

Melvin learned he couldn't just tell the city officials what he planned to do, that he had to have permits for everything which also meant getting architectural drawings from a licensed architect. After that reality check about what he couldn't do himself, he would hire a licensed professional to do what he couldn't. He and Chubby, one of the deacons, did most of the remaining work. The work was done during a very harsh winter with no heat in the building, and that took a toll on my husband's health and wellbeing. I suspect his overzealousness along with the scope and pace of the work also contributed to Melvin's back issues. He never wore insulated clothing or a back brace, didn't take much-needed breaks, and he wasn't sleeping well. Any, if not all, of those modifications would have allowed his arms, back, knees, legs, shoulders, hands, and neck to recuperate. He also didn't have extra workers to offset the heavy lifting, debris towing, and excessive pounding. Constantly kneeling, bending, climbing, straining, and falling all were further affecting his body. But every evening, although nearly frozen and exhausted, he would take a step back and marvel at the progress he and Chubby had made.

Melvin was determined to complete the job by spring so that we could move into our new church home. According to him, the Lord had laid it all out for him, he knew exactly where each room should go. With the help of others, the final product looked exactly the way he described. Melvin had done an amazing job turning the main section of that old garage into a beautiful sanctuary. We Cornerstonians were very proud.

Although they were successful, the work took a toll on Chubby as well. As they aged, they each ended up bent over at the waist and using walkers to get around. Yet the hardship never overshadowed the pride and joy the two of them felt as everyone praised their accomplishment. The members were not the only ones praising the transformation of the building. Melvin had promised to invite the previous owners back once the work was completed. When the Hoppe family entered the building, their eyes lit up. Appreciative and exuberant described their reactions. The place they loved had been restored and was once again a positive symbol in the community. According to his daughter, old man Hoppe would have been pleased.

A few of us decided to meet at the church one evening to discuss the type of celebration we should have in honor of our newly renovated building. Scattered about the room were a handful of leftover folding chairs that Melvin and his work crew used for breaks or lunch. Luckily, there were enough for the meeting. After one of the two deacons there opened the meeting with a prayer, we started tossing around several ideas including one that centered on the meaning of Spring... the season of new beginnings. I thought that was a great suggestion and was just about to say so when the discussion took a turn.

"The building is empty...where are we going to sit?" Asked one member.

Another replied, "Well, we can each bring a folding chair."

"What if we have visitors...where are they going to sit?" a deacon asked.

Somebody else answered, "Well, each of us should bring two folding chairs."

"How are we going to get some if we don't have enough folding chairs?" a second deacon chimed in.

How-are-we-going-to-do-this and how-are-we-going-to-do-that? Listening to all the back and forth had gotten on my last nerve. We all had decent-paying jobs, but it became clear to me that no one was willing to take on the task and responsibility of obtaining chairs. With a plan in mind, I excused myself and drove home. The next morning I picked up my phone and dialed a couple of familiar places to get pricing on new chairs. Then I went through the yellow pages and called several listed warehouses until I found one that had folding chairs for sale. It didn't matter if they weren't brand new, just that they would be in good enough shape to hold those in attendance.

I called Darren, announced that I had found a warehouse, and said, "Let's go to East Saint Louis." When we got there, we saw stacks and stacks of dusty folding chairs all around the warehouse. Luckily for us the folks were happy to get rid of them and were willing to negotiate. I don't remember what we paid but I do remember we bought two hundred chairs. The seller even agreed to have the chairs delivered to the church the following day. As soon as they arrived, everyone in the building pitched in to get them cleaned and arranged in the sanctuary. We were ready to have church!

Sidebar...

Not long after we were in our new building, the church held an open house so that friends and folks in the community could tour our partially renovated building. The members were encouraged to invite as many people as possible, and I extended an invitation to some close friends and my postal family who had given us plenty of support. I knew that, of the two hundred chairs we had purchased, some were in better condition than others. As the event got underway, unbeknownst to me, one member had picked out two of the better chairs for herself and her husband. Then she wandered off in search of her spouse who was already inspecting the place. Meanwhile, I spotted two very special guests and immediately directed them to the first available seats in my view... the same two chairs my church member had claimed for herself. The member returned to find her chairs occupied and demanded that our guests yield them to her. With a scornful tone, she explained that she had secured those seats for herself and her husband as justification for her lack of hospitality. She should have been playing host for the evening like every other member of the church and not sitting on her **blessed assurance** as my son would say. The stunned look on the faces of the two people I adored spoke volumes to me. I wasted no time in offering my sincerest apology as I located two more *(better)* seats for them. I was so ashamed of my church member's behavior that I don't think I ever invited my friends to anything else at church.

Moving For the Last Time

It was somewhat bittersweet the last Sunday at Ted Foster's because he had been such a great ally. My husband wanted the members to make the 20 block drive from the funeral home to our new church together as a show of solidarity. We piled into our vehicles, everyone aligning their cars along Grand Avenue, one behind the other, with Melvin's Caddy in the lead position. You could feel the excitement and anticipation in the air. The moment he pulled away from the curb, I watched through my side-view mirror as each driver repeated Melvin's every move. As he guided the front of his Deville onto the outside lane, merging with caution into the flow of traffic, so did every car in succession. It was like watching synchronized or precision driving.

Our motorcade must have resembled a funeral procession as we headed south on Grand towards our new home. Other drivers on the road would either slow down, speed up to get out of our way, or pull over completely allowing us to pass. Some commented later that the extended courtesy made them feel like dignitaries. Once we had arrived and parked at our destination, Melvin lined everyone up in close-order formation as though we were about to take part in a parade. He offered a quick and powerful prayer, then the soldiers-in-the-army-of-the-Lord marched into our building. What a sight to behold. We had traveled a long way and God had seen us through it all. From Washington Tabernacle to the Seventh Day Adventist Church to the Victory Center to the corner market then back to the Victory Center to Ted Foster's Funeral Home and now, finally, into our place of worship... home! It was a proud and happy day as we crossed that threshold. Once celebrated, cast aside, taken in, and bamboozled, we had survived the wilderness.

Even with only one side of the building finished, it was still ours, folding chairs, and all. What had been so very important to my husband was that everything in the restrooms had to be new. The men didn't seem to care or see the need and thought we should cut corners saving money wherever we could. Thank God Melvin didn't agree. The ladies got a restroom worthy of us as women. As part-owner of the building, I wouldn't have had it any other way. The pews and carpeting came later.

Along with some of my postal comrades I had been a long-time member of the NPAPM *(National Phoenix Association of Postal Managers)*. It warmed my heart that each one of them made a personal contribution towards our new place of worship. The Association's President knew of a building that was being renovated with all of its prior contents discarded in the process including some sturdy, well-made cabinets. You know what they say, one man's trash is another man's treasure and I'm happy to report that those cabinets are still in the church's kitchen. Another friend asked to help, and I told her that I was working on a room for the kids. She was well aware of my love and commitment to children's causes and assured me that she had things covered. Boy, did she! Our nursery and children's room was completely furnished with the best tables and chairs around. She splurged more on that furniture than she would have ever spent on herself. I thank God for these individuals who, even though not church members, served as angels in our time of need. I will always cherish their generosity and friendship.

Within weeks the pulpit, carpeting, and pews were added and each improvement drew a stream of members stopping by to see how it was going. I guess their curiosity got the better of them. Soon the workers were putting the finishing touches on our three classrooms and office & conference space for Melvin. I would often prepare lunch for the work crew and used that as my excuse just to get in on the thick of things happening at the church... my church. Melvin and I were discussing what decorative items he wanted to see on the main wall behind the pulpit and, though he didn't have an exact idea, he knew he wanted something special, sacred yet eye-catching. Keeping in mind what Melvin wanted, I volunteered to go shopping. I don't recall what store I was in, just that it was the last of many I had visited that day. As I began looking again for just the right *something special,* I had an aha moment: there was the perfect item that neither one of us could refuse. I had come across a plain wooden cross which, once mounted on that designated wall at church, would be large enough for everyone to see.

I knew that the plain wooden cross said it all. There was nothing fancy about Christ's crucifixion and I felt this was the perfect symbol to represent where he was nailed and died. I then located two smaller crosses in gold, each complementing the larger one. Together all three completed the look of the crosses that stood on Calvary's hill. My husband loved my choices and the crosses were mounted immediately.

I also bought the furniture for Melvin's office. He had two rooms, his office, and a small conference room. As I saw other members attempting to claim or assign the spaces as they saw fit, I felt I had to intervene and decided that both spaces should be his. Since it was my name on the loan and my credit that secured it, I felt entitled to make some *(if not all)* of the designations. And then I went shopping, making my rounds of all the local office supply stores but leaving each one more disappointed than the one before. The day-long search left me exhausted and I was ready to go home, yet my car seemed to have a mind of its own as I found myself on Forest Park Boulevard near a used office furniture warehouse that was not even on my radar.

"This had better not be a waste of my time," I scolded the car as if it had become possessed and driven me there against my will. Once I got inside the store, though, I noticed the old furniture right away. They even had what I wanted, office desks that were solid, well-constructed, and would last forever. And over in a corner was a round table that the salesman said had been there for a very long time. It was an extremely heavy piece and, to move it, you had to unscrew the top from its base. That alone intrigued me, and I examined it further before asking if, indeed, it was for sale.

The salesman seemed a bit surprised and asked, "Yes it's for sale but why do you want it?"

"It's perfect for us and unlike anything I found anywhere else." I responded.

I could see the advantage of Melvin having that round table because it would allow everyone to face each other. Plus it was strong enough and wouldn't be easily destroyed. The owner told me how much he was selling it for if I wanted it. The odd way he said, "If you wanted it," seemed strange and the price was a bit steep, but I was focused more on his statement than the price. So I asked, "If it's something that's been sitting here all this time and you don't want it, then why do you have this kind of price on it?" That's when they told me the table was an antique. People were generally looking for modern furniture one of them explained. They were shocked by my interest in such an antiquated piece of furniture, which I then bought and paid to have delivered. They happily got over their shock.

It was a perfect fit for the intended space, plus it pleased my husband. Melvin loved it when someone else took care of him especially when he didn't have to fork out any of his money. I could spend MY money, which was, in his opinion, HIS money. But he wasn't going to spend HIS money which, in his opinion, was not MY money.

I've never told the church members that I still claim ownership of that heavy wooden antique table. It was only loaned to my husband for his lifetime. I know that I'm being very selfish because I haven't a place to put it; nevertheless, I still believe it's mine.

Won't You Be My Neighbor?

From the outside of our building, no one could have ever imagined what was inside. I had hoped that, after witnessing such a spectacle, visitors would instantly want to become members. Converting the neighbors was also our desire but to have them accept the church as a part of their community was even more important. The neighborhood was plagued by unsavory activities that attracted occasional unwanted foot and four-wheel traffic. Some neighboring residents also expressed reservations about us occupying the building for fear we would take up all their parking spaces or add to already heavy traffic going in and out. Older residents were especially worried that they wouldn't be able to get to their homes safely if they had to park too far away because we were using *their spaces*, especially after dark. Instead of allowing discontent to spread, we took the opportunity to address their concerns. I joined the block unit to get a better understanding of what our future neighbors were dealing with and to show my overall support of the surrounding community. Getting to know the neighbors turned out to be beneficial for both me and the church.

I had been at the church so much while it was being renovated that it didn't take the folks in the neighborhood long to figure out that I was the Pastor's wife. In that time they had also determined I was a friend, not a foe, simply because of our casual waves back and forth in the course of my comings and goings. At my very first block unit meeting, there were only eight people in attendance including me. I noticed there were no 20-30-40 something adults there, even though the neighborhood was swarming with little kids.

I was in my fifties at this time and I was the youngest of everyone there *(all the other females well over the age of sixty)*. There was no agenda, other than the recording secretary reporting on what was happening in the neighborhood and the treasurer reminding everyone to pay their monthly dues before leaving. They asked me to introduce myself, so I stood and gave my name, church affiliation, and church title. Then I told them I wanted to become a dues-paying member. By their reaction, you would have thought I had won the lottery and decided to give them all my winnings.

Flattered yet fascinated by their favorable reception, I wondered about their reaction if I offered to pay dues for the entire year. I couldn't help but snicker to myself as I pictured those old ladies turning cartwheels around the room once I handed them my check for the full amount. My imagination, however, could not compare to the hilarity right before my eyes as I watched the treasurer count the money.

Ms. Washington was the block unit's oldest and longest dues-paying member. She loved being the treasurer and believed her utmost responsibility was to make sure every penny got counted. Unfortunately for her, she didn't have good use of her hands and fingers due to arthritis and it was evident to everyone *(including her)* that it was time to hand the reins over to someone else. But she was not about to give up the job.

Unfortunately for us, she also felt that no one should leave until all the money was counted. The last thing I wanted to do after a long and grueling day, was to sit there and watch Ms. Washington struggle to separate each bill or pick up every coin. There would only be about $25.00 turned in at any given meeting, but the count would take Ms. Washington 45 minutes or longer. She was so engrossed in what she was doing that I even thought about trying to make a fast-track to my vehicle before she finished. Instead, I sat there thinking, *If Ms. Washington was to join our church, she could never work in the finance room because it would probably be the next day before she finished adding up all our tithes and offerings.* Luckily, her membership was at a different church.

There were times I had to remind myself of my reason for being at the meetings in the first place – that I wanted to be a genuine representative of the body of Christ, bridging the gap between community and church. Ms. Washington was deserving of my patience and respect.

Changing the Climate

We held our weekly bible classes on Wednesday evenings at the church. Our building was close to what was once a popular hangout for prostitutes and, like our neighbors, the members had grown annoyed and concerned for their own safety. Especially since it was normally dark by the time bible class ended. Some of the church ladies and I decided to put our bible-thumping skills to good use. Each week we would go out among the **ladies of the evening** and invite them to join in on our studies. There was no discrimination in our efforts to save souls so we also extended the invitation to the male customers who continued to frequent the area. Young guys, new to the game, didn't want anyone seeing them, married men feared exposure, and neighborhood regulars avoided us altogether. We were relentless in our efforts and we became little pestering holy gnats that wouldn't go away. Heck, if they weren't going to go away, neither were we. Those ladies of the evening and their clients had no interest whatsoever in studying the bible and continued to shoo us away. Still, none of them had anything in their street arsenal that could repel us holy gnats.

We even installed barricades at the end of the block outside the church to stop drive-thru traffic completely. The neighbors were pleased by what we were able to accomplish, and the issue of parking was never a problem or ever mentioned again.

Chapter Ten
My ACADEMY Award – A
Dream Come True

I wanted to develop a curriculum for kids that would give them the tools to rise above their circumstances knowing their dreams could also become their reality. I knew that it would involve finding a location and even paying for the renovations if necessary. I wasn't hurting for money because, after I retired, I had worked under contract for my former employer managing two programs that I had developed. There was enough space in our church building that could be utilized and, even though it needed a lot of work, I couldn't wait to claim it as my own. I saw it as an opportunity to help my husband while doing what I had always envisioned... enriching the lives of young people.

The CIBC Westend Academy would be like no other, offering everything from academics, performing arts, food & nutrition, recreation, financial management, GED courses, and computer literacy. This task was designed especially for me, it's what fueled my momentum. Some of the parents needed just as much help with the same curriculum as their children which was an even greater motivating force that kept me going.

That motivation to some, particularly my husband, appeared to be self-serving but it wasn't, at least not in the way most dictionaries define the term. I had always sacrificed so much by putting

Melvin's needs ahead of my own, even when it came to starting the church. The time had come for me to do something for me... put my interests, my desires, on the front burner. Despite my many unfortunate circumstances, there was no denying so much good had happened for me. This was my chance now to give back, to sow seeds of wisdom and love into a child in need that was sown into me. I saw myself in so many of the kids that came through our doors. I knew first-hand what it was like to struggle, to live in a house with one parent, to have to care for younger siblings, to face ridicule by those more fortunate, or just to long for a simple hug.

Some people live a lifetime and never get the opportunity to make their dreams come true. My dream of having a program for children was finally coming to fruition and I could not have been happier.

As a child growing up, every penny in our household had great value. To earn extra money I used to run errands for the neighbors. Mrs. Womack, who lived close by, would often ask me to go to the store for her. Upon my return, she would have me sit down for **little talks** as she called them. She'd start by saying I was living at the beginning of my life. Then she'd tell me what happens at the middle and end of my life, that it was all up to me and that I needed to decide right then what I wanted for my future. And, if better was what I wanted, she told me, those pin curls had to come out of my hair whenever I was in public.

"What's that got to do with anything? I asked.

She said, "Rollers and pin curls are okay in your house but not okay out in public. You have to look like you care about yourself if you expect others to care about you."

Sometimes I still hear Mrs. Womack's voice when I'm not behaving or looking the way I know I should. Ruby, another neighbor, volunteered to become my godmother. She bought me a bicycle just so I would have what the other children had. Whenever she went shopping for clothes, she would go to the finest retailers to buy my clothes, outfits no one else had and which my mother could never afford. Mrs. Womack and Ruby never made me feel ashamed about being poor. Instead, they made me feel valued and, for that, I am forever grateful. That's the same spirit that I wanted to pass to these children and which I decided would be the Academy's main goal. We would feed any hungry child and dress any child who needed clothing. The generosity my mother showed when she had so little, coupled with Mrs. Womack's and Ruby's acts of kindness, set the stage for my desire to always pay it forward.

Staking My Claim

Like any good salesperson, I came prepared to pitch my ideas before a group of gentlemen from our church, specifically Melvin and Deacons Seward, Blumfield, and Johnson. However, after I began speaking, it did not take me long to recognize what I had felt so many times in the past – the uncensored expression of the male ego! That undeniable presence of arrogance, dismissive attitudes *(mixed in with a little bit of threat)* and envy was definitely in the air and most definitely coming towards me from every angle. It was clear that these men had no idea who was standing before them – someone who had trained with the "**best of the best**" bigots and egotistical a-holes the St. Louis Postal Service had to offer. I was ready and equipped with my well-defined, fully-developed, works-well-under-pressure mental biceps that could surely take on these four peons sitting before me. Blocking out any negativity, I continued by describing in detail the Academy's purpose, even sharing my carefully drafted mission statement. Then I told them my thoughts on renovating the unfinished side of our building, explaining it would be for the sole purpose of operating the CIBC Westend Academy. Right away the men smirked, making little or no effort to mask their condescending response to my proposal.

"What do you know about construction work?" asked Deacon Seward.

"I know a lot about construction work. I know how to spell it and to look in the yellow pages and find it if I have to. I also know that when you want a job done well you seek out a professional. What more do I need to know?" I shot back.

My answer might have seemed a little flippant, but they had earned that response. How dare these Doubting Thomases imply that I couldn't do what I had outlined. Then Deacon Blumfield made it a point of reminding me that the church had no money to make the repairs. Other than my husband, I understood the financial condition of the church far better than the deacon could have ever imagined. I was knee deep in the financial obligation of THE CHURCH! It was never my intention to make the membership responsible in any way for what I wanted to do. This was going to be MY special project. Mine and the Master. *I can do all things through Christ Jesus,* I thought to myself. I truly believed it then and it's still my motto even today.

When I said that the Academy would rent the space, it was pretty hard to ignore their positive reaction. RENT was the selling point! However, there was one other condition I needed to make clear to them. The church could not share ownership of the Academy. I wasn't about to have an entire congregation telling me what to do, not even my husband. With the pastor's and deacons' approval, it became official: the place was mine and I could now take the necessary steps to establish the CIBC Westend Academy.

My Proposition

I paid the rent, obtained our 501c3 not-for-profit status and went to work. I was a novice at most of what we needed to operate an educational program, so I sought advice from various folks who were in the business already. Then I made appointments with each of the churches in our surrounding area. The fact that we were of different denominations didn't matter to me. I just wanted to see if we could become an integrated resource for the community. One plus side to that was the churches were within walking distance of each other which eliminated the need for transportation. But, to my dismay, not one of the leaders from the other churches had any interest in working with us.

Undeterred and more determined than ever to do what I could, I reached out and requested a meeting with principals and administrators from three elementary schools and one high school. I wanted to look as professional as possible, so I dressed in my finest business attire. Experience had taught me that first impressions were lasting ones. After hearing my proposal, I received the same or similar pushback from all four schools which to me was quite shocking. Every school official reacted as though I was either accusing them of not doing their jobs, or of trying to usurp the entire school system by replacing them. Their attitudes made it clear that they were thinking *How dare you to come in here and tell us you can do more for these kids than we are.* Had I said something offensive? I took another look at my proposal when I got home, re-examining every word.

The CIBC Westend Academy will be opening soon. We propose a plan to assist children ages 6-16 with their homework to raise their academic scores ultimately preparing them for the next level. As you know many of our children are dropping out of school because of the challenges facing them. We want to help eliminate the dropout causes and support the children, their parents, and the school system wherever we are permitted. We understand we must obtain the parents' consent before you can release any information about the children. We are prepared to do so but want your agreement before we take the next step.

School officials were aware kids were dropping out before they reached eighth grade, others before turning sixteen, and too many already on the cusp of graduating high school. The numbers were staggering, and I knew that we, as a community, should want to do something about it. Whatever happened to the adage that **it takes a village to raise a child?** If one woman with a lawsuit could take prayer out of schools, surely I could keep a few kids in school. And so, in the face of disappointment and rejection but having faith the size of a mustard seed, my son and I opened with 10 children.

> *I say to you, if you have faith as a mustard seed, you will say to this mountain, 'Move from here to there,' and it will move; and nothing will be impossible for you. Matthew 17:20*

Following All the Rules

I had to adhere to all sorts of rules and regulations to get that side of our church building up and running. Aside from what was required to be licensed by the state, I had to also take care of any unfinished work throughout the entire building. The fire alarm system wasn't working properly, so I had to have that fixed. I installed a hood over the stove in the kitchen. The entrance had to be made accessible for everyone. The east outside wall that had deteriorated over the years needed to be secured. And, last but not least, some of the toilets with at least one sink for handwashing had to be lowered for use by the younger children. *(I also added a deep fryer in the kitchen because I wanted one. Heck, I figured if I had to go to all that trouble of giving the city, state, Melvin, and the church what they wanted, why not get something that I wanted — everybody knows food is never far from my mind, and I pictured myself frying fish, french-fries, and chicken wings. Plus, I paid for it.)* At times I could hardly contain my excitement watching it all come together. There were bumps along the way, however, because I trusted the wrong people and had to pay a big price for it.

Bumps In The Road – Peeden Construction

The east outside wall of the building was in bad shape due to neglect and little to no repairs over the years. Concrete particles and other debris frequently fell from the roof onto the sidewalk... a disaster waiting to happen. *(I always wondered why the city never cited us for the obvious deterioration after we bought the place.)* Our church sat on a triangular section of land between two streets. A resident, very influential in the community, became irate when he learned that we had purchased the building **as is**. He was waiting for the building to collapse so that he could get the property and turn it into some type of green space. Instead, he had to contend with black church folk who not only purchased the building but moved in determined to restore the structure he deemed as a ruin. The city started receiving a mountain of complaints shortly thereafter. It was obvious who was generating them.

One of the members of our church heard that I was looking for a contractor and recommended Peeden Construction Company. I had spoken with a few other contractors but, in the end, decided to go with Peeden because I trusted this person's judgment. I met with Mr. Peeden to discuss the work we needed. The crumbling wall was a priority because it had to be rebuilt as soon as possible for us to open the Academy. He examined the site and laid out a detailed plan of action. Peeden spoke with such authority that I have to admit I was impressed by what he said he could and would do.

According to the city ordinance, I had to get permits for everything and post them so that they were visible. Each time I mentioned that requirement, he'd interrupt by saying, "No worries, Mrs. Smotherson. I'll take care of everything and get back to you as soon as I write up the contract." I thought I had stumbled upon a real professional as I politely escorted him to the exit. The next time we met, he presented his written proposal to which I agreed as I paid the percentage upfront required for him and his team to get started. It felt good knowing the first of many tasks was complete.

Mr. Peeden was the only one who showed up on the day his crew was to begin work. At the time, I didn't think anything of it. I figured he was making a site visit to create trust between him and his new client. I expected that the rest of his crew would soon pull up outside in one of those heavy-duty work trucks. And then it all went downhill. He pulled me aside and said he had come to get the money so that he could buy the work permit.

"Work permit? Money? You don't have the work permit yet?"

"Mrs. Smotherson, the price I quoted you didn't include getting the permit to do the work."

The whole encounter had caught me completely off-guard. I knew we needed permits, so I didn't hesitate to give him the money, but I was not happy.

"You do realize Mr. Peeden, I am required by law to post the permit while the work is being done?"

"Yes ma'am, I know. I'm on my way now to take care of it."

My attention quickly reverted to my goal of marking off yet another task from my incredibly long to-do list. The much-needed and requested thing I sent him after had completely slipped my mind. When he got back from wherever he had gone, Peeden and his crew immediately started working. He never came back inside and was gone before I remembered I had forgotten to ask him for that darn permit.

Each day Peeden worked on our building I would remind him that I needed to get that permit posted. The city required it, but it wasn't as if he didn't already know that! Each time he'd have an excuse about why he didn't have it. He either left it in his other truck or it was on his desk at his office. And his all-time favorite... he would remember to bring it next time. Well, next time never came and I was getting more annoyed at Mr. Peeden. Instead of taking the bull by the horns and insisting he produce that permit, I stopped asking and moved on to other tasks that seemed more pressing. That's how badly I wanted the work to be completed.

(There was a television series that my children used to watch in the '60s called Lost in Space. The show featured a young boy named Will Robinson and his robot named Robot. One of its main functions was to warn the family of any imminent threat. It would flail its coil-like arms and flicker its flashing lights, all while bellowing, "Warning! Warning! Danger, Will Robinson! Only this time I was Will Robinson and, my inner robot had a different name... **Sinking Feeling.***)*

Peeden and his team continued the work without any further issues and that rebuilt outside wall certainly looked good when they got done. Then he suggested siding, explaining it would be the most economic and attractive exterior for the building. I agreed after viewing several pictures of other jobs he had done using the same material. The structures had such a clean look that I couldn't wait to see that same look on the outside of our building. Afterward, even the neighbors commented on how great the siding looked. Relieved that part of the building had been restored, I paid the contractor and was free to move on to tackle something else.

Several days later I met with the architect working on the plans for our accessible entrance. During our conversation, I mentioned that we had put siding on the east end of the building. "No, you did not! Not siding!" he exclaimed. His hair seemed to stand up on the back of his neck. I was caught completely off guard. The way I viewed it there was no need for alarm. I had done everything according to the book. I hired a professional contractor to do the work and obtained a permit approving the work. So what could be wrong?

Two days later I found out exactly what could be wrong. The city inspector who had either heard about or had seen the siding on the building broke the news. As he understood it and unbeknownst to me, our building was a certified historic site. That meant you could only use original materials for structural restoration. Nothing else. The inspector gave me some other facts. Mr. Peeden, as a professional contractor, should have been aware of the restrictions and various codes. And, if unfamiliar with the historic site requirements, Peeden would have learned when he applied for the permits before starting the work. "He did have the permits. I gave him the money and he told me he had gone down to your office and taken care of it." I told the inspector.

Not being sure of anything at that point prompted me to do a little investigating. The building division's permit section confirmed that they had no permit application as well as none pending. Nothing was found for Peeden Construction Company in connection with CIBC Westend Academy. Mr. Peeden had never obtained a permit despite him taking my money and claiming that he had. But what's even worse, I never suspected he was lying although I did call his office to confront him about the entire ordeal. He continued to deny my claims of his fraudulent misconduct. *I'm done with him* is what I was thinking. As I was writing this, I wished I had sued the man. Instead, I spent my time looking for another contractor because all that siding had to be torn down and I would need to get an actual permit to have the job redone.

Peeden was too much of a coward to come around anymore, not even to make things right for all the wrong he had done. And that was the last we saw of Peeden. He did send an employee who offered to remove the siding and haul it away, but I refused. The siding was mine; I had paid good money for it and wasn't about to let that swindler make more money by installing it on someone else's building. I called a young man that I knew who had started his own construction company. He was so happy when I told him he could have it. He didn't even mind that he would have to take it all down *(which only took him two days)*. I would have hired that young man from the start, but he was new in the business. Too bad he wasn't yet ready to take on a job of that size.

Luckily, I had another company ready to step in right away. They were also willing to accept time payments if I needed them, thank God. The new contractor went to City Hall to get the appropriate permit, then he went to the Historic District to get the second permit as well as the proper building material requirements. This professional was about his business. He brought me the permits and kept a copy of each one on file for himself. I posted them all in plain sight for everybody to see. It was a good thing my error in judgment only slowed down the progress and didn't sideline it completely.

It was an expensive lesson to learn. After that, I didn't leave one stone unturned... checking out everything and everybody.

CIBC Kids

Darren and I talked about our plans for the Academy with our good buddy Mrs. Mildred Boyd. She wanted to be a part of our planning and we were happy to allow her to do that. While Darren called her the **Warden** *(because she questioned everything)*, she was our biggest supporter. "What do we do first?" Mrs. Boyd asked. How to get started indeed. We knew we wanted to begin with a tutoring program for children in the neighborhood. We knew we needed tutors, and we certainly knew we needed children.

Mrs. Boyd's responsibilities as church clerk included reading the church announcements, so we agreed that she should add our solicitation for volunteers to her list of church news and happenings. It actually worked. We had four children from the church respond and later a few more signed up. That was so encouraging because we didn't have a single child in the beginning. Remaining optimistic, I printed up some really cool flyers. Darren rounded up some volunteers and off we went up two blocks in all directions placing advertisements under the wiper blades of every car parked on the street. We even rolled some up and, using rubber bands, attached them to people's doorknobs. We didn't dare place anything in the mailboxes because, as a retired Postal employee, I knew that was against the law. I also went door to door, introduced myself, and told neighbors about our plans for the Academy. I invited the adults along with any children in the household to visit us at our scheduled open house, making sure to mention we would be serving refreshments as an added incentive. Folks respond to FREE FOOD and the kids will come back again and again once they discover you have snacks.

For the refreshments, Mrs. Boyd made several batches of her homemade cookies. They were the best! Her lemon bars were so good folks would be ready to box one another for the last one. My husband and son, for instance, fought over those cookies every time she would bring some to church. Besides the delicious cookies, she also made these cute little bite-sized sandwiches. They looked every bit like those found in some quaint overpriced corner café. Those gems of hers were tasty, pleasing to the eye, and inexpensive to make. Mildred Boyd was a master at pinching pennies and cutting corners which made her a valuable asset to our organization. I admit the snacks were a bribe, but I was not ashamed. If it was going to get live bodies through that door then by-golly bribery it was going to be... and it worked!

CIBC Westend Academy Board of Directors

Setting up a program for children required the establishment of an oversight committee. We were fortunate to have several qualified individuals: a professor from the University of Missouri, Saint Louis; an engineer from the Missouri Department of Transportation (MODOT); a retired postmaster; a licensed family counselor; a member of the clergy in Pastor Smotherson; the secretary of our block unit; Darren, the board president; and me as the administrator. We became the CIBC Westend Academy Board of Directors. Such impressive credentials improved our chances of receiving grants, addressed neighborhood concerns about our professionalism and allowed us to broaden our reach to help families with domestic and family issues. Each member took a hands-on approach in their involvement with the Academy. This left an indelible mark on many of our children.

A good example of this deep involvement was the professor and the engineer: one oversaw our tutoring program, the other headed the math curriculum. Two successful black women... African-American females each possessing and sharing their wealth of knowledge and experience. They were tangible proof of the infinite possibilities that could await these young black people. Ten of them were selected to attend a six-week engineering workshop at the Missouri University of Science & Technology in Rolla, Missouri, which is known for its engineering program. Traveling outside the city limits of Saint Louis was new and exciting for many of the children, some of whom had never ventured further than a five-mile radius from their homes. One of the participants returned home after the first week not wanting to continue the program. The remaining nine completed the program with very high scores. That experience resulted in one of the Academy kids following that path to Rolla to become an engineer. Other Academy kids got a chance to take part in another higher-learning initiative that took place at the University of Missouri, St. Louis. We wanted all our kids to get a sense of college life and campus living.

As our numbers grew, it became clear that we had to get our hands on some real money and a lot more than the dollars I alone could provide. We knew we had to go hard or go home, and the latter was not an option. Everyone believed in our possibilities and, no matter what it took, they were willing to help move the

Academy forward. We were going to do whatever was necessary to make it work, so the entire board agreed on an assessment of $500 per member. That gave us a little operating money which included paying our rent. My job was to start looking for grant money, a few board members sought donations from individuals and companies they patronized, and others spearheaded fund-raising events.

My son, the President, has always had the gift of gab. He never hesitated to seek funds from wherever and whomever he could. At one social event, he harvested a $15,000 check for the Academy with only a handshake. Me, I enjoyed every one of my 12.5 hour days in the summer and 8 hour days during the school year. I spent my time overseeing the entire program, writing grants, attending required meetings, and soliciting volunteers. We were looking to address three needs... funding, staffing, and much-needed tutors.

Help Is On the Way – TUTORS

When we first opened the Academy, my help consisted of a few staff and a couple of parents. The most difficult subject for the older adults serving as tutors was mathematics. It took them a while to catch on to the *new math concepts* that had burst on the scene. These were church members and some parents who were used to earlier approaches of one plus one equals two. At that point, I knew we needed some younger tutors, ones who could connect with the kids and who understood how they needed to learn. Until I could locate these potential rescuers, I had to recruit some of the kids who were starting to show signs of real progress. I figured they could help the other kids who were still having some challenges. It yielded amazing results. Then I had these same kids teach us old heads their new math. They got immense pleasure from that. The climate in the Academy was starting to change right in front of our eyes. The trust levels were where they needed to be... us trusting them and them trusting us. And we were all benefiting from the experience.

I knew many of the children were still struggling in reading and mathematics. Truth be told, some were failing in every subject. In my mind that only meant one thing: it was likely that they would face a lifetime of struggle. These kids deserved a better outcome, so I made it my mission and went on a hunt for tutors.

I started by contacting the Community Outreach directors from local universities. I wanted to post the Academy's information on their student bulletin boards, and that meant I had to contact and get permission from each one to do so. Washington University was best known for academics and having great professors. The students also had an awesome campus life, so they were my first contact. The out-reach coordinator was more than gracious in posting our information and the students wasted no time in responding.

We were so pleased that the volunteers were both young men and women. After attending our orientation they were as eager to get to work as we were happy to have them. The tutors were always at the Academy before the children arrived... and always well prepared. On the days when we were short-staffed, they would even pitch in and help us set up the rooms if needed. I had heard rumors that the people at Washington University were pretty friendly, and I would have to agree. Pretty friendly, indeed.

We had the kids bring their homework every time they came to the after-school program. They knew help was always available, no matter the subject, so they were more than happy to do so. The kids loved having college students as tutors. Those well-rounded high-achievers weren't that much older than the kids themselves so that might've had something to do with it. Having these Black, White, and Asian successful college students also showed the kids that they, too, might follow their path.

A certain segment of our adolescent population loved having those young men as instructors. It tickled me so... but worried me even more. Not because of our tutors but because I was worried the girls were becoming too distracted and less interested in their work. The presence of the young men was also the reason our enrollment was on the rise. (*It didn't take a rocket scientist to figure that one out.)* For a while, the only students showing up were girls with schoolbooks in hand, all giggly, and googly-eyed.

I thought, *"Oh Lord!"*

These male tutors, however, weren't distracted by their adoring fans *(it seems they got that kind of attention all the time)* because they were there to broaden those underdeveloped minds and change the trajectory of those kids' future. I marveled at how they were able to bring about intrigue and inquiry, clearly shown on the faces of their unsuspecting little scholars. That's what those young adults did for our children. Not a day went by that at least two or three kids did not stop by after school wanting to brag about an improved test score or to tell us they'd read aloud in class that day... some for the first time. Many of them were thrilled because they had given the right answer when the teacher called on them. The kids continued to make progress in their personal and academic growth. It was exciting to see them floating along on newfound self-confidence. Every milestone for every kid was cause for celebration.

As our student numbers grew, our amazing volunteers recruited other university students. They, too, were as excited about the opportunity to help as were their colleagues. We were very fortunate to have had the chance to connect with some of the most amazing servants of the community. Everything that happened was simply confirming that we were on the right path doing what the Master had ordained.

MODOT

My sister, Wanda Diane, the engineer on our board, has been a great asset to me and the Academy. Her interest from the very beginning was in finding ways to improve the math skills of our young black boys and girls. We already knew how early some of the kids were dropping out of school and that made us both more determined to do what we could about it. She worked for the Missouri Department of Transportation (MODOT) where they had a community outreach program that she thought would be perfect for the kids at the Academy. TRAC™ was a hands-on learning tool that required students to use math and science to solve real-world problems. Wanda knew that engaging the kids in that process would improve their math skills. We also hoped it would spark their interests in science and inspire some to work toward a career in transportation and civil engineering.

I loved the idea of having actual engineers working with the kids because we needed as many visible role models as possible, especially ones who looked like the kids at the Academy. I had gotten a dozen used computers from a company that had upgraded their systems and had them installed in one of our classrooms. Wanda and her TRAC™ team did a quick inspection of the *used* machinery, then made the modifications needed for their program, which included designing bridges and traffic technology.

That next week we introduced the program to ten young people ages 11 to 14. They were so excited to find out that they were the first in the Academy chosen. Exactly why or what it was for was not a concern for them. They just knew that they were finally going to get on the computers and away from all the little kids. Using one of the *new* computers, a female TRAC™ team member gave a presentation on how to design a bridge. Then she printed it out from a drafting printer that they borrowed from work to use. The sheet measured 3 by 5 feet, large enough for everyone to see after she hung it on a nearby wall. By then the kids' interest had peaked. She went on to explain that their finished work would hang on a wall for their parents and visitors to see as well. That way they could explain their work to on-lookers. The project was also a way for the kids to develop their public speaking and presentation skills. Unbeknownst to them, of course. Kudos to Wanda J. and MODOT.

Grants

It became more and more important that I learned to apply for grants because the funds that I had set aside for the Academy were running low. I had never written a grant proposal before, so I took a class at the University of Missouri, St. Louis. Still, I felt that wasn't enough so, to serve as reinforcement, I had an instructor come in and teach grant writing to the Academy staff and to anyone else who wanted to learn. *(That gave me more practice before submitting an actual grant application.)*

The first grant I received was from the Boeing Aircraft Company to support the math program which was both instructor and computer-based learning. The funding took care of the children in the program and gave me the confidence to seek funding in other areas. Next, I received a large grant from the Department of Economic Development. Their contribution helped to pay for the remaining repairs and ultimate completion of the building. Once that happened, I thanked both organizations time and time again. Gussie Williams, one of our board members, was also successful in acquiring a grant, and she used that money to buy encyclopedias for the kids.

Then I began to wonder, *What should I go after next?* I loved the arts and, since art is a way to express oneself and comes in all forms, I thought it might be another way to reach the children. They were already dealing with so many issues they couldn't control. The Missouri Arts Council, (MAC) came to mind. I called them and got some information which convinced me even more that MAC was going to be my very best friend. I had always wanted a children's theater and, from what I read, that possibility was soon going to be my reality. I started working on a MAC application immediately.

Thankfully MAC offered what I called **pre-grant writing sessions** for all of us newbies, and this newbie was trying to absorb every piece of knowledge they were willing to share. One piece of advice I received was to state what I wanted, why I wanted it, and how I would use it. They also told me to stop begging, trying to sound so needy by claiming our kids were the poorest of the poor. I immediately tore up my original *(needy)* application and started again from the beginning. The result was that the Missouri Arts Council (MAC) funded our arts program for several years with the kids participating in activities from painting to theater performance and everything in between.

The MAC support, allowed us to hire professional artists to work with the children and Solomon Thurman, a visual artist, was one of them. Over time he proved to be a real friend and mentor to the Academy. He supervised the six-year-olds as they painted pictures that he hung on a wall specially chosen for them. The little kids loved seeing their artwork on display and every day the first thing they did was check to see if their paintings were still hanging on the wall. Solomon assured them that no piece of art was coming down until each child created a new masterpiece to replace the old one. That was all the kids needed to hear to get them started on their next piece of art.

Solomon's best-known work, Black Americans in Flight, a 51-foot mural hangs in the lower level at St. Louis Lambert International Airport. We took some of the older kids on a tour because we wanted to show them that talent comes in all colors. They, too, like Solomon, could achieve greatness.

Solomon has a special gift – creativity – and he knew how to engage each age group of children to bring out their creativity. Some of them became amateur sketch artists, some sculpted figurines, and some others painted large murals on huge canvases. I got so caught up by it all that I painted a picture myself, and I'm proud that it is framed and hanging in my son Bwayne's house. He was so surprised that his mother could produce such a marvelous piece of artwork. Actually, it was just an okay piece of artwork, but I was glad someone thought it was great. Each time I go to his house, just like the six-year-old kids at the Academy, I check to see if it is still hanging in its designated place.

Solomon, the Kids, and the Sculptures

In those early days many drivers sped through the neighborhood, running stop signs and generally creating a major safety concern for the Academy. In response I had the city mount large round concrete planters in the street near the corner to deter traffic in front of the church. Then people started driving their vehicles onto the sidewalk to avoid the planters and having to drive around the block. No one had any shame or conscience whatsoever and it had started to frustrate me beyond words. I was also terrified that one of our children could run out the exit door on the north side of the building and get hit by a speeding driver unwilling to take a slight detour.

The time had come for drastic measures. I had the planters placed on the sidewalk to block automobile traffic completely. I thought, *Finally... a dead-end corner that we could use for outdoor activities.* And we used it often. We put up basketball hoops which excited the kids and some of the older folks. The kids loved to engage in competitions of *b-ball* between different age groups or the boys against the counselors, or sometimes the girls against the boys. Other times we set up chairs for neighbors who loved to be entertained by the children's fantastic talent and step shows. The children's artwork was also on display for all to see. The corner of Washington Avenue and Walton *(renamed Rev. Melvin Smotherson Street)* was now safe. What a relief.

One day I overheard one of the group leaders say, "We should make this the children's corner." – what a great idea! My first thought was to design a large planter to replace the individual ones. We were tired of the streetscape arrangement anyway and this was another opportunity to involve the children. And I knew just who to ask — Solomon *(the professional)* — to see if he thought it was a worthwhile venture. He did!

Solomon and the kids began drawing figures of children in different positions and said they would form wire hangers into the shapes of the figures they had drawn. Neither the kids nor I were able to visualize what he was describing until he bent a clothes hanger to look exactly like the figure he had drawn. It was remarkable. After that demonstration and without questions or hesitation, everyone got busy. Clothes hangers turned into miniature shapes of children at play and became scaled-down models of the proposed sculptures. Solomon eventually formed the statues out of iron pipes which were then bent and welded into the shapes to replicate the wire hanger prototypes.

While Solomon worked on the prototypes I contacted the city officials. We needed permission to install a permanent decorative planter, one wide enough to block traffic with concrete

benches surrounding it for people to sit. There was some oppo-
sition from a man buying up property in the neighborhood who
thought a tall gate would be more appropriate so that it could
open to traffic when necessary. That was what we were fighting
against, the fast traffic right in front of our doors. And, with the
help of our alderman, the city approved the project. Now all we
only needed was a way to pay for it. The board members' assessment fees helped to pay for the planter and a grant covered the
rest. The iron pipe statues that we selected were of two kids
jumping rope and another of a kid tying his shoe. They would go
into the new street planter right outside of the Academy. The finished product looked amazing standing tall in that large planter.
Our alderman was proud to stand at our dedication ceremony
and declare it THE CHILDREN'S CORNER. That planter with
sculptures of children at play still stands today.

By the year 2000 the Academy was flourishing. After the dedication of the planter, we decided to continue the theme with
wooden sculptures adorning the outside walls on both sides of
the Academy's entrance. As you approached our building you
would see children studying, children working on the computer, a kid listening to the teacher, and another working on
a math problem. Solomon Thurman, with a few of the older
team leaders, made the sculptures for us and mounted them.
He was so strategic about the whole thing because he wanted to
create the perfect visual. The display piqued the interest of so
many that people were curious about what was happening on
the inside. The answer from one parent to an inquiring visitor
was that children were learning and growing into human beings
who would be sources of pride for their families and community.

Food Program

The City of St. Louis supported the After School and Summer
Food Programs. Children in the free lunch program during the
school year were eligible for this program as well. Ninety percent of the children attending the Academy met that criteria.
For me, knowing there was that kind of support available, was

crucial. The Health Department's guidelines for those programs stipulated that at least two staff members had to have or get the hepatitis A vaccine before taking part in the program. I felt it was my duty to be one of the two, but I had my concerns about who the other person would be.

Mrs. Boyd felt she was too old, and my son said he would be too busy working and couldn't guarantee he'd even be at the Academy during feeding times. That meant the two of them were out. We got lucky when one of our volunteers said she worked at a restaurant and had received both of her shots. She was also available to help during the scheduled meal breaks. I couldn't have been more pleased because I knew she would be a perfect fit for the kids.

Besides getting the shots we had to attend several classes on Food Prep & Safety. That was an enlightening experience as I gained a greater respect for food service workers and childcare providers. The most valuable piece of advice one of the instructors gave us was to make sure we kept a supply of food on hand, enough for two days, in case the food trucks got delayed.

The kids were never disappointed whenever the food trucks were late. When we did have to replace the meals, they got to enjoy their favorite indulgence: hot biscuits, large round sausage patties, jelly or syrup, and some milk. The kids would get home and go on and on about how good those biscuits were, thinking I made them myself just for them. A lot of parents asked me how I was able to make the biscuits so fluffy, and this is what I told them.

"First you go to the freezer, open the freezer, take out the box that says frozen biscuits, open it...."

I never could finish what I was saying because the parents would be laughing so hard that I would get tickled myself. One parent wanted to know how I managed to get all the sausage patties the same size every time. That was even funnier. The sausage I bought came in a large, long tube. Like the marks on a ruler or measuring tape, I would measure then mark the spots where I wanted to cut the tube. That's why they were always the same size. Baking them in the oven caused less shrinkage, too.

Whether on late truck days or normal days, the favorite midday snack was the banana pudding. Linda Tatum, one of our volunteers would make it special for them. Kids are appreciative of and fascinated by the simplest gestures, especially when they're served with love.

When to Make the Call

Opening the academy would present its own set of concerns. One of the most serious issues we had to confront was when/whether to call Child Protective Services, CPS. If we believed a child was living in an unsafe, unclean, or dangerous environment we had to act and I knew that reporting a case of possible neglect or abuse would be one of the hardest decisions I would ever have to make. I knew from personal experience that removing a child from one home was no guarantee that another would be better. While some foster parents are wonderful, I had been in some foster homes that caused me to wonder how the parents were ever approved for the program.

Some children who came through the academy showed signs of great need. Some of them lived in homes without running water. They were often smelly from not bathing or wearing unwashed clothes. My team started stocking up on essential supplies: underwear, t-shirts, socks, soap, deodorant, washcloths, toothbrushes and toothpaste. There were days when some kids would show up looking a mess and not smelling great, and we knew they were embarrassed by it all. We'd take the younger children into the restrooms, get them clean, and into clean clothes. The older ones got a toiletry kit so they could take care of themselves as well as clean clothes if needed. The kids may have arrived in rough shape, but we made sure they left looking and feeling so much better. I suspected our efforts sometimes caused a change at home as well because some of the children looked better the next time I saw them. It was the most rewarding feeling ever to have gained their trust. They'd see me and ask, "Mrs. Smotherson, how do I look?"

"Like an angel." I'd reply.

Challenging Behavior

I may have choked on that description of ANGEL if one child, in particular, had asked that question. Crystal was the youngest of three. Her mother had raised the older two differently from the youngest. That according to her older siblings. Crystal got away with everything. They did not. The two were quite embarrassed by their sister's continual misconduct. They didn't want anyone to know the three of them were even related. Crystal rarely faced disciplinary action. Nor had she ever received the directive... NO! She would hit and kick her brother and sister whenever she felt the urge. Which for them felt like every two seconds. They were to never, ever strike their little sister because they were bigger. The mother shared that tidbit with the Academy staff.

"I'm going to tell mommy if you touch me." Crystal would shout. But only after an ambush or massive assault against her brother or sister most days they were there.

All the kids had reached the end of their rope one day after dealing with Crystal's barrage of attacks. So I had to keep her in the office with me all day. That meant little to no interaction with the staff or other children. And forget about conducting any outside business. I was not a happy camper nor was I about to put up with any more of her behavior. And from the look on my face, Crystal knew it. When her mother came to pick her and her siblings up the staff directed the woman to my office. But not before informing Crystal's mom that her child had been in there with me all day.

As soon as Crystal saw her mother, she made a b-line towards her, eager to tell on me. This kid was a master at manipulating her mother. I watched in amazement the interaction between the two. For a few seconds, I couldn't tell who was the mamma and who was the child. Neither one had a clue of how tired of the both of them I had become. After listening to her daughter's complaint, Crystal's mom then turned and looked at me. I could tell she expected me to start talking. I didn't say a word, but I was praying she would say something so that I could let her have it.

Oh, oh! I can tell from the way her lips are all tooted up, she's about to say something. Come on say it! Ask me why I had your daughter in my office all day away from her siblings and the other kids. I said ask me! Then she did.

"Why are you treating my daughter **differently** from the other children?"

Thank you, God, for that question! "Because your little darling is **different**. You have made her **different**. So different in fact, she needs to be in a **different** program. Do you need me to help you find a **different** place for her?"

"What about my other children?"

"Your son and other daughter aren't different. They act like the other children... obeying the rules, enjoying themselves and avoiding this different child." Turning my head in the direction of her youngest.

The woman was furious with me but it didn't take her long to calm down after realizing she had to work every day and needed a place for her child to go. I made it CRYSTAL clear to both of them we did not have to put up with that type of delinquency. Crystal's mom had no choice but to make sure in the future her child was going to be **different**. Especially if her baby girl were to remain under the Academy's roof. Her sister and brother were hoping their younger sibling would completely disappear.

One Sunday several years later, a young adult choir had come to sing at our church. We were having an afternoon program of some sort. Standing in the front row of the choir was Crystal all grown up singing praises to the Lord. To God be the... Glory? As much as I tried to stay engaged in the singing my thoughts wouldn't allow me to do so. I thought about Satan. How it was said he was once in charge of the heavenly choir. And that he had a great singing voice. I wanted to believe Crystal had changed. It was hard to do given all the torment that child had put everyone through. Then I told myself what I know to be true. God can fix anything and anybody. After all, He was still working on me as well.

A Little Discipline Goes a Long Way!

I happen to believe that children want and need discipline. It's crucial in learning to function in the real world, learning to be respectful of others and complying with designated play/work/quiet times. Those were my expectations at the Academy and the children accepted those rules. There was always some activity in the building and, to avoid conflicts, we kept a tight schedule. Shuffling those little kids around reminded me of when I was in high school changing classes, only this time some of the moving parts were as young as six.

The main auditorium was where all the kids played tabletop games or sat and talked. It would get noisy, but I had grown accustomed to the sound. It filled the place with life, and I loved it. Sometimes I would stand inside a room's entrance and raise my right hand high enough for everyone to see. Not saying a word, I would just wait. Most of the time, it only took a few seconds for the room to get completely silent. Other times it took a bit longer but that wasn't happening as often as when we first started this exercise. That was the deal I made with the children and the staff: once I entered the room and raised my hand, activity should cease and the room quiet. This was so the kids could receive a word from *Mrs. Smotherson* or give their attention to anyone else who had the floor. I would show this skill off in front of parents and guests whenever they would stop by. I was just so proud of our children because they exhibited the life lessons we were trying so hard to instill in them, the value of good behavior and respect for those in charge.

CIBC's Production of The Wiz

I had always wanted a children's theater. I believed it would give children an escape from whatever might be haunting them. Many of the children in our community were suffering from so much: lack of self-esteem, inferiority complexes, all sorts of unhealthy environments, even a sense of not belonging. I thought that a chance to be somebody else or live in a fantasy world for a while might enrich and make their lives more bearable, at least for a while. It would also allow talents to surface that they never dreamed they possessed. All in all, I believed the theatre would be another outlet for positive expression, a likeness through which they could see themselves.

I had seen the stage production of The Wiz twice and thought it would be the perfect play for the kids. There were parts for all ages, even some of the adults who dared to try.

Since this was so important to me I called again on professionals to walk me through the process. I had gotten another grant from MAC which meant that we could hire two gentlemen from the Black Repertory Theater of St. Louis, both named Eric. Eric #1 took on the role of the director and Eric #2 was more of an acting coach who performed as the Wizard in our first presentation of The Wiz. Both Erics worked so hard with the children. They even crawled and hopped around on stage to show them how the monkeys and scarecrows in the play might act which never failed to make the little kids fall out laughing as they waited their turn to try it. The kids felt less apprehensive about performing after watching those big guys make fools of themselves. Many of them hid behind the walls they'd built up due to the harsh realities throughout their young lives. I was happy to see those walls start to crumble.

While rehearsals were going underway, two of the older kids joined me in making the costumes. Solomon and three older team leaders created the most realistic sets imaginable and seemed to have as much fun as those rehearsing on stage. I know they felt as much ownership in the process as anyone else. They were serious about the job. Those sets looked as real as possible. They also took care of the props, making sure everyone was in the right place at the right time, not an easy task. But they too handled that with great precision. It was all so captivating. The different activities going on at the same time and everyone with the same goal in mind gave me goosebumps. There was so much exuberance flowing throughout the Academy. I'd hoped the kids would remember it for a lifetime. In celebration of making it to the final rehearsal, the kids got to enjoy cake and ice cream. One of their many favorite snacks.

The moment had arrived. We were ready to present our version of the play. Solomon and the guys had the scenery all in place. The costumes hung in different rooms for easy access. Our makeup artists had everything they needed to do their job. They had practiced on each other for days. The sound system worked perfectly during rehearsal, but we wanted to check it again as a precaution. We even hired a local band to provide the music for the entire production. All we needed now was an audience to fill the seats in the auditorium ... for all three scheduled performances.

On the first evening when it was time to open the doors to the auditorium, we prayed that people would walk through them. It was a madhouse all over the rest of the building. That's where we were trying to contain all those noisy and anxious munchkins, and monkeys, and crows ... *"oh my!"* We understood their excitement and eagerness to get into their first costumes. The staff was just as excited but, of course, we couldn't let the kids know that. If we'd behaved in the same manner as the kids, there would have been no one in charge of keeping order. At least that's how we felt.

Much to our delight parents, neighbors, and friends were all waiting to enter. Even representatives from the Missouri Arts Council were in attendance. As I'm sitting here typing this on my computer, reliving what I felt at that time, my eyes are full of tears and it's hard to see through them. I thanked God for the marvelous gift of the evening. An outstanding production. Support from parents and the community. Positive feedback from a representative of the Missouri Arts Council. It was my dream come true. My friend and chef, JoAnn Williams, left work early to make sure she was at the first performance. After all these years she still reminds me about her reaction to the play. So I thought I'd call and ask if she wanted her comments to go in my book. Did she ever!

"The play was as awesome as the sun rising in the east. Seeing the neighborhood kids performing as if it was just second nature, speaking with clarity, and singing like angels is something I will never forget. I talk about it so much. It lingers in my mind how so much was done in such a small space with never a dull moment. Those kids kept it moving. They should have been performing on the Fox Theater stage here in St. Louis. They were as good as any performance I've seen there. The music was exceptional, and the costumes were just perfect. The entire show had to have been touched by God. That's it. It was touched by God."

The three nights of performance ended on a high note. Eric #1 thought the costumes were more realistic than he ever expected. He also thought that we had some real talent on that stage. Both Erics expressed pride in the project and both told me that I could call for them anytime. I appreciated their offer but, because we had limited funds I wouldn't have felt right doing so. Anyway, as we had talent on that stage, we also had talent all around the Academy. I'm blessed to have children and grandchildren who are multi-talented. They should be on stage. Fact is, most of them were in the play.

My daughter was then working at the Academy which to my mind was her being in the right place at the right time. I needed someone to direct the Wiz performances and, because she was up for the challenge, we were back in business. The show had to go on and it did with Pam directing and playing Glenda the good witch. People asked if she was a professional singer after hearing her sing **Believe In Yourself** and curious to know how I was able to get her for the part. They had no clue she was my daughter. I was itching to tell them, "It wasn't by artificial insemination." She did need to be on somebody's stage doing what she loved most, singing.

The kids performed the show for several years and were even featured in a local newspaper. I'm convinced that The Academy's performances were better than the last group of professionals performing The Wiz on national TV. I wish their sponsors had seen our children act. I also wish I could get the Academy kids to do it one more time before I leave this earth. They are much older now, some with children of their own who I'm sure would like to join them on stage. Wonder if I should use that logic to get them to perform again?

The Academy was open from 1997 to 2008. Every time I see one of the parents he talks about the marvelous change he saw in his son back then and all because of his time at the Academy. One young lady recently moved back to St. Louis, trusting that the Academy was still open. She was eager for her children to have the same rewarding experience she had had as a child. When her grandmother told her the Academy had closed, she threw up her hands and said, "That can't be, now what am I going to do?"

I still receive inquiries about the Academy and one of the reviews in this book is from a young man expressing what the Academy meant to him. His comments and feelings were quite meaningful and brought back so many memories. I miss the children and the challenges and wish I could have continued the programs.

Unfortunately, my husband became ill in the tenth year of the Academy's operation, and I chose to be home to care for him. Replacing myself as administrator was next to impossible because a salary was not guaranteed. Money was only available when we received grants, and I was also the grant writer. Further, having a regular retirement check from the USPS made it possible to endure the financial downtimes and there weren't many people around with that advantage. Since there was no one willing or in a position to take over, we limited our activities to assisting with homework on a call-in basis. Sadly, our temporary closure became permanent.

It's been six years now since his death, and I still haven't been able to muster enough of what it takes to get the Academy going again. I was 58 years old when I opened the Academy. At 81, I needed a different kind of challenge. So, I wrote this book.

Chapter Eleven
Sins of a Father and a Mother – God Wasn't Through With Us Yet

*M*y husband didn't do a particularly good job of hiding his indiscretions. In his arrogance and self-ishness, Melvin wasn't paying attention to the fact that his sons were growing into their manhood, often attracting the same women that he was pursuing. On occasion, Melvin and either one of his adult *single* sons would show up at the same woman's house. He was also oblivious to the woman his daughter was becoming. During one of our in-depth mother and daughter conversations, my adult daughter asked me if her father ever really loved me. That question shook me to the core and made me ask myself, *What example had Melvin and I set before our girl child?* The thought of being **a poor example** was so disturbing I don't even remember if I answered her question.

Whether Melvin was ever remorseful or not about his wrong-doing, the guilt of my indiscretion was, at times, too painful for me to bear. I should have gotten out of my marriage once I realized I had fallen in love with someone else, instead of continuing to betray my marriage vows. Melvin had given me plenty of reasons and justifications for leaving him, yet I couldn't find the courage to do it. To me, getting a divorce would have felt the same as getting a failing grade and I hated to fail. I let my fear cripple me because I couldn't fathom watching my children grow up without a father, or me struggling to work and take care of them at the same time. I was haunted by the thought of experiencing the same type of ridicule and hardship that my mother had faced. It was easier for me to turn a blind eye to Melvin's infidelity *(always blaming myself for my marriage being an unhappy one)* than to be honest with myself and stop pretending to be okay when, in fact, I had grown to resent him for the hurt he was causing me.

Because I allowed my fears to keep me prisoner and accept being blatantly mistreated, I compromised my integrity by succumbing to that immense need to fill the void in my life. I never imagined that outside of my ex-boyfriend, Burgess, there would be another man who would want to love me, take care of me and protect me until I met Logan. Much to my regret, however, I became what I loathed and knew it was time for me to turn matters over to the Lord and expect something good to happen. I had to do some serious soul-searching and praying because I, too, was broken and in need of repair. My way and Melvin's way weren't **the right ways** to solve our problems. For me to stay in my marriage, I had to start loving myself and surrender my desire to fix my husband, accepting that no matter how hard I tried, the dilemma was not mine to remedy... it was God's.

1 John 1:9 states, *If we confess our sins, he is faithful and just and will forgive us our sins and purify us from all unrighteousness.*

Over the next thirty-plus years, the Lord replaced my pain with a purpose, my failures with focus, my despair with a renewed determination, and my void with a vision. I still faced challenges and still made mistakes, still even needed forgiveness, yet God continued to bless our union.

That statement, **what God has for me, is for me,** manifested itself in ways I never imagined. Doors continued to be opened or lifted off their hinges as opportunity upon opportunity allowed me to stay engaged and productive. My husband and I also got involved in activities that we both enjoyed, including our love and responsibility to minister to people. We felt we needed to be more transparent because folks needed to understand that we were just as human, as vulnerable, and as flawed as they were, but that we all were still worthy of God's love. The Lord continued to reveal Himself to me and I was realizing daily my true calling… helping people.

It was all starting to make sense. My focus should have never been on what I didn't have, how insecure I was, or who my husband was not in our not-so-perfect marriage. God was showing me all along the abundance of blessings and favor I did have if only I had opened my heart to Him completely. Truth is, I stayed with Melvin because I did love him and I never stopped hoping things would get better between us. Over time, they did. And for that, I thank my Heavenly Father.

In 1982, I became a grandmother for the very first time and, when I got the chance to hold my granddaughter, a feeling of jubilation had consumed my entire being. There wasn't a problem big enough to overshadow my joy that day. I felt whole again. *Work, Lord Jesus!* Until you're a grandparent you can't imagine the depth of that kind of love and I was fortunate to be able to experience that feeling eight more times. My grandchildren were a welcomed and exhausting distraction that I wouldn't trade for anything in this world. I gained a total of thirteen grandbabies in all and a slew of great-grandbabies. But the Lord wasn't through with me yet.

We were together for 48 years by the time Melvin's physical health had begun to deteriorate. Over the next nine years, as he continued to try to keep our church going, he went from a cane to a walker to a wheelchair. It was challenging for both of us. Kidney failure was only one of his many illnesses which required him to go to dialysis three days a week. I used to transport my husband until it became too difficult for me to handle him by myself. The last time I tried to help him into the car, he slipped and fell underneath it. Luckily, one of my grandchildren drove up, and together we managed to pick him up and get him into the car. Melvin was always so stubborn about me getting more help, and whenever I did, he would constantly tell the caregivers, "My wife can do it." He either didn't realize it or he didn't want to accept the fact that not having the help was starting to break me down. Even when he was in the hospital he would tell the nurses not to give him a bath because his wife would be there soon to bathe him.

Melvin had three back surgeries, stents for his heart, and arthritis, along with kidney failure. Because the medications he was taking were causing hallucinations, memory loss, and paranoia, my husband felt he needed to keep a gun right next to his bed. At 3:00 AM one morning, I was awakened by the sound of gunshots because Melvin thought two men were in his room, one tall and one short, about to attack him, so he shot them. Thank God the bullets went into the wall in his room and not out his door into the hallway where I often was either headed to his room or going into the bathroom. I immediately collected all his firearms and called the police the next day to have them picked up. Melvin felt I had no right to get rid of them because he was only trying to protect his family. He stayed angry with me until the next crisis occurred. His lengthy illness took its toll on both of us.

No Heir to the Throne

Melvin still wanted to remain the pastor of Cornerstone despite his pain or the **PAIN** he was being to everyone else. Now wheelchair-bound, I wanted him to turn the church over to our son (who had been ordained by his father) but he thought he should stay to try and rebuild a congregation that was getting smaller. My husband feared he was no longer able to keep the members' interest yet at the same time he couldn't see that his anger and frustration were part of the reasons why he could not. He simply refused to let the pulpit go – he would not, even for his own son.

Another church was considering appointing Darren as their pastor, but Cornerstone was where he wanted to be. He even asked his father's help and guidance, hoping his father would say, "Don't leave, I need you here to take over." Instead, my husband told his youngest son to go and that he would be going with his blessing. After years of working long and hard in support of his father, our son was heartbroken by his dad's reaction and viewed his response as a rejection, not a blessing. Darren felt he had no other choice but to accept the appointment at the other church. It was extremely painful for me to see the sorrow in my son's face and the tears that he shed the last Sunday he attended his home church. My baby boy was leaving and any hope of Melvin reversing his decision to turn the church over to his son faded the moment Darren left the building. My husband reck-lessly discarded a rare gem that awful day.

Me, I prayed, "Lord, please take care of my child." And He has.

Cornerstone Institutional Baptist Church is now in its for-ty-first year. We came out of darkness to become one of the most popular churches in the surrounding area and now one that is on the upward climb again. It's not our memories that keep us going, it's the grace of God. It is HE that continues to bestow favor upon us. So many, like my husband, have gone on to a better place leaving behind the proof of their labors. Now it's time for me to look inward and ask myself, *What will I leave? What proof is there that I, too, was on the Lord's side and know exactly where I stand with the One above? Have I been a good steward over what I've been given, or do I truly love everyone? And... have I forgiven those who have trespassed against me?* That's a hard one. After careful review, I may be able to one day answer those questions.

Our Last Time Together

I know that I took good care of my husband when he was ill but I do regret having to put him in a nursing home near the end of his life. He didn't get the same kind of care I had been providing and he suffered because of it. Melvin had developed one large bedsore that covered his entire backside that I didn't know about and, once I discovered it, I felt awful. I knew I should have been inspecting his body myself instead of trusting the staff to care for him properly, especially when he kept complaining about the pain. From that point on, however, I visited longer and insisted that the staff turn him more often.

One day he said, "You don't have to stay here so long."

To which I replied, "I would rather be here with you than anyplace else."

In a very weak voice, he said, "Me, too."

Those two words meant more to me than anything he had said in years.

Melvin had grown tired of suffering and knowing that he would die, he decided to stop his dialysis treatments. It was too painful whenever they transported him from one bed to another. **He had had enough.** On our last day together, I was going on about much of nothing to keep us both engaged.

Because he was hurting so much he looked at me and said, "I know you want to talk but I just don't feel like it."

I understood, kissed him on the forehead, and promised him that I would be back. About four hours later my home phone rang. When I looked at my caller ID, I immediately regretted leaving my husband in that nursing home alone. I had no idea what the voice on the other end would say to me but knew they were calling to either urge me to get there right away because his health was declining faster than expected, or that he had actually died. My worst fears were confirmed the second I answered my phone. The caller let me know that my husband had made his transition. I did go back as promised. He was there lying in the same position that I'd left him in, but he was not there. He had gone where we all must go.

I kept my word that Melvin would have a full Masonic funeral which was held on Saturday, January 24, 2015, at Austin Layne Mortuary. The Grand Master spoke, the burial team was perfect with their presentation, and all the brothers were present. Melvin had on his black tuxedo decked out with his Masonic regalia. He would have been proud. The Homegoing Celebration was held at Cornerstone on Sunday, January 25, 2015. This time Pastor Smotherson was clad in his pastoral robe. His wardrobe change was a pleasant surprise to those who had seen him the day before. Our friend and Funeral Director, Austin Layne, was gracious in honoring our wishes and was more than willing to dress his friend in the attire suitable for each service.

My husband's homegoing was an amazing music-filled celebration. The choir stand was full of current and former choir members who, for many of them, had not been together in years but sang as if they had never been apart. Our son, Bwayne, sang, "If I Can Help Somebody." Our daughter, Pam, sang her father's favorite song, "I Know the Lord Will Make a Way." Even some of our grandchildren sang one of the songs their Grandpa used to sing with the Gospel Keys, "God Is Taking A Record *(Of Everything We Do)*" while our three percussionist grandsons did their thing on the drums. Every musical selection was appropriate for the life celebrated. Then our baby boy, Rev. Darren K. Smotherson, delivered the eulogy to a packed house of loving family and friends. For the experience of it all, I was grateful to God and humbled by those who supported us. Failing to videotape the service was my only regret.

Chapter Twelve
Friends Along the Way

Throughout my 35 years at the Post Office, I worked with a lot of folks. Some people I have forgotten completely, while others became lifelong friends, like Donna Balsano. When her Postmaster selected her to be a Trainer at the Florissant, Missouri Post Office, she was sent Downtown to my office at the Main Post Office to be trained for the job. That was 51 years ago in 1970.

Donna, a proud Italian, was fearful at first of having to come to the City because Downtown St. Louis was a bit foreign to her. She had also heard rumors that various crimes were being committed in the area, even though she didn't know exactly how close in proximity to the MPO those alleged crimes occurred. It didn't take her long to relax after she realized much of what she'd been told was exaggerated. She even looked forward to her training sessions. One day the staff was ordering lunch from one of the local restaurants, so I asked her if she wanted a sandwich.

"What kind of sandwich?"

"Fish," I replied.

"Sure, I'd like a sandwich."

When our food arrived, it didn't take long before the aroma from the large greasy brown paper bag began to spread throughout the unit. It barely took another minute or two for us to make our way to the break area and take a seat at either of the two tables inside. One by one, each person retrieved their sandwich then passed the sack to their anxiously waiting co-worker. The sandwiches usually came double wrapped in wax paper which helped keep them warm but, once the unwrapping began, conversations most definitely stopped after we each took our first bite.

Donna said, "This is good, but it's a little chewy." Then asked, "What kind of fish is this?"

"Tripe," I answered with a slight giggle.

"Never heard of it." As she finished her sandwich she asked, "Why are you laughing?"

"Tripe is not fish; it's the stomach lining of a cow. Did you like it?"

"I loved it!"

Now she buys tripe sandwiches on her own.

In 1974, the Florissant training operation was relocated to the Main Post Office, Downtown, which made Donna a part of my immediate staff. I could not have had a more loyal person working with and for me. We went through some challenging times together but came out on top even though some of Donna's behaviors were a bit bizarre. She worked in our unit from 10:30 PM to 7:00 AM. One night I went into the office just to check on the training activities and found Donna down on her knees, in a corner, on the floor. I never would have guessed what she was doing which was replacing rat poison with granola. We had a serious rat problem in the building and I had asked the maintenance people to get rid of the rodents. Donna, on the other hand, was feeding, capturing, and then releasing them to the outside. She said I was trying to murder the poor animals.

"Would you rather I murder you?" was my question.

It didn't take long for us to become part of each other's families, and we remain family to this day. My mother used to keep a chunky whisky shot glass in the refrigerator because she liked it chilled before pouring her daily hit of 1843. Just one shot glass full and that was all for the day. Mrs. Balsano, (Donna's mother), however, could drink any man under the table without showing any signs of intoxication.

My mother, my teen-aged son, and I were visiting the Balsano home when Donna's mom graciously asked, "Lula do you drink?"

"Sure!" My mother answered with a twinkle in her eyes.

"What's your pleasure: wine, vodka, gin?"

"1843!"

Mrs. Balsano enthusiastically replied, "Oh, you're a whiskey drinker, I think I have something you'll like!"

And then the drinking began.

Mrs. Balsano–"Lula, do you like this one?"

Mama–"Sure!"

Mrs. Balsano–"Lula, you want another?"

Mama–"Sure!"

My mother (*with her one-shot-a-day habit*) and Donna's mother (*who could drink all night and not have the slightest hangover the next day*) were both having a grand old time. Mrs. Balsano kept right on supplying liquor to my mom and laughing her head off because she could tell after the first hit of whiskey that Mama wasn't a real drinker. Donna caught on to what her mother was doing and humorously hinted that it might be time for us to go home. But when my mother tried to stand, she could not.

Mrs. Balsano, as she continued to chuckle, asked, "Lula are you all right?"

Donna, trying hard not to burst into hysterics herself, rolled her eyes at her mom, hoping it would signal her mother to cool it with the clowning around, but it changed nothing. When we were ready to leave, my son helped his grandmother up from the chair and pointed her in the direction of the front door which was already ajar, however, my inebriated mother still could not find the opening. With each attempt, Mama wound up staggering toward the walls on either side of the door. We all burst into laughter once she became tickled by what was happening to her. Our mothers had a lot of fun together during that one-and-only encounter they shared, a memory that I will always cherish. Whenever I tell people about my friend Donna, I always talk about the time her mom got my mother drunk. Before she passed, Mrs. Balsano gave ME her fur coat and, of course, I tease Donna about it every chance I get.

I enjoyed baking and introduced Donna's family and friends to my baked goods, like sweet potato pie and coconut cake. *(They are the best if I do say so myself.)* After introducing my Italian friend to tripe, I got the girl eating chitterlings, too. Whenever she has Thanksgiving dinner with other folks, she demands that I save some for her and I do, because she's family. Donna B. will eat and enjoy everything I cook, but she refuses to taste my spaghetti. I guess she feels she would be betraying her heritage but I just want her to taste the *#%*# spaghetti. It may not be Italian but it, too, is the best.

Irma Cannida and I went to school together, then ended up working at the Post Office, together. However, I would rather write about our time in school. We had a special relationship, particularly in our French class where we sat close together and covered for each other. Irma could correctly speak in French, and I could read it and write it but didn't do well speaking it. I don't remember everything we did to make it through but, without each other, we would never have gotten good grades. I am so proud of Irma who made a career change *(when many of us were afraid to even think about it)* from the Post Office to the pulpit at the Greater Truevine Church. She believes in saving souls and caring for those who need help raising themselves out of despair. In the pulpit, my friend speaks with authority just as she did in our French class.

Irma Castro *(the other Irma in my life)* is my former bowling partner and co-worker. In the Annual City Bowling Tournament *(she nor I can remember the year but it was between 1968 and 1970)*, I bowled three games, a 221, 209, and a 206 for a total score of 636. I bowled a lot of strikes, but I also picked every spare that dared to test me. Irma also did well and we won first place in the DOUBLES competition. That win was no surprise to us because we were already bowling every week in the Post Office League and knew we had the skills to win. That victory, however, was a shock for many who did not look like us because in the 60s and even the early 70s you didn't see or hear of black women holding the top bowling spots. A short time after the tournament, winners from each category *(singles, doubles, and teams)* gathered at a local hotel to take photos. When Irma and I arrived, we stopped at the front desk and asked the attendant where to report. He pointed us in the right direction then proceeded to announce over the loudspeaker that two Hispanics were on their way over. We looked at each other shaking our heads at how ridiculous it was that white people would rather say we were Hispanic than accept the fact that two black women beat the pants off of every last one of them. Why was that so hard to acknowledge and why did ethnicity have to play a part in it at all? We won and it was as simple as that.

My mother made wool jumpsuits for both of us (yellow for me and pink for Irma). She thought we looked so cute in them because at the time, Irma weighed 90 pounds and I weighed 105 pounds. We were so tiny that we never imagined the disturbance that it caused on the workroom floor the night we wore them to work. Sure, we got a lot of attention but we weren't trying to create any problems because the jumpsuits covered our entire bodies. Before the night was over, however, we knew we had caused a major crisis when the manager posted a sign on the bulletin board that read... NO JUMPSUITS ALLOWED. We laugh about that every time we see each other and also agree that it would be nice if we could get back in them.

Tillie Cuffie was part of my staff for a while and the first to learn sign language because she wanted to communicate more effectively with our hearing-impaired employees. She even taught some of our American Sign Language classes so that more of us could communicate just as efficiently.

Tillie is a very light-skinned African American who is often mistaken for white – and, **when it amuses her,** she allows. We once attended a Missouri Postmasters Conference about 50 miles from St. Louis, as representatives of the PEDC *(Postal Employee Development Center)* and where I was scheduled to speak about special training sessions available to Postmasters and their employees. I was the only **OBVIOUS** black person in a room of approximately 300 people seated ten per table. A white female Postmaster at our table, while looking at the printed program, leaned forward and asked me, "What is this PEDC, some Poverty Program?"

Tillie immediately kicked me under the table... hard! When I looked at her, she had an amused smirk on her face due to this woman's inference. Then, acting as if she wasn't black, Tillie whispered to me, "You're the **ONLY ONE** here."

Mary Hendricks Dailey had two weeks' seniority over me, and we were working as substitute distribution clerks but looking forward to becoming regular employees. As subs, we never knew how many hours we had to work or if/when we would have a day off, but becoming a regular meant getting set hours and bidding rights. The list of names in seniority order was posted on a bulletin board for everyone to see. If five regular positions became vacant, the five individuals at the top of the list made regular. Mary and I would check our position on that list daily. If I was the ninety-ninth person on the list, she'd say, "I must be number 90." One day I looked and Mary's name was gone along with the six other names ahead of me. I had made it to #2 on the list so I knew my time was coming soon. Two weeks later I heard that several more people had made regular and I was certain my name wouldn't still be on the list. When I checked, I could see a long name at the top of the list... Geraldine Smotherson. Turns out only one person had actually made regular so I was now #1 and the next to be promoted which finally happened one month later.

Mary and I had become best friends despite her teasing about seniority. She also teased me for being so careful about leaving the break area on time to avoid problems with my supervisor. Mary, on the other hand, was and still is fearless. She also had the best figure of any woman in the entire building on any of the tours. With her tiny waistline and broad shoulders clothes just laid on her body without a flaw and she knew it. I liked her anyway.

As my best friend, Mary knows where all my skeletons are buried, even the ones we promised to bury forever. More than that she is now both a friend and family because her older daughter married my older son. That also makes her grandchildren, my grandchildren. We never even suspected those two would end up together, yet they have been married for over 25 years. Of course, we talk about them and their children but now we mostly talk about ourselves as we compare notes on how fast our bodies are falling apart. That's what friends do.

Gwendolyn LaZard and I belonged to the same postal organizations but had never worked directly with each other. She was quite a proper lady, meticulous both on and off the job, who added a certain class to whatever she was doing. When I was preparing to open the CIBC Westend Academy, I knew that we needed someone to handle the money. Gwen immediately came to mind and, lucky for us, she said yes. This quickly made her, in my opinion, the most valuable person on our staff. The Academy audits were conducted each year without error because Gwen knew where each dime originated and had the documentation on exactly where it went. She kept us out of trouble by making sure every city, state, and IRS report was prepared and submitted in a timely manner. Because of her, I looked like I knew what I was doing. Even if I mustered the strength to reopen the Academy, I wouldn't do it without Gwen. I would trust her with everything I have... and I did!

Ruth T. Scott was a miracle woman who was late for everything including work yet she somehow managed to keep her job long enough to retire from the Post Office. The Lord took good care of that child. Some mornings the first thing Ruth would do when she got to the MPO *(before heading to her own work assignment)* was to stop by my office. She'd call her manager to say she had some business to take care of in the training unit and that she would be there shortly then sit down and chat with me for a while. Once Ruth made it to her desk, she would do her work and I'm sure that helped to keep her employed. Ruth, Mary, and I, despite how polar opposite we are, will remain friends forever.

On August 12, 2020, Ruth wasn't feeling well and was admitted to the hospital where they told her that she had liver cancer. My prayer and desire for her then were that she be returned to good health but she was preparing for whatever was to be and I'm proud of her for that. Our dynamic trio was reduced to just two,

Mary and me, when our friend passed away on August 27, 2020. I love you, dear friend.

Joann Williams (Dee Dee) is a friend who enjoys my cooking even though she cooks far better than I do. She is a chef working at an upscale grocery store where you can buy specialty food items, many prepared by Dee Dee. She and her staff keep the shelves stocked full of delicious ready-to-eat items. Her soups are to die for. Now and then, on her way home from work, she will drop off something special for me to sample. I hope she reads this and continues to do the same.

Dee Dee catered my son's Heaven & Hell wedding reception some years ago and people are still talking about it. In Heaven, she served prime rib, shrimp, and fruits & vegetables galore. Hot buttered bread, twice-baked potatoes, and two kinds of pasta were also available. In Hell, she served hot & spicy foods too numerous to name. Guests said they had never seen anything like it, nor had they ever had as much fun, especially when they visited Hell. Dee Dee's dream has always been to open her own restaurant and my prayer is that one day God grants her the desires of her heart.

Mildred Boyd Carr was our church clerk and also my confidant, road buddy, friend, and someone for whom I had great respect. She was a senior citizen who lived on $369 per month. Mrs. Boyd lived in an apartment building owned by her brother and paid $100 a month for rent. Her church tithe was $40 per month. From the remaining $229 she paid her utilities, bought groceries, and saved as much as she could for emergencies. All from $369.00! She knew the price of every item in the grocery store and which stores had the best sales weekly. At 55 she learned how to drive and even bought a car. Some would question whether she did in fact, learn how to drive because riding with her caused your heart to skip several beats and your right leg to tire from putting on brakes.

Mrs. Boyd showed me what to do with those inexpensive Banquet frozen fruit pies. They were not as flavorful and much cheaper than the other brands but she knew exactly what to do to improve their taste and quality once she got them home. First, she would lift off the top crust, then add butter and seasoning. Next, she'd replace the crust, bake it, and have the best tasting homemade pie without the expense. The Banquet Company could have used her as a consultant. Mrs. Boyd also introduced me to Rally's hamburgers. She said it didn't make sense for me to continue to buy the more expensive hamburgers when Rally's was cheaper and tasted just as good or better. She was right about the burgers as well as so many of my other costly practices.

When I opened the CIBC Westend Academy, Mrs. Boyd was right beside me every step of the way. She claimed ownership *(kept a watchful eye)* of the Academy and everything that was connected to it. At the start of each computer class, she made sure she got **HER** computer before anyone else arrived. She'd get jealous if other students got more attention and felt that they should wait, especially when she needed help. She was hilarious. I thanked God for Mrs. Boyd because she arrived at the Academy each day at 5:45 AM sharp just so we could enter the building together. Never having to be alone was a real comfort for me. Children would start coming in about 6:30 AM and with her help, we were always ready. The Warden, as my son used to call her, would start directing traffic, telling the kids where to go and what not to do.

The Academy was not her only support of my projects or initiatives. My husband would frequently host meetings of 25 to 30 preachers which always included a complimentary dinner that I had to cook. Mrs. Boyd was with me all the way and together we prepared the best FREE all-you-can-eat buffet any group of hungry men could ever imagine. We served everything from short ribs, baked chicken & dressing, ham hocks, and pork chops to macaroni & cheese, candied sweet potatoes, black-eyed peas, cornbread and I'd better not forget the green beans and collard greens. For dessert, they had a choice of chocolate cake, coconut cake, or peach cobbler. Not only did they eat all they wanted, but they also took plates home to their spouses. One of the wives enjoyed the food so much that she started coming to the meetings with her husband just so she could eat afterward. This went on for several months and was getting expensive so the next time, after everyone had gotten their fill, we distributed a flyer that read, "Dine-In or Carry-Out Meals *only* $15.00."

Much to my surprise, their response was "Oh no, we can go to Old Country Buffet for a lot cheaper than $15.00." Nobody took into account the cost, time, and effort we put into providing those free meals for months. Rev. White was the lone defender of our cause who told the group that their reaction was outrageous and they should be ashamed of themselves for being so ungrateful. I appreciated Rev. White's efforts and support. Mrs. Boyd and I weren't disappointed when they changed their meeting place to Old Country Buffet.

On a very hot day one summer, Mrs. Boyd didn't come to the Academy. Worried, I called and got no response then told my husband that something had to be wrong. We agreed to meet at her house and, although we saw her car parked in front she didn't answer the door when we knocked. We called the police who kicked in the door so we could enter. We found her lying naked on the floor just outside her bathroom where she had been all night and half the day, unable to get up. She had tried to crawl to the telephone but had been unable to do so. It was also very hot in her apartment because she wasn't using the air conditioning. Many seniors get in trouble when they try to keep their electric bills low by not turning on the air. We believed this was the reason she got overheated and lost consciousness. The paramedics worked on her for a while before offering to take her to the hospital which she refused. We refused to allow her to stay in her apartment alone so we took her home with us. She loved the pampering and had fun ordering me around. Mrs. Boyd called all her family letting them know where she was.

"I'm staying at my pastor's house with Geraldine." is what I heard her say over and over.

It was a pleasure having her with us and seeing how much she enjoyed being served after she had spent so much of her life waiting on others. Before that unfortunate event, she had always been so independent and proud that she could take care of herself. As years passed that, too, changed. Her diabetes got the better of her and she had to live her last days in a nursing home.

I would visit often until my husband got so sick. Whenever I did get the chance to see her, Mrs. Boyd would always ask, "How's my pastor, are you taking good care of him?"

On my last visit with her, she gave me permission to stay home and take care of him instead of driving out to see her. I will admit that did make my life easier because leaving him meant that I had to have someone else stay with him. One of her sisters later said, "Mildred started going downhill when Geraldine stopped visiting her." Sadly, I didn't find that out until after Mrs. Boyd's death and it broke my heart.

My Classmates, of equal importance, are my friends from grade school and high school who still include me in their lives. They each have their own life stories that should be shared in book form. We have all been blessed to live to the ripe old age of 80+, still functioning in our right minds and able to take care of ourselves. We didn't get to this point on our own. We had family, friends, and the Grace of God for whom we are all grateful.

To my dear friends Jeanette Cofield, Sandra Goins, Nancy Harris, Joy Johnson, Yvonne Ray, and Sandra Stephens, THANK YOU! *May God be merciful unto us, and bless us, and make his face to shine upon us. Psalm 67:1*

Chapter Thirteen
Epiphany

*O*ne day I was in the shower thinking about what I had been writing and why. I really wanted to sit down in the tub and soak because showering, no matter how refreshing, wasn't as relaxing. When I was about 60 years old, it started getting harder for me to bend my knees as I sat down in the bathtub. Using those same knees to get out of the tub was even more difficult. Once, I tried for about 30 minutes to get to my feet so that I could get out of the tub and failed with each attempt. The entire time, I kept turning the hot water on just to keep the water temperature comfortable while I figured out what to do next. Finally, I managed to turn over onto my hands and knees and crawl out of the tub. I haven't taken a bath since. As I showered this particular day, I had an epiphany to the question, **WHY**?

If my mother having five children and no husband had a bad effect on me, then **why** did I recklessly choose to have unprotected sex, get pregnant, and not expect it to have a bad effect on my mother? **Why**, if I became a master at justifying my husband's poor behavior, was I so devastated by all the infidelity. **Why**, if I stole from others, would I be shocked or hurt because someone stole from me?

Life Lessons Learned

1. Have faith in God, yourself, and humanity despite your circumstance.

2. When you pray, start to walk in the direction of the answer.

3. In times of stress remember that there is always an angel somewhere in the mix and that this, too, shall pass!

4. Some people think kindness is a weakness. They can only keep you down if you chose down as your destination.

5. ALWAYS be the best you that you can be, stay true to yourself, be responsible for your own happiness and, NEVER say never!

6. Never be too proud or too afraid to seek help when you need it.

7. If you're not careful, there's a chance that you will do bad things you never dreamed you would or could do.

8. No one is without sin or mistakes. Learn from yours as well as those of others.

9. All that seems might not be. Awareness is the first step to growth.

10. There is a fire inside each of us, but we must control the flame.

11. Give the other person and yourself room to breathe.

12. There will always be someone smarter and better looking than you so accept it and move on with your life.

13. Respect the knowledge and wisdom of others, no matter their position.

14. Practice forgiving yourself first, then others.

15. People are not gods, so don't give them that status.

16. If I don't love myself, how can I expect others to love me?

17. No two people love the same way... but they can still complete each other.

18. It is amazing how your early limitations, if you are not careful, can cripple your mind and block the limitless possibilities in your life and your future.

19. Be grateful for every breath you take and every friend you make. Learn to appreciate the small things in life.

20. Every day offers a new beginning, another chance, so get up!

One Last Thing

Now that I am more aware of my flaws, my justifications, and my sins along with the Grace that I have been granted, I can do better. And it's not because I'm old and can't do the things I used to do that compels me, it's because I still have life. Each new and precious day gives me a chance to live better, do better and be better.

Who am I? I am Geraldine Jackson West Smotherson, specially chosen for the journey that is my life, good and bad. I wasn't sure at first if I even dared to share my truth, but writing this book has helped me to: heal old wounds; let go of the shame of being fatherless; forgive both my parents; repent for my wrongs; accept that I can't be everything to everybody; and know that, no matter how imperfect I am, it's okay to be *Unapologetically Me.*

Afterword

Finally, brothers and sisters, whatever is true, whatever is noble, whatever is right, whatever is pure, whatever is lovely, whatever is admirable—if anything is excellent or praiseworthy-think about such things.
Philippians 4:8 NIV

I have had a lot of titles throughout my life: daughter, sister, wife, mother, granny, aunt, in-law, boss, friend, First Lady and so many more. As a result, I wanted to give those who are closest to me the opportunity to share their thoughts about me being a part of their lives even if that meant I was nothing but a disappointment. It would be their truth, experience, or perspective regarding GERALDINE.

My Mother, Geraldine Smotherson

It's really hard for me to pour out my feelings for my mother because it's something I just am not used to doing. I'll try because she asked. She is the person that named me Bwayne.

My mother is my source of reason and calm. My mother didn't get honors and degrees until later but has always been smart and resourceful. She knows how to talk to people and knows the right approach to a problem. My mother is my speechwriter if I get in a rut and my editor who corrects my mistakes. My mother is why I know now that a shirt looks better than a T-shirt. My mother is why I love vanilla ice cream and shortbread cookies. Sweet potato pie, pound cake, chitterlings, dark meat chicken, grits with butter, and more things than I should say. What I'm telling you is I knew she loved me. She would say it every once in a while, but I just always knew it. Just like I always knew she was with me even though she wasn't there. Let me explain.

I can vividly remember that my mother didn't attend a lot of the things I did between sports and music and I knew why. My mother was working 8, 10- and 12-hour days taking care of her family. To this day, I have never been bothered about that. I have never felt neglected and ignored because I always knew she cared about me, supported me, and loved me. I knew by the clothes I wore and how Vaseline made my face shine. I knew when she would allow me to play the drums in the house. That feeling of her being with me began in elementary school when my mother would show up at school and catch me doing things I wasn't supposed to be doing or didn't wear my sweater at recess as I was told. I never understood how she always caught me.

I do feel that I was not prepared for life like my friends were and completely lost at college. I bring that up because I've never blamed my mother for it and understood later why that was.

Finally, because of her love, honor, and reputation, I have worked to be a better person and regret a period in my life that didn't reflect well.

So, what does my mother mean to me? Love!

Bwayne Alexander Smotherson – *Your First-Born*

My Mother (The Most Important Woman In My Life)

When my mother asked me to write something for her book describing what it's like to have her as a mother I was a little hesitant at first to say, "Sure!" I knew, that by doing so, it would take me on an emotional journey of ups and downs *(mostly downs)*. I wanted those memories to remain in the back of my mind.

I remember when we lived on Maple Place in St. Louis in the early 1960s. I was around three or four years old and my mom had me sitting in a make-shift highchair *(chair stacked with phone books)* in the kitchen. The stove was on the North wall of the kitchen and the kitchen table sat against the South wall. She was frying an egg for my dad's breakfast. I love fried eggs *(as long as you don't break the yolk)* even then, which is probably why the memory of what happened is so vivid. I remember how fixated I was watching her crack that egg, put it in the skillet, and hearing the crackling sound of the raw egg white when it hit the hot grease. When it finished cooking, my mom scooped the egg from the skillet *(using that same spatula)* and proceeded to carry it across the kitchen to my dad's plate that was sitting on the kitchen table in front of me. I'm looking with great interest thinking, *Wow! My mom can do everything!* But before she could get that egg onto my dad's plate, it hit the floor. We both looked down at the egg on the floor – my mom looked up at me and I make eye contact with her. I don't remember being alarmed and I guess it was because when the egg hit the floor the yolk was still intact. My mom, however, sure did look flustered. She quickly scooped the egg from the floor, placed it neatly on my dad's plate, looked at me again, and then put her pointer finger to her mouth. I knew exactly what that *"shhh"* gesture meant but I guess to make sure that I did, she said, "Don't tell your father what just happened!" I was just happy that she had saved the egg.

When I was growing up, for me, it was an extremely lonely time. I always felt that I was different from everyone *(brothers, schoolmates, everybody)* but couldn't figure out why. In addition to feeling isolated, shyness was an even bigger hurdle for me to get over. It was years before my parents even learned that I could sing. But there was one thing that my mom knew I could do well. I could memorize any poem or script she put in front of me. And she did exactly that! My Easter speeches were always the hardest and the longest to learn. She also knew I loved to dance. Boy, could I dance! Despite my extreme shyness and with a lot of prompting, my mom was the one who could get me to dance at birthday parties. It was even her idea to enter me into a dance contest while we were aboard the S. S. Admiral cruising up and down the Mississippi. *(Anybody who lived in Saint Louis in the 60s knows about the excursion steamboat.)* I won that contest by doing a dance called the DOG and my mom loved it! I don't think she realized just how much her encouragement meant to me.

Here's where I get emotional.

I mentioned previously that my childhood was a lonely one. I was the only girl and my brothers wanted nothing to do with me, and rightly so. They were the ALL-BOY kind of fellows where sports, sports, and more sports consumed most of their time and attention. *(I was not having any of that nonsense.)* I spent a lot of time in my room watching musical movies starring Sammy Davis Jr., the Nicholas Brothers, Doris Day, Gene Kelly, Fred Astaire, Donald O'Connor, Debbie Reynolds, and my all-time favorite, Gregory Hines. I also loved musical comedies featuring Dean Martin and Jerry Lewis. My room was my performance wonderland, a place where I could be any entertainer I wanted to be. I knew all the lyrics to every Gospel Keys *(my dad's singing group)* song plus any song from Aretha Franklin's 60s and 70s R&B hit list. I could sing them effortlessly but, only in my room. I was too afraid of letting my parents and brothers in on my secret or even my *embarrassment*. My self-confidence was sorely lacking.

The one thing that was a constant for me growing up was when my mom was home. Maybe it was because there was another girl in the house. I remember feeling less anxious about everything around me whenever she was nearby. As a kid, I would've loved to have had a "June Cleaver" situation going on in our household, with me coming home from school every day greeted by my mom and chocolate cake. Because of her sweet disposition, Geraldine Smotherson would have been perfect for the role of Mrs. Cleaver but, unfortunately yet, fortunately, she worked full-time. My "Leave it to Beaver" fantasy would have to remain just that... a fantasy.

I can still picture my mom sitting in our upstairs hallway surrounded by hundreds of index cards with postal addresses and zip codes that she had to memorize. Even though she couldn't devote all of her time and attention to me, I remember how good it felt just having her home. But I also remember the car rides to the MPO all those years ago. That's when my mom would kiss my father goodbye, climb out of the car, and walk up a gazillion steps *(when you're little it seemed like a lot of steps)* in front of the building then disappear through these heavy glass doors. Sadness would sweep over me each time and I was back to feeling lonely with just my dad and my brothers as we made our way back home. Nobody knew that but me.

1 Corinthians 13:11 (NLT) says, When I was a child, I spoke and thought and reasoned as a child. But when I grew up, I put away childish things.

I began this story with the egg incident because I thought as a child. I wasn't aware of my mom's age, her maturity level, or the extent of her cooking skills *(she did save the egg)*. All I saw in that kitchen was a woman who I knew to be my protector and who loved me dearly. Nothing else mattered. She was a young woman no older than 22 with a husband and three children who, not too long before that, was just a child herself! No wonder she tried to carry the egg to the plate instead of bringing the plate to the egg. Still, she was AWESOME to me.

Because my mother worked all the time, I told myself it was because she needed a break from us. I had even convinced myself that she loved her job, travel, and school more than she loved us. The way I saw it, work was her temporary escape yet for me, I felt trapped, abandoned, and alone. There were times when I even resented her for leaving me home to deal with my dad's ridicule. Nothing could be further from the truth and it wasn't until I became an adult, wife, and mom *(facing my own life experiences and hiccups)* that I came to fully comprehend the hard choices and sacrifices my mother had to make. She demonstrated her love for us in the most selfless way imaginable. I love and respect her for that AND I pray she does not burden herself with useless guilt. Her courage and strength are remarkable. That's why she will always be the most important woman in my life!

If I were to list a few reasons *(there are hundreds)* why I am grateful to/for my mom it would be as follows:

- She loves the Lord and demonstrates His Word every day.

- She loves UNCONDITIONALLY.

- I appreciate her dedication to any task, project, or commitment.

- I'm thankful for her transparency and candidness– my brothers and I can talk to her about ANYTHING!

- I am proud of the acts of kindness she exhibits to all who encounters her and I am even more proud of her for instilling that in her children.

- She is NEVER judgmental and never makes me feel stupid for the STUPID things I do.

- She, without question, adores, cherishes, and protects her family.

- She served as a buffer between me and my dad–even when she didn't know she was doing so.

- She was the BEST SUPPORT SYSTEM any daughter facing a battle with breast cancer could ever ask for.

- She trusted in my abilities to assist her with this book.

What I want most in the world for my mom to stop doing is:

- Apologizing for things that **ARE NOT** her fault or responsibility.

- Fixing everybody's problems and issues (**NO** is an okay word even when you're saying it to me).

- Feeling guilty for making herself a PRIORITY... sometimes!!!

Pamela Jean Smotherson–
*Your Second-Born **and** only Daughter*

My Mother the SUPERHERO

My mother is the SUPERHERO in my life because of her strength, her brilliant mind, her willingness to share, and how she has always found a way to make a difference. I call her my SUPERHERO because she doesn't fight with her fists or her words, she fights with her heart, with her actions. Those qualities continue to impact my life to this day.

My SUPERHERO mother is like Robin Hood, the fictional character that took from the ones who had and gave to the ones in need. She doesn't take from anybody other than herself... always putting the needs of others before her own. I remember on occasion going with her to deliver Thanksgiving turkeys or to drop off Christmas gifts to my father's family members who were in need. She would always make sure my siblings and I had money to buy my father and others something for Christmas but one year she didn't receive a gift from anybody including us. Even though it was probably my mother who insisted we not spend our money on her, I can still remember how heartbroken I felt for her.

I was an outstanding athlete my entire life, especially throughout high school and college. I can remember my glory days on the fields of University City High School and Lincoln University. Sadly, I reflect on instances that literally could have caused me serious physical harm and some that did cost me the greatest opportunities of my football career. During practice, one of the white coaches used to make us do a drill called **suicides** *(running full speed, head-on into each other crashing and smashing our helmets together)*. He believed the exercise would make us tough but I viewed it as something that would give us concussions and proceeded to protest against the reckless approach. I said, "Coach we don't need to do this. This won't make the players tough this will make them scared." I even saw stars one time when it happened to me.

My unsolicited nickname given to me by another coach was **Waterhead** because of how hard and strong I would hit people with that helmet on my head. He also knew I was capable of unleashing tremendous pain and agony on my foes, especially during **suicides**. That's when my teammates became my opponents. Whenever we practiced this ridiculous and hazardous ritual, many were afraid to express how reluctant they were to have to go up against me. I became the team's advocate vocalizing my concern for everyone's safety even to school officials but to no avail. I also continued to warn the coach that someone was going to get hurt and get hurt badly if he didn't stop. He finally listened after I almost decimated one of the players. I felt awful for having to do that to my teammate and let down because the coaches and school didn't heed my warning.

My mom had the difficult task of having to tell me that she couldn't afford to send me to college. I somewhat had a clue given the fact that she was already struggling to keep herself, my father, both my brothers and, my sister all in school at the same time. I told her, "Ma, don't worry about it, I got this covered." I had made 154 tackles, played the most positions, and was sure to be named MVP my senior year of high school. Plus, I was getting stacks of letters from prominent Division One colleges like Oklahoma, Mizzou, Nebraska, and Texas all looking to recruit me. I was confident that my goal of securing the most lucrative scholarship to a division one school was firmly in my grasp and that her worries would be no more.

Unfortunately, that same coach decided to blackball me after I raised the issue about the team having to do *suicides* and made it his mission to sabotage any chances of me receiving an athletic scholarship to a major university. The MVP award was given to another player on my high school football team who had only played two positions and made 54 tackles. I was offered a scholarship to attend a school that, in my opinion, was beneath my skills and abilities. That was devastating; my hopes and dreams were shattered, and I was convinced all was lost. My SUPERHERO, however, urged me to accept the scholarship to Lincoln University anyway and, I did what my mother asked. At the time I was fully unaware of the fact that it was God's opportunity to break me, melt me, mold me, and re-make me.

I was recruited to play linebacker but soon became one of Lincoln's top football athletes. Still, I was unable to shake the resentment of Lincoln being my only option in reaching my goal of becoming a professional ball-player. But I remained dedicated to the game, practicing hard and playing even harder. In no time, I was considered one of the smartest players on the team. One of the assistant coaches, however, thought I should play lineman because of my size. Reflecting on the times in high school of playing six other positions because I had agility, brains, and muscle to go along with my size, I respectfully declined the offer. But, I guess, just like in high school, I must have stepped on this college coach's toes. From that moment on, he launched an all-out personal attack on me by coercing some of my weak-minded/envious teammates to try and cause me physical harm by cutting my legs from under me.

Thankfully, even though he tried, he could not diminish my talent or contribution as a player. I went on to break all the records with most career tackles during my time at Lincoln. I became an advocate for former teammates who had lost their scholarships because the school was unwilling to house or feed them. I even had an article written about my contributions entitled *A Little Glimmer... a Lot of Gloom.* Though I hated the circumstances surrounding me ending up at Lincoln, I was blessed to be able to get an education and earn my degree.

You intended to harm me, but God intended it for good to accomplish what is now being done, the saving of many lives. Genesis 50:20

My mother is the source of so many teaching moments for me. She told me to always look out for people and to help them. Also to try and make a difference in someone's life because that was more important than fame or fortune. AND, to find a way to take care of myself. Those times when I was feeling inadequate or insecure, she would remind me that God made me just the way He wanted me to be. She'd say, "Smile in the midst of trouble. Even though you feel you're on the losing team *(facing obstacles and hurdles)*, keep fighting and never quit." She is my living example that it's not about how people treat you, it's about how you treat them. That even though when you try to take care of the people in your life it is no guarantee that they will take care of you. She continues to remain behind the scenes still propelling people towards their greatest potential.

If anyone thought my mother may have appeared weak whenever someone tried to talk down to her or talk bad about her they would be wrong. Only STRONG people can look the other way and not retaliate. That is my superhero. My wish is that I can be half as thoughtful, smart, and giving as she is. What I appreciate the most is that my mother's stewardship has rubbed off on me.

As a little kid, I used to be told constantly that I looked just like my mother. I hated hearing it because I thought people were implying I looked like a girl. I was way too much the alpha male to even entertain such a thought. I'm honored to say I do indeed look like her and even prouder to say I am most definitely my mother's child.

Darren Keith Smotherson – *Your Baby Boy*

Geraldine Smotherson... My Mother

When I was growing up, things were kind of complicated in terms of who I was and where I fit in. My life was in no way sad or uncomfortable. Just the opposite. I was always happy and loved.

As I grew, I knew that I had a mother and grandparents who loved me and cared for me, but I also had a father, stepmother, brothers, and a sister. I love them all. It was always a thrill to be around them. That's where Geraldine Smotherson came in.

My stepmother has always been my "Mother." She never made me feel unloved or "outside" of the family. Yes, I am the son of another mother but, Geraldine will always be my mother. She is a beautiful woman who possesses an even more beautiful spirit. I am so proud and blessed to have you as my mother and prayerfully you are proud of me as your son.

When God sanctioned Mary to carry Jesus, He sanctioned Geraldine Smotherson to be the matriarch of our family.

Favour is deceitful, and beauty is vain: but a woman that feareth the Lord, she shall be praised. Proverbs 31:30

I praise you mother, and I love you forever. God Bless You!

Charles Melvin Smotherson

Big Sister, Friend, Mentor, Advisor, Confidant, Consoler, Counselor, Guardian, Role Model

How have I seen my sister, Geri? All of the above that I can think of right now. Having a 15-year age difference places a varied viewpoint from this little sister. Now, seeing her as the Pastor's wife and First Lady of the Church, are views that I've witnessed through the eyes of others. Yes, I have respected her in those positions but she's first and foremost MY SISTER.

That 15-year difference …. Looking up to my big sister was natural … she's always been beautiful, both inside and outside. My jealousy of her is a good jealousy … I recognize beauty and have always thought my sister to be prettier than me. I can remember being out with her, maybe shopping, somewhere where people were.

We'd be walking ... oh I guess I should say I was probably in my early teens, but we'd be walking, passing
some fellows who I thought should be noticing me,
but they were looking and gawking at my sister as we'd
pass by. They were not being disrespectful; they were
just noticing what they thought was a good-looking
woman. And of course, the woman part was probably
what attracted them to her instead of me. But still, that
younger me noticed those guys noticing my big sister
and not noticing me. I wasn't mad, just wished I looked
more like her at that time. She was and still is a Beauty.

That 15-year difference ... my sister took me to my first
gynecological visit. Oh, was I not happy with that. I was
getting ready to go to MIZZOU and she convinced my
mother that I should have birth control pills. I was hurt
... I told her I was not "doing anything". And why she
didn't think I was still a virgin really hurt me ... I gave
her no reason to not trust me. My word was my bond,
it always had been (still to this day) ... I was telling the
truth. I didn't need birth control pills. But she took
me ... I had my first exam, got on birth control, went to
MIZZOU, and lost my virginity. Oh well .. since I had
pills, I thought I had permission.

That 15-year difference ... my sister was my role model.
Truth, honesty, and the American way. My Hero. She
never lied and I believed everything, E-VE-RY-THING,
she told me. For years, I thought her middle name was
Jeraldine. Because she told me it was Je-Ral-Deen. Yes,
one day I got up the courage to ask my sister what the "J"
stood for. She always went by Geraldine J. Smotherson.
And why I didn't know my big sister's middle name was
embarrassing to me, so I finally got up the courage to
ask. I didn't believe my sister lied and I truly didn't
get her sense of humor. So as I received her response,
unbeknownst to me as to what she was really doing,

she went into this long dissertation of how her middle name was Je-Ral-Deen ... she actually spelled it out "J-E-R-A-L-D-I-N-E". You'd have to hear the influx in her voice as she pronounced Geraldine Je-Ral-DEEN. I intently listened to my role model, my big sister, my hero and took in her explanation. I carried that knowledge for a long time until I shared my expertise ... don't even remember where we were ... but as I corrected the crowd on what "J" stood for, you would have thought I was doing the greatest comedic performance of all times ... laughter, tears, from others; but from me, a little humiliation realizing how gullible I was, but more than anything else, that was when I realized my sister did tell lies. I was in shock.

That 15-year difference. This story is not from my memory, but one that my sister shared with me in my older years, so I may be mixing up the details. Anywho, she always used to tell me that I was her baby. That I was always with her. Remember 15 years between the two of us. I don't remember these other babies entering my life, interrupting my natural flow ... but my nephew is 3 years younger, and my niece is 4 years younger. And I can only imagine that this 3/4-year-old ME received Bwayne and Pam as just another playmate/sibling that was always around when my sister was there. But this memory has to do with Geri and Melvin moving into their own place. I guess Pam wasn't here yet ... but this ME, this 15 year younger than Geri ME, always been Geri's baby ME, entered that lodging with such amazement and excitement that I finally had a home ... think I may have referenced having a dad. Don't remember but as I look back at this story, I wonder how that little girl transitioned from being Geri's baby to Geri's little sister. I don't remember, but I can just imagine that it was hard, not hard but confusing ... I'm quite sure I didn't understand why I wasn't living in the same house with Geri. I had to accept that my mother lived at 4319 Saint Louis Ave and that I lived with my mother. Geri had her real babies and I had to accept that, and I had to move forward, realizing, and understanding that Geri was my Big Sister.

I have another sister, who's 5 years older. My relationship with her was much different than my relationship with the sister who's 15 years older. Oh, if I had to have conversations that involved talking about someone, cussing about someone, talking down, needing to provide a beat down to someone ... Geri was not the one to help reason me through that situation... Debbie was. Geri didn't curse, Geri didn't fight, didn't talk about people, Geri didn't lie, Geri didn't ... Geri didn't watch Young & the Restless, Geri didn't drink, Geri didn't look at the cute boys, Geri didn't change into the blue jeans and tee-shirts which was the proper attire required to give the necessary beatdown to those neighborhood kids ... Geri didn't do those things.

Even though the level of respect and admiration never fades, that relationship gap has changed from Big Sister to Sister, and the 15-year gap in age doesn't seem like 15 years anymore. There's a level of respect that I feel from Geri ... and this is attributed to her respect for people. She shows me on a regular basis that she believes I have matured into this adulthood category. She actually asks ME questions for advice. Every time that happens, I try to rise to the occasion by giving adult level-headed rational responses ... of course, I don't want to disappoint my big sister by saying something stupid. Remember, I said she's a role model, and to disappoint her with a stupid response would be disrespectful to how I see her, a role model. Her being in my life makes me a better person ... well at least it makes me want to be a better person. I miss the mark

at times ... I recognize that because the honesty in Geri
that I want to emulate, makes me check myself and recognize my downfalls.

In case you're wondering if Geri has ever hurt me ...
can't say it happened much. Well, there's one situation that used to really hurt me. Don't know what was
actually going on with Geri, but she used to jokingly
say she was not going to live to see her 73rd birthday.
She would just randomly say this ... not sure why or
how she thought it fit into the conversation. We could
be in a group conversation; I could be overhearing her
saying this to someone else; I would respond by telling
her to stop saying that ... I knew how I felt when she
said it, but I don't think she knew that that statement
brought anxiety to my spirit ... it hurt me to hear her
say that. Once I asked her if she realized what she was
saying ... she did. But of course, her response to me
seemed flippant, like it was natural for her to think
that she would not have more years in her life than
our mother. I never thought she was trying to hurt me;
I just couldn't understand how she could make those
words pass through her lips and come out of her mouth
... it hurt me. And finally, one day, I think I got my message across ... when she said it this last time, tears came
to my eyes and I walked away from her ... letting her
know that I can't look at you right now. It's been several
years since that time, but I didn't hear that from her
again and we've gotten past that 73rd-birthday.

I love family but sometimes, growing up, it didn't seem
that family loved me at the same level I loved them.
I've had my moments when I just didn't understand
WHY .... And there was no explaining WHY. Unlike
my other siblings, I never had a combative relationship with my 15-years-older-than-me sister. She was
always supportive. Always encouraging the best of me,

the best for me, always there no matter what. That's the way it seemed. Family, she shared her family with me. I have a snippet memory of her allowing me to pick up her new baby. That had to be Darren ... I think I'm 6 or 7 years older than Darren. She allowed me to pick him up, she put trust in me, and I have that memory of holding a baby for the first time. I see my SMILE and I see HAPPINESS. Another memory I have of Geri sharing her family, was when she allowed her teenage daughter to drive with me to Kansas City when I relocated there. Mind you, I was relocating to KC to work for EPA while taking a sabbatical from MIZZOU. That had to be 1976/75, I was 22/21 years old, that would have made Pam 18/17. I guess she wasn't as young as I remember ... any who ... Geri allowed Pam to ride with me (a new car owner) across the state of Missouri for my relocation. Pam helped me find an apartment, she met a new coworker of mine, named Jaime, and then had to get on the Grey Hound for her return trip to the STL. Geri has always made me feel I was her family.

It's been some 15+ years, that my sister's reference to age 73 brought discomfort and hurtful discord to my spirit, so my sister's mention to being age 80 is received by me, differently ... this is her comedic acceptance of getting older. I haven't quite figured the real point, but she is quick to tell me that she is 80 ... well as of May 13, 2020, she's 81 ... so will it be "I'm in my 80's" or will she continually remind me that she's the big sister, that she is 15 years older. Yeah the relationship gap has changed and I'm good with that ... Geri's my partner in crime, my casino buddy, my confidant ... guess what, after all these years, Geri is now looking at Young & the Restless. Geri gets hesitant about asking me to take her places, she tries not to be a burden. But I keep telling her that I plan on being this 90-year-old driver taking her to the Casino when the mood strikes ... so stay ready.

I wanted my sister to be Soror, but her life was not in the place where she could add another organization to her resume. She did not understand my love for my sorority and why I wanted to call her Soror. I even investigated if she would have been honorarium material for membership. At the time she would have. I even found some old papers showing that I had presented Geri for membership into AKA by way of Omicron Eta Omega chapter, but I guess that's when she told me she could not be a member of another organization. Membership, to her, meant commitment and participation, and her personal time was already spread thin. Remember, 3 kids, Pastor's wife, USPS executive, etc., etc., etc. I understood her reasons and accepted it, but it hurt ... because I truly wanted my Sister to be My Soror. I love my Sorority and wanted to share that special Sisterhood with my Sister. Oh well, now I blame her because two of HER granddaughters chose different paths ... and not the same path ... one's a Delta, the other is ZPhiB. I've somewhat resolved those feelings, gotten past that hurt, and accept that my family is a Devine9 family. We have Kappa's and Que's, too, by way of my Sister. Oh, and let's not forget her husband was a member of Alpha Phi Alpha .... 06 ... 08.

I'm VERY proud of my sister's accomplishments. I'm proud to proclaim that my sister was the highest-paid female postal employee, at that time. I'm proud to say that my sister was asked to be photographed and included in an advertisement for the University of Missouri, St. Louis that was published in the St. Louis American. Probably advertised in the St. Louis Post Dispatch too. I'm proud to proclaim that my sister was the best Special Grand Associate District Deputy that developed the bestess criteria for that position ... even though no one after her followed that lead. Such a loss. I'm proud to know that if she had wanted to, she could have been the Grand Worthy Matron of the Order of Eastern Star for the State of Missouri. I'm proud to know that her philanthropic spirit successfully launched the Westend Academy that was housed out of the Cornerstone Institutional Baptist Church. I'm proud that my sister, has been First Lady at three churches ... First Baptist Church of Creve Coeur, Washington Tabernacle Baptist Church, and Cornerstone Institutional Baptist Church ... and now holds the title of FLEA (First Lady Emeritus Always) at Cornerstone. She doesn't like the title, but I understand the level of respect that our now Pastor has for his FLEA ... she's going to have to let him have this one. I mentioned her being an UMSL grad. Well, this degree was, or should I say "these degrees were" earned while being a full-time employee at the USPS, a full-time mother of three children at the Smotherson household, a full-time wife to the Rev. Melvin Smotherson (that had its own challenges), a fulltime stepmother to the Rev's other kid, and being the sole provider, breadwinner for the Smotherson household. That 1980's song that says, "I can bring home the bacon, fry it up in the pan, and never let you forget you're a man!" ... well that's my sister in a nutshell and more. I am proud to call that woman My Sister.

From Wanda Diane (Sister)

Sidebar...

My sister Wanda Diane was in tow when Mama and my aunt moved me and Melvin into our apartment. Because she thought she would be moving in with us, Wanda was just as excited as we all were. "Now I have a mommy and a daddy!" Exclaimed my 3 ½-year-old baby sister. What she said tore into my heart, and a happy day instantly turned into a sad one after hearing those words. I can only imagine how my

*mother felt realizing how much not having a father around
had affected Wanda. Now I had to let her down too. She
couldn't live with us; her place was with her mother who
loved her very much. How do you mend the broken heart of
someone so young and fragile or even help her make sense
of it all? I struggled with that for many years and sadly so
did Wanda.*

My Granny

As I sit at my desk typing this, all I can think is *Where
do I begin?* The immense love and patience my Granny
has for me are sometimes hard to understand. I am not
the greatest first-born grandchild. I've tried to be and
failed many times but even in my lowest moments, my
Granny always reminded me how much better than
that I was. She may not know this but when I disappoint her, it's a heavy feeling and it breaks my heart.
Crazy thing is, she never makes me feel like a disappointment, so why the heavy feeling? I believe it's
because I see my Granny as Godsent. She's just not the
one you'd want to hurt in any way.

I cherish the many memories I have with her. Two of
those memories I share quite often with friends and
family. My Granny took me skating at Saints Skating
Rink when I was about 10 or 11. She actually got out
on the floor with me. I was in total shock and awe!
I'd never seen her skate before nor mention that she
had, but she did it for me. My second and FAVORITE
memory was getting to go to work with Granny, sitting in her big office, watching her do her Powerful
Black Woman thang, and eating in the cafeteria which
gave me such joy. Seeing her behind that big desk was
such an inspiration. Knowing now the struggles that
came with that job infuriates me. Again, she is not the
one you'd want to hurt. She is God's chosen and her

strength is unmeasurable. How can I be this great of a woman is the question?

Now, there have been times of disagreement and that's hard to have to acknowledge. Even when I felt disrespected or misunderstood was it ever proper for me to have ever made her feel the same. Luckily for me, never was there any love lost as hers is unconditional. Plus, you can't stay mad at Granny longer than 5 minutes because she'll be offering you a meal, some cake, or any kind of comfort you don't deserve. Granny is still a mystery to me. I sometimes wonder about her experiences in life and how they molded this extremely kind and forgiving woman.

More than anything, I am truly grateful to have known Granny for almost 39 years of my life. Heck, that's all my life. I will go to war for her, so please folks out there, choose your words wisely when speaking about my Granny. There's no other woman like her. *(Oprah doesn't even come close and that's real!)* If it's one thing I've learned from my amazing grandmother it would be to *kill people with kindness.* Granny... not everyone is deserving of your glow and positive energy.

Peace & Many Blessings!

Jaymi Lynn Smotherson *(First-born Grandchild & First-born Granddaughter)*

My Granny

You asked me to write something about you, whether it be good or bad. So I'll start with the good first!

I don't even have to talk about the money you used to leave all the grandkids in the Christmas stockings

EVERY Christmas. But you would leave me a little extra and write "MFG" (My Favorite Grandchild) on it! Never told anybody our secret, until now!

Granny, there are too many good things that I can say about you, but your willingness to give and to be of service is amazing! Even when people (and ME) are not deserving of it, you still go above and beyond. That's what makes you special, and I didn't realize it until you and I did the yard sale at the church! Once you and I finished hauling, loading, and setting everything up, then the rest of the congregation decided to conveniently show up! I was so pissed nobody was there to help, but you were so excited, and happy and so calm! I was getting mad that you weren't mad! Then I talked to Big Pam about it and she was just as calm as you. She explained to me, "Nathan, this is who your granny has always been"... at that point is when I realized she was absolutely right! That's why there are no bad memories or anything bad to say about you. Maybe when we were bad in church, you use to pinch us with *them* nails! Then give us peppermints to soothe the pain!

The only time I got mad at you was when I was in college and you called me one time and asked if I was okay. I said yes, and then you said, "Because your dad said you were down there, on them DRUGS!"... which consists of so many different things I've never done. But at the time, that was just someone's uneducated, asinine opinion about what I was doing, and you got caught in the angry grandchild crossfire! 😟

Granny, you mean the world to me! You are a beautiful, strong (mentally & physically), dependable, trustworthy woman of God, and I couldn't have asked for a better Granny!

I LOVE YOU.

Nathan Alexander Smotherson–*Your Firstborn Grandson and "MFG"*

My Granny

Dear Granny,

How much do I love thee? Let me count the ways. I've always marveled at how you continue to be such an awesome person day in, and day out and you never seem to get tired. While you're a classy, dynamic, kind, and all-around great human being, you're also the absolute best grandmother a guy can ask for. I can't thank you enough for everything you've done for me personally as well as my family. You will always be loved and appreciated as long as we're around.

Love you,

Chuck *(The coolest "Grand" of the bunch)*

My Granny

My Granny asked me to rate her performance as a grandparent. To be honest, it has taken me some time to get my thoughts together because I didn't want my review to be cliché. "Oh, Granny is so sweet!" or "She is smart, she is wise, she is kind, and makes great pancakes." Yes, all of those are spot on and true but listen here! There is a side of her that you all do not know and have never seen and I was skeptical about sharing. Granny is sweet, but *chile*... she could be so ***mean***! Let me tell you why.

When I was a kid, my mom would drop me off over to Granny and Grandpa's house ever so often on a Saturday. It was great! Granny would make me pancakes, bacon, and eggs and Grandpa would slip me a few bucks. I was living large on a Saturday morning ok! Until the "J" word... Jenga! Yes, yes the game. We played that game every time I was there, and Granny cheated EVERY time we played by not letting me win... EVER! That is the worst thing any grandparent can do to their grandchild. My lovely pancake-flipping, sweet potato pie baking, homemade chili-making Granny had the nerve to play fair. In my childlike mind, I was certain that grandparents were terrible at board games. The unwritten rule was that kids are smarter and play games better. Well, I was wrong. Yes, I lost every time... yes I got mad... and yes she laughed at my pain. I mean she was tickled. Even to this day, she gets tickled whenever we talk about it and I'm sure she's just as tickled right now reading this review. It took me some time to get over it because I was an extremely competitive kid but I never loved her any less. Almost 20 years later I realized that in life you're not going to win at everything, and you will encounter people who are better and smarter than you at something. AND, that is ok. Just work harder. Thank you Granny for the life lesson, taught in such a unique way!

Now that I'm older and an adult, my views and opinions are completely different. This grandmother of mine doesn't have a mean or firm bone in her body whatsoever and it can drive me crazy at times. Let me clarify that a little more. I'm not wanting her to be a mean ol' witch *(can't say the other word)*, I just wish she would be a little more selfish. Put herself first 99.9% of the time and be ok with it. Doggone it, put that foot down! But of course, we're talking about Geraldine Smotherson who would probably cringe at that percentage. As a kid growing up, it has always disturbed me to watch my Granny constantly give and bend over backward for people *(family too)* who wouldn't even think to lift a finger for her. To do it with no complaints and a smile says a lot about her character in general. All of these things are great traits for a person to have *(I have some of them)* but you best believe I have a cutoff. It just becomes too much for a grandchild to witness when her good deeds seem to never be reciprocated. She gives so much and when you know the kind of grandmother you have, **EXCEPTIONAL,** you expect her to be treated as such. These are things that have always concerned me but I never felt the need to say anything to her about it or, that I could. She's the grandmother and I am the grandchild and I sure as heck *(again, can't say the other word)* cannot tell her how to live her life. If it makes her happy, then I accept it.

Speaking of giving too much. Granny is always trying to give me stuff that she bought from HSN. I don't know how many times I have gone to her house and left with things I did not need like cookware, veggie chopper, plastic cutting boards, a comforter, suitcase, I mean the list goes on! Yes, these are all great things a young person should have but, I still haven't used the first set of house-hold items she gave me a week before! This is what she says, "How much time do you have? I want to show you something!" Of course, I say, "Sure, I have time" knowing exactly what is about to happen. She shows me a little gadget of some sort and I "ooh" and I "aah" and then she proceeds to ask, "You want it?" Then tell me, "You can have it, I bought two!" It became a routine and I had to start telling my sweet Granny… "NO!" I was convinced that she wanted my house to be like hers… a collection of stuff. No thank you, Granny, I'll pass, love! Her giving me things is just a constant reminder of how much she cares and loves me and wants to always make sure I'm never in need of anything. The same applies to everyone she encounters. This is the kind of grandma-ma I have, and I wouldn't change or trade her for anything in the world. I love you, Granny.

Joii Alexandria Williams *(aka the favorite Grandchild..*
that's my story and I'm sticking to it!)

Aunt Geri–Not Granny

I remember the first time I realized that my Aunt Geri, was really my Aunt Geri, and not my "Granny." I mean, I knew biologically that she was my mother's sister, technically making her my aunt. But my mother is one of the youngest of her siblings and is closer in age with Aunt Geri's children, which resulted in me growing up with all of my first cousin's children. If you couple that with my last living grandparent passing when I was 8, you can see how the "Granny" illusion developed itself in my brain. I had a grandparent void, but I was never made to feel slighted. On Christmases, I would have the same money stocking hanging like all of the other grandkids. When it was time to dress all of the grandkids in plaid, or sailor outfits and take grandkids' pictures...I was always included. She came to every birthday party, pageant, recital, game, or whatever life celebratory thing I was having at the time. And I got the same Granny pinch for acting up in church. (Though when we talk about it, she swears she's never pinched me and graciously offers to show me what she did. I pass every time but realized I have only ever gotten one, and that's enough to last me a lifetime...scared straight, I guess.)

In 2004, I was set to receive my bachelor's from UMSL, of course, I was super excited and sent her one of the first graduation invitations because "Granny" is always there to lovingly celebrate me. So when she called to congratulate me and begrudgingly told me that she wouldn't be able to attend, I was crushed. Unfortunately, my graduation date fell on the same date my cousin Jaymi was set to receive her bachelor's. Jaymi is Aunt Geri's first grandchild, and if there was a conflict between attending her first grandchild's graduation and mine, of course, attending Jaymi's would be the obvious choice. I had (and have) no animosity or jealous feelings, but the realization hit me like a ton of bricks. I realized I had been "Granny" loved so well that my subconscious brain really made her my grandparent, and in a moment she was Aunt Geri. That's not to say that it is a lesser relationship or love, or that I am bitter about her not being able to attend. But it is definitely a testament to how my Aunt Geri loves hard with her actions and her presence, and so selflessly has filled the "Granny" void for me over the years like she has I'm sure for so many others that I randomly hear call her Granny.

With much love and respect from LaKeisha McKeown
(Niece and Honorary Grandchild)

My Granny

Geraldine "Granny's an angel, our angel Granny" Smotherson has been and always will be my role model. When I was younger, I spent so much time with her and felt it was because I was an only child and had no one to stay home with like my cousins did. I generally enjoyed our time together but did not enjoy the chores, the trips to SYMS Department Store, or the early days of Michaels or Garden Ridge. I loved family reunion trips but did not like my automatic relegation to the age group that is five years younger than me all the time. I felt like the babysitter. I felt like I spent so much time with her working for and with people in some way and that is not what I imagined childhood to be about. She was always so patient with me in a way that made me feel silly for having an attitude about some of these things, but sometimes I couldn't resist. She just demonstrated a calm with me that I have not seen in anyone else that eventually, I saw what was really happening.

It is from her that I learned to truly care for others and be of service in my daily doings. Her dedication to making things better is something that I hope she sees in me. I now find joy in helping, especially without being asked. Sometimes I wrestle with what happens when no one notices it, but then I think of how much she has done for me and others, that goes without a thank you in words or actions. Then I remember that this is simply what she has taught me about love. Love is using your gifts to nourish others. I watched her love through using your creativity and talent for business, people, and art (and craft) and create/run CIBC Westend Academy. I watched her love by extending kindness even to the most arrogant of us in a way that undeniably demonstrated her integrity. I still watch her let God lead her as she leads us, always ready to help however and whenever she can. The initiative she shows in doing what needs to be done and not waiting for permission or acknowledgment is something of which I have become very protective. Watching her do these things is watching a front row to her heart and it is the most beautiful one I know. Granny is how I know that God is real.

Brittany Smotherson *(Second-born Granddaughter &*
Your Twin)

My Mother-in-Law

Mrs. Smotherson *(I call her Granny)* was always patient with me. I am thankful for her always having an open mind when it came to marriage advice. Being that I am married to one of her sons I know it had/has to be hard for her to have discussions with me.

She reminds me so much of my grandmother Leola Hendricks. All of Leola's daughters-in-law would come over to our home to ask her for her advice about their own marriages. They also knew that whatever they spoke about stayed between them. This too is Geraldine Smotherson. It has been an honor to have known her my entire life.

Granny, you have made me a better woman, wife & mother. You are truly a rare gem.

Love always, Rose Marie Smotherson *(Your oldest son's wife and your best friend's daughter)*

Granny

I have had the pleasure of knowing Mrs. Geraldine Smotherson for most of my life. I am pleased and fortunate to refer to her as Granny. Granny is a woman of stewardship, strength, poise, and grace. She always has a caring and willing spirit to help others. Even if helping others means putting herself last. She has been blessed with so much wisdom, kindness, talent, joy, and positivity that you can't help but smile and laugh when you are in her presence. Granny has this giving/passionate spirit that captivates your attention. You know that she can always be trusted and counted on for whatever you are needing.

Granny has always been one of my biggest cheerleaders and the first to congratulate me when achieving my goals through life's journey. She is not afraid to hurt your feelings with truth nor is she stubborn/stingy in providing and teaching crafts to get you through your trials/tribulations. She will be in your corner to fight with you in love, consistency, and strength. And even when you stumble, she is certainly there to encourage you to get back up!

Proverbs 11:14 NASB states, "Where there is no guidance the people fall, But in abundance of counselors there is victory."

God has a divine purpose over our lives. We are his vessels to not only spread His love and lessons but to provide teachable moments to those we meet. To one of the most giving and loving people I know, thank you for being who you are and teaching me so much. I love you, Granny!

Halston E. Hutchison *(Grand-daughter)*

My Grandmother "Granny"

My grandmother is a person who cherishes family over everything except for maybe God. The way I have seen her care for her family and others outside of it has influenced how I have treated everyone I have met. To this very day, I still have not come into contact with a more loving and kinder person than my Granny.

Correy Alexander Smotherson *(Last-Born Grandson)*

My Grandmother

I am the youngest granddaughter and although I have not experienced my grandmother in my adulthood as much as my older cousins might have, who she was in my childhood is to not be forgotten. Her warm spirit is something that I can feel with my eyes closed. It is undeniable, potent, unmistaken, and unwavering. Her infinite love is what breathes life into the Smotherson family. Her will to be kind, to be just, and to be a virtuous woman is what she has exemplified to those around her since my earliest memories of my Granny. My Granny has a voice that will soothe a soul, re-energize the weak, and give peace to your mind. My Granny is a home to those who are lost, a meal to those who are hungry, and a mother to those who are without. My Granny is an angel gracing this earth when at times we don't deserve her. My grandmother is appreciated, loved, and unforgettable.

Sydney Smotherson – *(Youngest Granddaughter)*

My Granny

Her poise expresses both dignity and grace
When she speaks, although meek, so full of wisdom
Her spirit is gentle and God Fearing
Her style? Classy, Elegant, and Glamorous all
come to mind
I have still yet to meet a person as creative and
resourceful as she
She loves me and I love her
She is my Granny

Alexes *(Grand-daughter #3)*

Granny

Blood doesn't always make you family. So I must say I have the most loving granny a person can have. Very soft-spoken but means what she says, especially during a church service. I think she had to pinch me a few times, but all while sitting so pretty with her fly hats.

I love you and thank you for being my Granny

Elona *(Grand-daughter)*

Aunt Geri

You and I have had our disagreements, but all of this is still my honest truth of how I see you now and how I saw you then as my beautiful Aunt and a strong black woman. When it comes to our family, you were and still are the same... A GIVER. I admire always how you handled yourself as a wife and an amazing First Lady.

Pamela Jaquess, Niece

Granny

She's not just a woman, she's the epitome of a lady. Just by me watching her, she showed me what it means to have class, how to behave in certain settings, how to dress, and how to speak in the best manner were some of the many lessons I got from her.

She created CIBC Westend Academy where young people like me at the church and in the community could have a place to express themselves talents and just be children. No other summer camp was like that camp because that camp was an extension of who my granny is. Her spirit of giving to help others is a blueprint of how I want to walk in my purpose in helping others and giving back.

Granny is like an action word... she didn't just talk about stuff and hoped for the best, no, she did it. She instilled in me the mindset to strive to one day be as much of a loving, kind, and classy lady that gets things done just as she has done and continues to do.

LaTrisha *(Granddaughter)*

Impressed with your breakdown of your virtues. ALL apply.

I may not know all the interpersonal actions of some of these designations/relationships however your interactions with me as a friend, family member, co-author, and all-around good person...NO faults. These are all honest assessments of you in my life. I am hard-pressed to find fault as I think we have had a long-time relationship of truthful, loving, and forthright conversations and interactions. Oh, wait... I know what I have an issue with NOT having enough time to spend together.

Cousin Toni *(Chicago)*

My, Aunt Geri

I am grateful to my aunt for showing me and encouraging me so much. When I didn't want to deal with the abuse of the family growing up, she was one of the few people that was by my side at every moment, even when I needed to be taught a lesson myself. I always hated asking either of my parents for help, so when I needed some extra money to get through to the next paycheck, and I knew I had to work for it, she would oblige every time. I enjoyed doing what I could for her and the lesson of putting in hard work to earn what I had/have was invaluable. I'd be a lot more of a lazy individual if it weren't for that. Whenever I needed her, she was there.

James Burrell – *(Nephew and Honorary Grandchild)*

The saying goes, "Give people their flowers while they can still smell them."

I am thankful for the opportunity to have a moment to celebrate one of the true giants and influential figures in my journey. Since before I can remember most things, Mrs. Geraldine Smotherson has impacted my life. I was drawn to her from the first time I saw her. Even as a very young child, I recognized her light. Her way was loving, easygoing and her actions were always intentional. She has been and remains a quiet force in my life. Two things that are most powerful when modeled correctly are love and leadership. True leadership begets more leaders. Add to that, a dash of love, and you get a servant leader. This definition captures the essence of Mrs. Smotherson. She was my first Sunday School Teacher, the First Lady of my home church, and even my first employer at the CIBC West End Academy. Her ability to model love and servant leadership are two of her most admirable qualities, among so many others. To say that she's made an indelible impression on me is an understatement. From teaching me early lessons about faith to signing the very first check I earned, I am eternally grateful to Mrs. Smotherson for sowing into my life.

ELBERT JAQUESS *(EJ)*

Our Neighbor... Our Friend

Geraldine Smotherson is one of the most gracious, honorable, and awesome ladies that I know. Our families have been neighbors for over 50 years. First, she has the most beautiful smile and always looking for a way to bless folks. She loves to cook and always thinks about us even sometimes more than she thinks about herself. Many times she has prepared meals and called me to come over to get dinner or she would bring the food over herself. My mother, Jewel Ford stated that Mrs. Smotherson was her angel and that's what she is. One time in particular I remember when my mother had surgery on her foot Mrs. Smotheson brought breakfast over, not just for my mother but for the whole family. My baby daughter at the time was about 3 years old and she looked forward to those scrumptious breakfasts and probably got spoiled after a week. One day there was no breakfast delivered so my 3-year-old daughter, while her grandparents were sleeping, unlocked our front door and went next door to the Smotherson's. She knocked on the door and asked Rev. Smotherson, "Did Mrs. Smotherson forget to give us our breakfast this morning?" Rev. Smotherson brought her back next door and explained that Mrs. Smotherson was at work. This was years ago but we all still laugh about the 3-year-old going after what she wanted. Mrs. Smotherson and my mother have become great friends over the years and enjoy talking to each other about everything. She seems to always look out for my mother and me. Mrs. Smotherson is an excellent cook and we just love being included. It's not just the cooking but she is also a woman of God who shows the love of Jesus Christ in her life every day. She is the epitome of love to her family and to us. She is a blessing to this neighborhood, her church, and most of all to the Kingdom of God. Proverb 31: 29-31 states, "Many daughters have done well, but you excel them all. Charm is deceitful and beauty is passing, but a woman who fears the Lord shall be praised. Give her the fruit of her hands, and let her own works praise her in the gates." Mrs. Smotherson your worth is far above rubies and gold. You are a virtuous woman of God. Please now take your bow and always know that your neighbors next door, the Ford family, truly loves, adores, and admires you. With all honor and respect, always and forever.

Gaile Ford, Next Door Neighbor

Mrs. Smotherson

My experience with the CIBC Westend Academy was awesome. When Mrs. Smotherson asked me to help at the Academy, my first thought was to say, "no thank you." I wasn't a people person, I was private, although I had attended the church for some years. I thought about it for a few days because I didn't know what I could bring to the Academy or how to help. I did not know the children nor their parents and wondered how I could be of any assistance. I came to Mrs. Smotherson and asked, "What is it you want me to do?" Her response was to make snacks on Tuesdays for the children, but she did not give me a menu or an idea of what to make. When Tuesday came, I met with some of the children, the camp Jr. Leader and some of the parents. I realized that the best way was to let the kids be a part of making the snacks. Letting the kids help proved to be a very successful project. We learned how to work as a team, how to measure ingredients and the most important outcome was having fun. After about three weeks I realized I was getting to know the children and the adults and was coming out of my shell. I found myself. I started talking more to the congregation of the church, found many friends and a god-child and even an adopted family and a love for being a servant by way of cooking for others. This experience challenged me, and I really enjoyed it. I thank you for the experience with the CIBC Westend Academy and the love and connection with kind, sharing, and godly people.

Sincerely, Linda Tatum

Mrs. Smotherson

I can remember back in the 80's I would occasionally visit Cornerstone Institutional Baptist Church with my mother-in-law Retia Stewart. I would always see this beautiful well-dressed fair-skinned woman sitting in front of the church who always had a smile. Me being a PK *(preacher's kid)* myself somehow I knew she had to be the first lady. I never went up to her to speak but I would see her from a distance and smile. I was looking at a woman full of grace. Well, some 30 years later, I'm now a member of this church and we are not only friends but I think of her as my godmother. I appreciate our relationship and what we have in common.

There have been days through the week when I would feel down and before I knew it, the phone would ring, and it would be her on the other end. It seemed she could always sense whenever something was wrong. All I could say was "Wow! So glad to hear your voice." Mrs. Smotherson would have a kind word to say and tell me that my favorite dessert was ready for pick up. To me, that's what makes her God sent. Thank you, Mrs. Geri, for being my friend and confidant. May God bless you with your best seller book.

Love always, G. Michelle Norman

About Ms. Geri's Smile

When I was asked more than a decade ago by the youth of the CIBC Westend Academy to write something to honor you, I believe that what I wrote then I could have written five decades ago, and I can offer it today with consistent relevance. Though the depth and breadth of your smile are unparalleled in adaptability to life's struggles, pains, celebrations, and pleasures, your smile itself remains a constant. I sometimes muse at whether your smile is a mechanism for your internal consumption and a shield for your comfort and protection from a harsh world, or if it is truly and purely a light shining outward. Whatever the case, there is power in the grace of your gift and I am personally grateful for the light of your smile, even when (or, especially when) it has shone on my life to adjust my darkness.

Ms. Geri's Smile

Usually, when I speak I don't say what's expected
This time I'll be straight and see if straight's accepted
When asked to write about what you mean to me
I came up with something using the letters L–O–V and E

L is for your smile–a blessing for a mortal to behold
O is for your smile–that light from the depts of your soul
V is for your smile–a cyclone touching like a breeze
E is for your smile–when it puts a low spirit at ease

Jesus Christ the Savior taught lessons from heaven above
Your smile is a small reminder of Christ's agape' Love

Rev. Rick

Mrs. Smotherson

Mrs. Smotherson this is Lisa, you know the one you refer to as "teacher." I am sending you a note of thanks that I hope you can use in your book. It's real and from my heart. I remember when my grandmother died I was on the verge of a nervous breakdown... But God stepped in! The Lord sent angels to guide me: my family and you, my First Lady. He steered me to Mrs. Smotherson thru this ordeal. Well, no nervous breakdown! She counseled me, she prayed for me, she sought help from God FOR ME and MY FAMILY! For this and more... I Love You!

Respectfully, Alisa Lewis

Geri Smotherson

In 1995, I, being asked to participate in a newly conceived project with two individuals I did not know from totally different postal backgrounds and geographical areas was met with ambiguous expectations. It has been years since my work experience with Geri and Marlene Mohamed on the Community Development Project, yet this single experience became the most fulfilling and proudest of my many postal career activities.

From the beginning, it was Geri who took charge, found our strengths, and led us into one of the most successful projects ever undertaken by the training and diversity development group. Geri's background in training and development was the source for creating the training program, getting the course accepted as a continuing education credit from the University of Missouri.

You only have to give her an idea of what you want as a project or outcome; then stand back and watch her 'create magic' in short order that will 'knock your socks off.' Yes, that is who I found her to be–a professional, timeless worker that did not settle for second best! She had such a quiet way about her that upper managers did not feel intimidated by her seeking outrageous support and budget for her project. And since the outcome was outstanding, by the time they realized she should not have had such latitude, they were too busy taking credit for their successful outcome and all was right with the world. And Geri just smiled, not needing the accolades. She was 'just Geri':

(Goodness, Excellence, Righteousness, Readiness, Infinite Information, Great Leader, Excellent teamwork, Realistic, Role model, Ingenious, Smooth, not flashy, Model of calmness, Others first, including the job at hand, Thorough with work projects, Honest and keeper of secrets, Enjoy life and people, Ready to incorporate new ideas, Share the accolades of her work, Open to people differences, Never has a closed mind)

Although no one person can be everything to all people, she became first a Co-worker, then a Mom, and always a Friend that I will honor, respect, and love forever.

Your friend,

Henrietta Clark Goldsby

Sis. Geraldine Smotherson

Sis. Smotherson *(as I call her)* has been a part of my life since I was a youngster attending First Baptist Church of Creve Coeur. Even though she has always shown me love I was shocked when she asked me, Arvella "Val" Edwards-Campbell, to write something for her book.

What I remember most about my early years is when I was about six or seven and Sis. Smotherson along with our mothers worked together on special activities for the kids at Creve Coeur. For one performance, we were all dressed in white and wore white gloves as we did a pantomime to the Lord's Prayer. I still remember how we practiced over & over again; how excited I was the day we performed; and the wonderful feeling I had after hearing the church members applauding. I wanted to always feel that joy! Working with young children and developing their minds appears to be an important part of Sis. Smotherson's makeup. She's able to pull out of you the abilities you didn't even know you had which showed every young child she encountered that any-thing was possible. The memory of that pantomime came to my heart here recently when Sis. Smotherson and Pam organized an event for young girls called 'The BEST'. The practices (and there were many) were, as the kids say, "off the chain." The young ladies dressed from head to toe in all white just as we had been all those years ago, walked with such grace. I was whisked back down memory lane from the experience of it all as I recalled the magic of my youth and my joy.

Sis. Smotherson has a style about her that makes me stand back, watch, and take note of the example she may not even be aware she is setting. Whether she is in her role as the Pastor's wife or simply Sis. Smotherson, she is the same. Watching her interact with her friends is awesome. They correct each other when they're wrong, cry with each other when they're in pain, rejoice with each other when they're happy, and stand up for each other when they're down. My mother, Peggy, and Sis. Smotherson were friends. My mother would say 'Oh Geri she don't mind' or 'Oh I'll see if Geri wants to do this or that', 'Geri, just talk to her, she'll show you how to do it.' That is how I remember their friendship until the day my mom passed away in 2018. Now here it is 2020 and Sis. Smotherson is still being my mom's friend by looking after her children whenever possible. Knowing that my brother loved her pies, Sis. Smotherson would always bake one for him. Even though Peggy made the same pie, Peggy's baby boy would WAIT for Sis. Smotherson's pie to show up and it was the one pie my mom allowed in the house.

If you're wondering why... it's because she and Geri *(Sis. Smotherson, that is)* were TRUE FRIENDS!!!

Arvella *Val* Edwards-Campbell

What You Mean to Me

I have always called her "Mom," not Mrs. Smotherson because I've known her and have been a part of the family since I was 15 years old.

My mother's name was Ida Mae Harrison, a feisty spitfire of a woman who loved to cuss! She would cuss when she was happy, sad, partying, instilling wisdom & knowledge, or yelling at me and my four siblings for something we did wrong. There was, however, no doubting my mother's love for us even amid her very colorful swearing. "Mom" Smotherson is nothing like Ms. Ida Mae. I don't think I've ever heard her say one bad word... EVER! I would probably contrast the two in this way... my mother was the wind and "Mom" is the calm. Without hesitation, "Mom" was there for me when my mother *(may she rest in peace)* passed away in January of 2020. Two very different personalities sharing a common bond... ME.

I consider "Mom" Smotherson my hero especially whenever things would go wrong in my life... something she probably didn't even know. She was and still is always so cool, calm, and collected! I also have never seen her get mad about anything. She just appeared to have everything together. What I love the most about her is that she is very easy to talk to. I can sit and tell her anything that's on my mind. She is always so positive and encouraging about whatever it is I tell her I want to do. Mom just makes you feel comfortable... I can totally be myself.

When I first joined Cornerstone, she was at the helm of all the church functions. If you needed clothes, furniture, props, and oh yeah, HATS-for-days she was definitely the go-to person. "Mom" had whatever anybody needed to make the function beautiful.

I remember when I moved into my new apartment after returning to St. Louis and "Mom" came over to see my new place and, to make sure everything was okay. I told my best sister-friend that I needed a stove and refrigerator and before I knew it, my best sister-friend had told her mother, which is "Mom" that I needed those things. "Mom" and my best sister-friend got those things for me before I could blink an eye. They would do anything to help anybody. Whenever I visit "Mom," she always has a smile for me and that makes me feel really special. She means the world to me and I love the fact that I have "Mom" Smotherson, my second mom, in my life.

Dollie Ianke

This is such an honor.

When Mrs. Smotherson asked me to write something about her for her book, what came to mind was my very first encounter with her at Washington Tabernacle. I didn't know anybody there, but I remember it was Mrs. Smotherson's young smiling face that drew me in. It didn't take long before I started to take a liking to her. As I continued to grow in the church, she became someone that I could trust and even my sister got very comfortable with her. Mrs. Smotherson is a very kind woman and now looking back, I can truly say she loves children. She didn't know me, my siblings, or my mom but got us involved in a lot of church activities. She would even pick me and my sister up and take us to the youth meetings and afterward get us home safely. I would often ask myself why is this lady doing this for me? I didn't know anything about the church but as I got a little older and learned a few things, I now know for sure my First Lady, Mrs. Geraldine Smotherson did what she did because she wanted to.

It was around Christmas time and as little girls my sister and I wanted to do something special for Mrs. Smotherson because she was so special to us. We each only had a little money, so we put our funds together and bought a purple bracelet. We felt proud we were getting Mrs. Smotherson a gift. She was someone who had been doing things for us since we'd been at the church and we wanted to not try and repay her but show we were just so appreciative of her. The church had a Christmas service where everyone exchanged gifts. Being the First Lady, she received lots of presents from members of the church and in her normal fashion graciously and publicly thanked everyone for their thoughtfulness including us. We were glad she didn't say our names probably because we weren't sure if our gift was good enough. She didn't look down on us or our gift. After that, we knew we could trust Mrs. Smotherson with anything.

Mrs. Smotherson, I'm sure there are a great many women, men, boys, and girls that will tell you how much of a positive impact you have made on their lives. I'd like to say I'm one of them. Kudos to you for writing this memoir. God Bless you in your endeavors.

Luv–Kim Morton

She often said, "Who would you miss most if they were gone for a month? The top executive or the Custodian?"

Does No mean No?–Having worked for Geri for many years, I learned quickly that it doesn't in terms of work product. If her bosses told her, "No", I knew that we would need to work that much harder. She would go under the obstacle, over it or around it; but would get it done. Sometimes it was the simple act of waiting. Timing is everything.

Things are not as They Seem–For ASAP time, a certain Senator headed the Postal Committee in Congress. Because he represented St. Louis, he and the then-District Manager were doing many illegal moves including hiring constituents from the Senators area: promoting individuals who were not the most qualified but were cronies of either the Senator or the District Manager. The hiring and promotion at that time were predominantly Black to appease the Senator. To me, any time the racial balance was so obviously unbalanced, I felt the disparity was wrong. At one point, when I didn't understand the situation, I, unfortunately, called Geri a racist. I never heard her curse before; but, she quickly told me, "That's crap, get out of my office." Sure have wished I hadn't said that.

While working for Geri for many years, I was amazed at the selections she made for jobs in our unit. Many of the selections she made resulted in complaints of discrimination; some allegations were due to the selection because they were white, some because they were black. The selections were rarely the folks I expected. One day, I asked Geri how she made her selections. Her answer made complete sense. She selected the people who had skills that the current staff didn't have. With each selection, she built a more well-rounded staff. As a result, we became known as one of the best training units in the country.

We were seeking volunteers to key on a new piece of letter sorting equipment. It had an upper and lower keyboard much like a musical organ keyboard. Successful completion of the aptitude test was challenging. One of our employees who had been hired through the Handicap Program wanted to volunteer. The guy had missing fingers on both hands; he had perhaps three on one hand and two on the other. I thought there was no way he could qualify because of his missing fingers. I decided it just wouldn't work and delayed him from entering the program. He was persistent in his quest to try. I complained to Geri that this guy continued to bother me. Her response caused me to be ashamed of my behavior and humbled me. It was a short question that said it all, she asked, "Well, is he able to key?" I responded, "I don't know." Geri said, "Why don't we find out." I started him in training, and he qualified.

Donna Balsano

My thanks to everyone who added their comments to my book.
I am extremely grateful.

My daughter Pamela worked tirelessly editing my book.
Thank you, Pam.
I am also indebted to Sandra Shaner for her expertise.

To those who read my book, *Unapologetically Me*,
thank you for your interest.
God bless you all.